INTERCULTURAL THE

Intercultural Therapy: Challenges, Insights and Developments examines the impact of the work of the Nafsiyat Intercultural Therapy Centre in North London, which focused on providing free, psychodynamic therapy.

Set up by Jafar Kareem, the centre was the first psychotherapy service with the specific task of offering psychodynamic psychotherapy to Britain's Black and ethnic minority population. The editors of this book have invited a number of Nafsiyat therapists and colleagues to give their view on what has changed, or not changed, in regard to the integration of intercultural issues into mainstream therapy.

Intercultural Therapy will be of interest to all psychotherapists working in multicultural practices, as well as practitioners and social workers.

Baffour Ababio is a psychoanalytic intercultural psychotherapist and clinical supervisor in private practice and at the Nafsiyat Intercultural Therapy Centre, where he has also worked as head of clinical services.

Roland Littlewood was associated with Jafar Kareem at the start of Nafsiyat and retired a few years ago as professor of psychiatry and anthropology at University College London, where he is now a research fellow.

INTERCULTURAL THERAPY

Challenges, Insights and Developments

Edited by Baffour Ababio and Roland Littlewood

LONDON AND NEW YORK

First published 2019
by Routledge
2 Park Square, Milton Park, Abingdon, Oxon OX14 4RN

and by Routledge
52 Vanderbilt Avenue, New York, NY 10017

Routledge is an imprint of the Taylor & Francis Group, an informa business

© 2019 selection and editorial matter, Baffour Ababio and Roland Littlewood; individual chapters, the contributors

The right of Baffour Ababio and Roland Littlewood to be identified as the authors of the editorial material, and of the authors for their individual chapters, has been asserted in accordance with sections 77 and 78 of the Copyright, Designs and Patents Act 1988.

All rights reserved. No part of this book may be reprinted or reproduced or utilised in any form or by any electronic, mechanical, or other means, now known or hereafter invented, including photocopying and recording, or in any information storage or retrieval system, without permission in writing from the publishers.

Trademark notice: Product or corporate names may be trademarks or registered trademarks, and are used only for identification and explanation without intent to infringe.

British Library Cataloguing in Publication Data
A catalogue record for this book is available from the British Library

Library of Congress Cataloging-in-Publication Data
Names: Ababio, Baffour, editor. | Littlewood, Roland, editor.
Title: Intercultural therapy : challenges, insights and developments / edited by Baffour Ababio and Roland Littlewood.
Description: Milton Park, Abingdon, Oxon ; New York, NY : Routledge, 2019. | Includes bibliographical references and index.
Identifiers: LCCN 2018038467 (print) | LCCN 2018038684 (ebook) | ISBN 9780429459788 (Master) | ISBN 9780429861741 (ePub) | ISBN 9780429861758 (pdf) | ISBN 9780429861734 (Mobi/Kindle) | ISBN 9781138625594 (hardback : alk. paper) | ISBN 9781138625600 (pbk. : alk. paper)
Subjects: LCSH: Cultural psychiatry. | Cross-cultural counseling. | Psychiatry, Transcultural.
Classification: LCC RC455.4.E8 (ebook) | LCC RC455.4.E8 I572 2019 (print) | DDC 616.89–dc23
LC record available at https://lccn.loc.gov/2018038467

ISBN: 978-1-138-62559-4 (hbk)
ISBN: 978-1-138-62560-0 (pbk)
ISBN: 978-0-429-45978-8 (ebk)

Typeset in Bembo
by Taylor & Francis Books

To the memory and example of Jafar Kareem

CONTENTS

List of figures   ix
Notes on contributors   x

Introduction: process and development in intercultural psychotherapy   1
Roland Littlewood and Baffour Ababio

1 Intercultural therapy and neoliberalism   10
   Inga-Britt Krause

2 Who's being assessed? Post-modernism and intercultural therapy assessments: a synergetic process   24
   Oye Agoro

3 Not yet at home: an exploration of aural and verbal passing amongst African migrants in Britain   40
   Baffour Ababio

4 Group psychotherapy with Turkish-speaking women at Nafsiyat: migration, gender and ethnic difference as catalysts to growth in the psychodynamic group   60
   Dilek Güngör

5 Finding our voice across the Black/white divide: race issues in therapy   71
   Eugene Ellis

6 Racism in the room: internal working model of the 'non-white' introject 83
   Deri Hughes

7 Intercultural psychotherapy, intracultural psychotherapy, or just good psychotherapy? 94
   Peter Cockersell

8 Postcolonialism and countertransference in two cases of the sexual abuse of women by doctors 105
   Roland Littlewood

9 Inferiorisation: approaching a stigmatising reality in therapy 111
   Antony Sigalas

10 Face to face: psychotherapy in black and white 119
   Charles Brown

11 Embodied intercultural ground 126
   Carmen Joanne Ablack

12 Intercultural psychoanalytic psychotherapy and generationally transmitted trauma 137
   Lennox K. Thomas

13 Beyond the famil(y)ar: the construct of the self outside the dyad – intercultural therapy as an opportunity to explore the social self 152
   Francesca Zanatta

14 The challenge of racism in clinical supervision 167
   Isha Mckenzie-Mavinga

Index 178

FIGURES

13.1	Destiny's family	157
13.2	Destiny's family (members responsible for children in grey)	157
13.3	Destiny's systems (members responsible for children in grey)	158
13.4	Anna's presumed family	160
13.5	Anna's system of care	161
13.6	Attachment conducing to development of healthy self	162
13.7	System in interaction with Anna's self	163

CONTRIBUTORS

Baffour Ababio is a psychoanalytic intercultural psychotherapist and clinical supervisor in private practice and at the Nafsiyat Intercultural Therapy Centre, where he has also worked as head of clinical services. Alongside his clinical role, he also developed a career in managing mental health services, integrating a community-based response to support recovery from a broad range of mental health problems. Having completed his training at University College London (UCL) and the Guild of Psychotherapists, he is a member of the United Kingdom Council for Psychotherapy (UKCP) and the British Association for Psychoanalytic and Psychodynamic Supervision.

Carmen Joanne Ablack is a group, relationship and individual psychotherapist, trainer and supervisor who has published on clinical contemporary practice (intercultural communication and dilemmas) and on regulation. A UKCP honorary fellow and former trustee, she is currently president of the European Association for Body Psychotherapy. She is a faculty member of the Gestalt Centre, London and a member of the Black, African and Asian Therapists Network Leadership Group. Website: www.cjablack.com

Oye Agoro is a cisgender woman of Yoruba ancestry, currently practising as an integrative therapist and clinical supervisor, who studied sociology and social anthropology and trained at UCL/Nafsiyat Centre. Oye previously worked as a psychotherapist at the Forward Project – a Black mental health resource in west London. She was director of the Lorrimore, a charity based in Southwark providing social support to people with mental health difficulties. Oye co-founded the Multi Ethnic Counselling Service in London and currently manages counselling services in south London. She has her own practice in south London, Waddon Ponds Therapy Practice.

Charles Brown is a psychoanalytic psychotherapist, clinical supervisor and supervisor of supervision. He trained at the Guild of Psychotherapists, London. He is also a specialist addictions therapist and an experienced group facilitator. Charles works across the public, voluntary and private sectors. He is the founder of BeMe Therapy, a counselling service for Black and ethnic minorities. Charles is also a training therapist and has lectured in psychotherapy training organisations. He has a particular interest in identity and race and has published papers in books and journals. He has a small private practice in south London.

Peter Cockersell is a psychoanalytic psychotherapist, supervisor, and consultant and trainer in psychologically informed environments. Peter trained originally with UCL/Nafsiyat Centre, and did his doctorate with Metanoia, Middlesex. He currently works in private practice, as a supervisor in the voluntary and private sectors and in the NHS, as a lecturer in psychodynamic theory and practice at Surrey University, and as a consultant for various organisations working with mental health, social exclusion and homelessness. Peter is married with two children; the family has two cats, two gerbils, two rabbits and a goldfish, and is proud to share the roof space of their home with a group of pipistrelle bats.

Eugene Ellis is a psychotherapist and founder of the Black, African and Asian Therapy Network, the UK's largest independent organisation to specialise in working with Black and Asian clients. Eugene trained as an integrative arts psychotherapist and has worked for many years with severely traumatised children and their families in the field of adoption and fostering as well as working in private practice. He has a special interest in sensorimotor psychotherapy, somatic experiencing and other body-orientated therapies and has over 15 years of meditation and mindfulness practice in a Buddhist context.

Dilek Güngör is a UKCP registered senior psychotherapist, who has been working at the Nafsiyat Centre since 1993, working with individuals, couples and groups. Her background is nursing, teaching and community development. She has many years of experience working with the NHS, social services, Family Action and the Women's Therapy Centre. Dilek lectures and runs seminars in Turkey and some of her clinical work with therapists and clients is via Skype. She is a writer and an artist. Her private practice is in north London. Email: dilekfridakahlo@hotmail.com. Blog: dilekfridakahlo.wordpress.com.

Deri Hughes is a psychoanalytic intercultural psychotherapist who trained with UCL/Nafsiyat Centre. He has worked in the NHS as a principal psychotherapist and clinical supervisor and runs his own private practice in Rochester, Kent. He has worked extensively as a psychological expert witness in asylum cases and has supervised the clinical work of psychotherapists at Freedom from Torture, London. He was clinical director at the University of Kent, Canterbury on master in clinical science training in psychoanalytic psychotherapy leading to UKCP registration. He has an MA in linguistics for English language teaching, an MSc in intercultural psychotherapy, an advanced certificate in eye movement desensitization and reprocessing therapy and a post-graduate certificate in higher education. He is a UKCP registrant and a senior associate member of the Royal Society of Medicine. He is interested in the pragmatics of psychotherapeutic discourse and how it informs understanding of unconscious communication. He has lived in South Africa, Iran and Spain and has worked in a number of other countries. He speaks and works in both English and Spanish.

Inga-Britt Krause is a social anthropologist and consultant systemic psychotherapist. She has carried out ethnographic research in Nepal and with the Punjabi community in the UK and helped set up cross-cultural psychotherapy services in London. She is currently Training and Development Consultant in the Tavistock and Portman NHS Foundation Trust where she also works as a child and adolescent mental health services clinician and is the lead of the professional doctorate programme in systemic psychotherapy. Her publications include papers on cross-cultural psychotherapy as well as books such as *Culture and Reflexivity in System Psychotherapy: Mutual Perspectives* (2012) and with Begum Maitra *Culture and Madness: A Training Resource and Commentary for Mental Health Professionals* (2015).

Roland Littlewood was associated with Jafar Kareem at the start of the Nafsiyat Centre and retired a few years ago as professor of psychiatry and anthropology at UCL, where he is now a research fellow. He is a past president of the Royal Anthropological Institute and was a consultant psychiatrist and psychotherapist in Bloomsbury. He has also carried out ethnographic fieldwork in Trinidad, Haiti, Lebanon, Italy and Albania. Currently looking at Dalit ('Untouchable') conversion to Christianity in India, he has edited five books and written six, and around 200 academic papers. Email: r.littlewood@ucl.ac.uk.

Isha Mckenzie-Mavinga is a published writer/poet and psychotherapist, lecturer, trainer and supervisor. She has published chapters in a variety of counselling anthologies. Isha has worked in mental health, with women impacted by violence in relationships and as a student counsellor. She facilitates online transcultural supervision and therapeutic support and presents workshops supporting her books: *Black Issues in the Therapeutic Process* (2009) and *The Challenge of Racism in Therapeutic Practice* (2016). Website: www.ishamckenziemavinga.com

Antony Sigalas is a senior psychoanalytic psychotherapist and clinical supervisor who has worked at the Nafsiyat Centre for 15 years and as a consultant clinical lead of its newly arrived refugee family service, before he undertook the clinical responsibility of running the north London drug and alcohol counselling services in Enfield. In the same borough, he set up and has continued to run for 18 years the Let's Talk culturally specific service for the Greek-speaking community. He trains and lectures on the themes of clinical assessment and therapeutic effectiveness of intercultural psychotherapy.

Lennox K. Thomas was formerly a clinical social worker and probation officer with children and families and now works in intercultural psychotherapy with refugees and trauma. He is trained in psychoanalytic psychotherapy, child and family psychotherapy and couples therapy and is a training therapist, clinical supervisor and fellow of the UKCP and a former clinical director at the Nafsiyat Centre. His interests include attachment and relational therapy and organisational consultancy.

Francesca Zanatta is a psychologist and lecturer in childhood studies at the University of East London. She completed her doctoral research reviewing attachment theory from a rights-based perspective. Francesca has developed her practice working in the education and voluntary sector. She is an advocate and campaigner for children's rights and member of the Children's Rights Alliance for England. Her current research projects focus on the concept of the agency of children and the use of mobile apps to support children and young people's mental health.

INTRODUCTION

Process and development in intercultural psychotherapy

Roland Littlewood and Baffour Ababio

An Indian psychologist in London, in the 1970s, was approached by an African Caribbean young man with this story. Jonathan, the young man, had previously been in psychotherapy with a well-known white British therapist; a pillar of the psychoanalytical establishment in north London. Jonathan came from a successful middle-class professional background (his stepfather was a doctor) and was about to proceed from school to university, when he experienced periods of anxiety and uncertainty and a loss of interest in study; his parents had encouraged him to seek therapy. One day, waiting at the bus stop on the way to his session, he was confronted by a group of white youths who insulted him in racial terms. He missed his bus as the encounter degenerated into physical violence. The police were called. Eventually, Jonathan escaped and, followed by the police, arrived 20 minutes late at the house of his therapist bloodied and bruised with his normally smart suit torn. He was ushered in and collapsed into his usual chair, sweating and panting. The therapist simply remarked that his coming late perhaps had something to do with unresolved issues from the last session. After that, Jonathan had looked for a therapist who had some greater empathy with the Black experience.

The Indian psychologist was Jafar Kareem (1930–92), born in Calcutta, who after joining the anti-colonial movement had studied in India, practised there and then had two training analyses in Austria and Israel before coming to work in Britain in the Nation Health Service. Jonathan's story, which Jafar recounted to us and briefly summarised in a variant account in Kareem and Littlewood (1992), brought to a head issues that had bothered him for some time. Unless they were professional or wealthy, Black and ethnic minority people were unable to access psychotherapy to deal with their personal difficulties. If they were middle class they might conceivably find therapy but this seldom met their personal dilemmas. With some like-minded colleagues, Kareem set up, in 1982, the Nafsiyat Intercultural Therapy Centre in north London, the first psychotherapy service with the specific task of offering psychodynamic psychotherapy to Britain's Black and ethnic minority population (Kareem 1992). Their psychological health had then become a matter of concern with high rates of psychotic illness diagnosed and frequent use of pharmaceutical and, compared to the white British population, other physical treatments such as electro-convulsive therapy, higher rates of compulsory hospital treatment and internment in secure state hospitals, and with a general absence of psychotherapy or counselling for less severe psychiatric illnesses (Littlewood and Lipsedge 1982). Nafsiyat was set up by Jafar Kareem to provide free (we were funded case by case by different London boroughs), brief but psychodynamic therapy (the therapists had previously qualified as psychotherapists or psychoanalysts) but with a less rigid approach to timekeeping and self-disclosure than was then current (missed appointments we did not regard as a grave matter, and so on). Contrary to psychoanalytical dogma, services were free to the user and we did not practise ethnic matching of therapist and client except when language differences merited it. So, then, not counselling but a psychodynamic psychotherapy which acknowledged the interpenetration of internal and external worlds and with a flexible practice.

Nafsiyat was set up against a set of psychotherapeutic assumptions, notably that non-Europeans would not benefit from a theory which valued psychological interpretation of internal motivation (Littlewood 1992), but an empirical PhD by Sharon Moorhouse at University College London showed that Nafsiyat clients, who typically had issues with anxiety and personal identity, benefitted from Nafsiyat psychotherapy (Moorhouse 1992). Some of our early therapists had also studied social anthropology, whilst their analytical training had included the Freudian, the Kleinian, the Jungian and others.

Jafar died ten years after he started Nafsiyat, just after we published the first book in Britain on 'intercultural therapy', as he had called it (Kareem and Littlewood 1992; Kareem 1978). Since then there have been many British publications on psychotherapy and counselling across cultural and 'racial' borders, contributions which we have listed rather partially in the Further reading section to this introduction.

That first volume sketched out for us a then unexplored field. Jafar's chapter is still the best introduction to the area (Kareem 1992). Now, 25 years after his death and that book, we have invited a number of Nafsiyat therapists and colleagues to give their view on what has or has not subsequently changed, with some examples from their own practice. At the level of the NHS mental health service, there has not been much change: people with Black Caribbean and Black African ancestry still have higher rates of major psychoses, they are more likely to be compulsorily detained in hospitals and to have poorer long-term outcomes, whilst those of South Asian origin are now experiencing high rates of attempted suicide and eating disorders.

What then of psychotherapy? There has been much development of intercultural and anti-racist therapy since Nafsiyat was founded. Compared with the more theoretical work in France and other European societies (e.g. André 1987), our concerns have been more pragmatic and less historical. In the first chapter, Inga-Britt Krause, an anthropologist as well as a systemic psychotherapist, argues that Nafsiyat was founded amidst a general turn to issues of subjectivity and agency in the social and human sciences associated with a movement in the wider society to more inclusive social policy which was significantly anti-racist. But by 2017, 'multiculturalism' was under attack across Europe (see Chin 2017). Racial attacks still occur frequently and she observes they are now included in the less specific category of 'hate crimes' as part of a resurgent neoliberalism which continues an emphasis on individual self-sufficiency, now the subject and rationale of current capitalist economics, along with the privatisation of healthcare and a decline in the activity of our public health services. The individual has been detached from society and their identity as a citizen fragmented. Krause offers the practice of systemic psychotherapy as a way of preserving the individual as an individual who can exist only in a social framework; all of those components (including the therapist) are an integral part of the wider social system including past history, present meaning and the culture of all the participants. She outlines the advantages and disadvantages of a commonly used checklist (see Krause 2012) and shows how in the clinical case she presents here, the professionals involved had a rather limited idea of what constitutes a 'father' or a 'husband' for a Bangladeshi man in Britain whose own emphasis on his culture of origin was seen by them as an individual (and maladaptive) psychological deficit. To understand what family relationships meant she needed to understand the background of Bengali colonial and postcolonial history in its relationship to Britain far beyond some simple presumption of Bangladeshi identity. Agoro (Chapter 2) is more optimistic about the emphasis on the individual in our postmodern turn, and notes that the traditional Western epistemology which still pervades psychotherapy derives in part from our old colonialist perspective which privileges the white and the male. By contrast, the 'postmodern' perspective continues the project of high modernism in allowing the patient or the client to determine the direction of the therapy. This is of course more problematic if patient and therapist exist with differing world views. Like Krause, she calls for a greater acknowledgement of the patient's social and political life outside the therapy (particularly as this is often oppressive) and of their own subjective understanding and response to it. Using the Marxist theorists Gramsci and Fanon, we can begin to understand how dominant structures create a defensive internalised oppression in which the dominated seek scapegoats among themselves. Recognising and confronting this in therapy, the case illustration suggests, it may be more helpful to exercise this anger than to deal with it internally (inside the self and inside the dominated group) and she outlines a sequence of therapeutic stages in which therapist and client can deal effectively with these issues. So, activism? Maybe.

In Chapter 3, Ababio takes up one of the defences Agoro describes and examines the psychological and social phenomenon of 'passing' for immigrants from Africa. The other Black African descended community in Britain, the West Indian, is larger and probably more homogenous than the African British and has come to represent the popular idea of 'Black Britain'; this leaves the African, who comes, perhaps, from a more middle-class background in their country of origin, to adapt not only to the white British majority but to seek a place in the Black (i.e. British

Caribbean) world. He designates the response within the Black communities to internalised dominance as a maladaptive strategy for surviving in a postcolonial racist society, Ababio emphasises the dilemmas of the 'doubly marginalised'. Back in Africa, the more privileged African could identify psychologically with the British, whilst in Britain they could not because they were seen primarily as Black and their aspirations had to work through a British West Indian/Black British culture. This leaves the patient in the example he outlines, a middle-class Ghanaian, being wary of taking on a presumed shared identity. Another example illustrates the transferences of a female West African client in which she replicates her earlier traumatic experience and perceives Ababio as a woman, as a gentleman and as an African. Using Fanon and Baldwin, he shows how the African situation repeats that historical situation in which many Africans were transported as slaves to the Americas but some were not. Each group has had to adjust in their own way to white dominance and racism, now as then. He signals second- and third-generation Africans in Britain deconstructing the tyranny of 'soft power' and forging a syncretic cultural path.

The next two chapters concern therapeutic groups. One for Turkish-speaking women run by Dilek Güngör illustrates the hopeful, initial expectations of the women for clear direction from their 'expert therapist'. She describes how the group developed into one of mutual support, more generous and 'gentle' than that generally offered to a rather more robust white English clientele. She describes how solidarity in the group emerges with a shared concern over religion, communal honour and traditional female subordination, and how she intervenes to write letters on their behalf in a way not found in traditional group therapy. Yet this is psychotherapy not counselling and she describes transference (and countertransference) reactions to her which are realised and interpreted in the group. She writes about her own role as both inside and outside the group with subtle accounts of her motivation and doubts. Ellis takes up in the fifth chapter the issue of the subjective effects of domination and race for the therapist in describing his work with two groups, one for the therapists and one for the trainees: in particular, the black/white dichotomy in therapy and in counselling. Issues which came up included the hurt engendered by covert prejudice and ambivalence experienced by white therapists who were supposedly able to deal with this hurt. Like Ababio and Thomas (Chapter 12), he emphasises how history has left its residue in the individual and how the current generation is still coping with the defences and denials of its own ancestors. This results in contemporary denial, but also hurt with shame and physical symptoms when the issue of 'race' reveals itself. This Ellis terms intergenerational race trauma. He describes associated issues raised by the groups and the facilitators, constantly pointing out the link between that recognition and the individual's bodily state and movements.

The next three chapters all deal with issues for the white European therapist when acknowledging and confronting racism. In Chapter 6, Hughes considers the discomfort he experiences when his Sikh patient, 'G.S.', assumes that he, the therapist, is intrinsically more skilled and valuable simply because he is white:

overidealisation is not uncommon as a response in therapy but one which gathers power here because it is coupled with ethnic difference. Hughes makes sense of it in dynamic terms by invoking the idea of projective identification, in which the receiver internalises the unconscious fantasies of the projector, the patient, who is trying to get rid of them (Klein 1946). Hughes feels excluded by his patient and this resonates with the feelings of fear he had experienced when he was an isolated European in revolutionary Tehran. And G.S.'s assumptions of his own racial inferiority had followed his own putting down by his Sikh family and relatives. Hughes associates this man's subservient attitude with the popular use of the term 'non-white', which he argues reinforces the white person as the reference point, the determining rhetoric of discourse and action in reaction to the 'other'.

Like others in this volume, Cockersell (Chapter 7) argues that any individual psychotherapy is not merely dyadic for it happens in the interface between the social and the individual. And this is of course most overtly recognised in the practice of intercultural therapy. As he posits, 'all psychotherapy should be intercultural psychotherapy'. He points out that social anthropology has become uneasy with the idea of 'a culture' as a discrete entity distinguished from all others. Individuals in different 'cultures' may resemble each other more than they do fellow members of the same 'pre-regulated' culture. Yet background is of vital importance. He illustrates this by a client who, although a white British male like Cockersell, comes from and lived in such a different social world as to question the very idea of a shared culture for the two. By contrast, he finds that he shares his sensitivities and values with an Egyptian woman from a similar class background to his own. But in both cases, he sees his task as helping them as individuals, to experience and find spaces within their own milieus in reconciling their inner and outer worlds. Chapter 8, by Littlewood, is perhaps unusual in that he – a white Anglo-Swiss – comes out and expresses an intense dislike of an Arab and an Indian – two men with whom he had brief therapeutic contacts (neither was in formal psychotherapy). Whilst that raised interesting – too interesting – issues of how their transgressions might become translated into some aberrant new 'culture', his major concern then and now is with the postcolonial assumption he makes and with his own countertransference. Did their crimes facilitate some contempt of his for their societies, militaristic and hierarchical: crimes without which he could not have permitted his own prejudice to emerge? His contempt? Theirs?

Beneath what might appear as a 'neurosis', Sigalas argues (Chapter 9), we can often detect a state of chronic anxiety and depression, often generated or compounded by what he terms 'inferiorisation': a set of complex personal social experiences such as extreme poverty or trauma which reinforce futile feelings of inferiority, leading in the adult to feelings of worthlessness and often to guilt. The person accepts themselves as justifiably inferior to others. This is further compounded by the situation of being a refugee, effectively powerless and subject to the demeaning demands of the immigration officials and the Border Agency. The popular media and the medical profession amplify this by regarding them as 'a victim'. The whole situation offers questions to Western societies which have presented themselves to the rest of the world as affluent, civilised and liberal, countries where people can achieve their own inherent potential. Dealing with such situations effectively may involve not only formal therapy but 'therapeutic care' of the sort more familiar in counselling such as assistance with housing, educational, medical, financial and asylum problems ideally without compromising too much, the therapeutic interaction.

Brown, in Chapter 10, considers skin colour in two patients' transference dreams of the therapist. He suggests these are particularly common when patient and therapist are from two different ethnic groups and thus are possibly seen as psychologically distinct (as is of course specified by popular perception). In one case, the recollection of him in a dream by a white patient, evidently as Black (as he actually is), enables the therapist to more easily address issues like white guilt and Black rage. A second patient dreams of him as a white woman, a presentation which, when discussed in therapy, opens up issues of sexual desire by the woman (and her repression of it) as well as wider issues of attachment. In both cases, the dream of the patient, whether the dreamed-of therapist is black or white, the specification of colour open up the opportunity to explore the psychodynamics of race and power within the transference and resistance to it.

In Chapter 11, Ablack notes the importance of feeling *with* the patient as well as interpretations *of* the patient. She outlines her Gestalt/phenomenological approach and how it evolved in the practice after she grew up in northwest London struggling with racist abuse and violence. She describes the not dissimilar experiences of her own parents but with which they could not deal. Two of her poems presented here emphasise her complete embodiment in two contrasting situations which illustrate the twin poles of dignity/ignominy. Ablack discusses Surita, a doctor diagnosed with ME (myalgic encephalomyelitis, chronic fatigue syndrome). She encourages her to stay mentally and physically attached to the immediate situation; but then Surita recalls a childhood experience of feeling detached and isolated from her mother who is unable later to join her in her wider life. Ablack ends with a comment on how recollected sounds and voices are often 'heard' in the body and how she herself physically resonates with the patient.

Lennox Thomas, one of the original members of Nafsiyat, reviews in Chapter 12, the legacy of intercultural therapy and Jafar Kareem's earlier work with the child survivors of Nazi extermination camps. He argues that trauma is a central concern in psychotherapy and whilst the immediate response may be physical survival and dissolution of the traumatic memory, such experiences as New World slavery, the Irish potato famine and the Holocaust echo in successive generations who became the 'container' for dilemmas their parents and forbearers could not solve, leaving the child with unprocessed emotions. He offers us one case of lifelong depression which he attributes to the patient's Dutch mother losing her whole family in the Shoah (Holocaust), whom she mourned for the rest of her life, raising her son 'in a mausoleum', as he himself put it. Thomas argues that a long-term legacy of child rearing in the West Indies, following from the slave mother not getting too attached to her children (who could be sold away at any point), is a relative lack of affection in African Caribbean families. Another of his examples concerns an Indian middle-aged professional who discovers some old family letters and realises that she had been conceived in a rape at the time of the partition of India – a fact her own family had been able to hide from her and from others outside the immediate family. He describes a West Indian family in Britain where extreme physical chastisement by parents has passed down the generations and argues this is not an uncommon issue which needs to be addressed by Black psychotherapists in their own family of origin.

Many of the chapters, such as this by Thomas, support the psychodynamic understanding of 'attachment' as described by John Bowlby, but in Chapter 13, Zanatta critiques this in its usual form by citing various feminist writers to argue against the exclusivity of the mother's or the mother-substitute's role. In this the child's subsequent failure (or success) has become the mother's failure to parent: in particular, it is the African Caribbean mother who has been blamed by social workers and other authorities. Detailing some of her own ethnographic field work with West Indians in south London, she shows how a whole complex of people, both biologically related and not, are intimately involved with a young girl's celebration and future career, not only the biological mother. And similarly, the worries of the social workers in another example that a child, separated from her own mother through the mother's illness, is 'at risk', are misconceived. Zanatta supports the argument by returning to the question of how the self is inherently a social product (as in Chapter 1 and Chapter 2). This recalls Jafar Kareem's description of his own patient who had multiple mothers (Kareem 1992).

The last chapter in the book considers many of the issues the volume as a whole has looked at but here in the context of the clinical supervision of therapists. Failure to address in supervision the impact of racism and social disadvantage, or the internalisation of racism, or at least Eurocentrism, will inevitably have reflections in the therapy itself. McKenzie-Mavinga's own terms are defined: 'recognition trauma' of the powerful feelings associated with the recognition of the impact of racism; the 'ancestral baggage' of both in the 'Black empathetic' approach allowing fundamental issues to be dealt with in therapy. Supervision can be a relatively open place to explore issues which might have previously been too difficult in the therapy itself. She ends with a checklist of concerns and strategies that can usefully be raised in supervision.

Whilst our writers each approach intercultural work from the different perspectives of their own personalities and training, two general issues emerge with clarity from their chapters, one theoretical and one practical. The different terms used by them – 'internalised oppression' (Agoro), 'internalised colonial objects' (Ababio), 'inferiorisation' (Sigalas), 'recognition trauma' (McKenzie-Mavinga) – all refer to a very similar process: the unconscious taking in of prejudiced and racist assumptions by others of a subdominant status resulting in a subdominant identity which is compounded by depression, guilt and anxiety. The other general issue is what Sigalas terms therapeutic concern: that without sacrificing psychodynamic rigour, the intercultural therapist may provide practical assistance with issues of education, employment, healthcare, housing and so on, as well as a more flexible approach to the therapeutic sessions.

Although dealing with these two therapeutic issues, both reference the outer world beyond therapy and which may prove difficult for a classical, conservative dynamic therapist to work with, the example of Nafsiyat has shown them to be both practicable and efficacious. The outer world, unfortunately, is not necessarily benign.

The integration of intercultural issues into mainstream therapy is still at an early stage. Compared, say, with feminist issues, intercultural therapy is not yet another sort of dynamic therapy with its own paradigms and procedures, classic cases and accepted body of training and interpretation. It is quite simply psychotherapy which takes account of the outer world and its issues, both globalised and emergent. As Cockersell argues in Chapter 7, perhaps 'all psychotherapy should be intercultural psychotherapy'.

Acknowledgements

Chapter 8 was previously published in 2006 in the journal *Transcultural Psychiatry*, volume 43, pages 235–42.

Patients' names in the book are all pseudonyms. In addition, minor details of their personal biographies which could identify them have been altered. We are grateful to them all for allowing us to share their personal stories and for their often courageous endeavours to resolve dilemmas which are common for all of us in our present society. Thank you all.

References

André, J. (1987) *L'Inceste Focale Dans La Famille Noire Atillaise*. Paris: Presse Universitaire de France.

Chin, R. (2017) *The Crisis of Multiculturalism in Europe: A History*. Princeton, NJ: Princeton University Press.

Kareem, J. (1978) Conflicting Concepts of Mental Health in a Multicultural Society. *Psychiatrica Clinica*, 11: 90–95.

Kareem, J. (1992) The Nafsiyat Intercultural Therapy Centre: Ideas and Experience in Intercultural Therapy. In J. Kareem and R. Littlewood (eds), *Intercultural Therapy: Themes, Interpretations and Practice*, 14–38. Oxford: Blackwell.

Kareem, J. and Littlewood, R. (eds) (1992) *Intercultural Therapy: Theories, Interpretations and Practice*. Oxford: Blackwell.

Klein, M. (1946) Notes on Some Schizoid Mechanisms. *International Journal of Psycho-Analysis* 27: 99–116.

Krause, I.-B. (ed.) (2012) *Culture and Reflexivity in Systemic Psychotherapy*. London: Karnac.

Littlewood, R. and Lipsedge, M. (1982) *Aliens and Alienists: Ethnic Minorities and Psychiatry*. Harmondsworth: Penguin.

Moorhouse, S. (1992) Quantitative Research in Intercultural Therapy: Some Good Methodological Considerations. In J. Kareem and R. Littlewood (eds), *Intercultural Therapy: Themes, Interpretations and Practice*, 83–98. Oxford: Blackwell.

Further reading

D'Arden, P. and Maton, A. (1969) *Transcultural Counselling in Action*. London: SAGE.
Fernando, S. (ed.) (1988) *Culture and Family Therapy*. London: Routledge.
Fernando, S. (1998) *Mental Health in a Multi-Ethnic Society: A Multi-Disciplinary Handbook*. London: Routledge.
Fletchman Smith, B. (2003) *Mental Slavery: Psychoanalytical Studies of Caribbean People*. London: Karnac.
Krause, I.-B. (1998) *Therapy across Cultures*. London: SAGE.
Krause, I.-B. and Maitra, B. (2015) *Culture and Madness: A Training Resource and Commentors for Mental Health Professionals*. London: Jessica Kingsley.
Lago, C. (ed.) (2011) *The Handbook of Transcultural Counselling and Psychotherapy*. Maidenhead: Open University Press.
Lago, C. and Thompson, J. (1996) *Race, Culture and Counselling and Psychotherapy*. Maidenhead: Open University Press.
Littlewood, R. (2000) How Universal Is Something We Can Call 'Therapy'? In J. Kareem and R. Littlewood (eds), *Intercultural Therapy: Themes, Interpretations and Practice*, 39–58. Oxford: Blackwell.
Kareem, J. and Littlewood, R. (eds) (1992) *Intercultural Therapy: Theories, Interpretations and Practice*. Oxford: Blackwell.
Lowe, F. (ed.) (2014) *Thinking Space: Promoting Thinking about Race, Culture and Diversity in Psychotherapy and Beyond*. London: Karnac.
McKenzie-Mavinga, I. (2009) *Black Issues in the Therapeutic Process*. Basingstoke: Palgrave Macmillan.
McKenzie-Mavinga, I. (2016) *The Challenge of Racism in Therapeutic Practice*. London: Palgrave Macmillan.
Papadopoulos, R. (ed.) (2002) *Therapeutic Care for Refugees: No Place Like Home*. London: Karnac.
White, K. (ed.) (2006) *Unmasking Race, Culture and Attachment in the Psychoanalytical Space*. London: Karnac.

1
INTERCULTURAL THERAPY AND NEOLIBERALISM

Inga-Britt Krause

Introduction

Twenty-five years ago, Nafsiyat and its association with intercultural therapy were a focus for budding optimism and energy not only in race relations and in the field of medical anthropology, but also in cross-cultural psychotherapy and in psychotherapy generally. The centre with its related activities was a hub for cross-cultural thinking and for a specific kind of gentle, albeit tenacious, anti-racist activism. With the textual or biographical turn in social sciences (Clifford and Marcus 1986; Giddens 1991, 1992) came a more reflective mood with some possibilities for self-examination for researchers and professionals and this was beginning to find some, although for some time limited, expression in psychotherapy. We were excited, not least because this promised a field of application for anthropology with an interdisciplinary collaboration, which would be progressive for both anthropology and psychotherapy. For anthropologists, this promised a framework not only for turning our attention onto ourselves and the cultural conditions, contexts and biases of our own assessments which were presented in ethnographies and other writings. Eventually, it also heralded a turn away from the Durkheimian influence which considers individual persons as mere expressions of social rules and norms to an approach which can recognise and attempt to capture the multitude ways of thinking and enacting agency outside, and in spite of, social constraints in all societies and social contexts. For psychotherapy, the collaboration promised a turn away from considering the internal world and life of individuals against a prototype, which reflects a particular theoretical, and sometimes hegemonic, set of developmental and psychological theories.

In the UK, this development was helped by supportive developments in legislation and in the political environment. The Commission for Racial Equality still existed then, and the Macpherson Report into the murder of Stephen Lawrence

(1999) with its emphasis on institutional racism was another progressive development. Institutionalised racism recognised the racism hidden in ideas and actions, which may be outside awareness, and it thus addressed the problem of racism not as an individual issue but as an issue of the very fabric of relationships, attitudes and ideology. It became unlawful to neglect to address these issues, and public institutions were required to demonstrate what was being done in order to address discrimination on grounds of 'colour, culture and ethnic origin' (Macpherson 1999: 28).[1] It seemed that these developments in thinking and in theories in the social sciences and in clinical mental health work (Gilroy 1987; Hall, 1996; Littlewood 1991; Kareem 1992; Thomas 1992), while not reflecting majority views, did hold out hope for stirrings on the margins. The Race Relations (Amendment) Act 2000 certainly assisted myself and my colleague in attempting to engage both with the institution in which we had been employed and with individual clinicians. Though even in this atmosphere affecting some changes was an uphill struggle and often felt more like 'whip' than 'carrot', the resistance being articulated in terms of established theory, training and tradition, but no doubt also sometimes reflecting deep personal prejudice.

What seemed to hold a promise of progress in race relations in the UK has not materialised. The number of racist incidents reported to the police have increased since the 1990s. This has risen from 10,997 in 1993 to 51,187 in 2011 (Burnett 2012: 92). During this period the geography and profile of racism has also changed. The intensity and number of attacks have moved from the inner city to rural areas, and in the criminal justice system racist incidents are increasingly being classified and reframed as 'hate crimes'. Burnett explains the implications:

> what the amalgamation of hate crime definitions into the workings of the state has done is to avert the gaze from the world to the individual. 'Hate crime' displaces racism ... from the social (and political) to the psychological – and thereby resolves the state from institutionalised racism.
>
> *(Burnett 2013: 13)*

This is a racialisation of politics combined with a personification of racism (Giroux 2004: 57), which is characteristic of neoliberalism in which a continuous fragmentation of ever new subject positions, through which individuals and the informational power they represent can be capitalised and tied to profit, and attached and reattached in ever new combinations. Neoliberalism thus focuses on individuals rather than collectives and this also implies a different role for the state and its various institutions. McFalls and Pandolfi refer to Foucault's final five lectures (Foucault 2008) and conclude that for Foucault neoliberalism is a therapeutic mode of government. This is:

> one that legitimises its authority with claims of benevolence, of expertise, and even of empowerment of those whose conduct it guides. Whether it be civil society or the entrepreneurial individual, the neoliberal subject ideally takes

charge of its life through a panoply of practices of the self from self-help and self-reliance to self-marketing and self-governance.

(McFalls and Pandolfi 2014: 173)

At the beginning of this chapter I applauded the move away from social determinism which the rapprochement between anthropology and psychotherapy afforded and which also was spurred on by the turn to 'the self' and 'self-reflection' in social anthropology in the last decades of the 20th century. I am now pointing to a contrary and more invidious process, which has changed the race relations in the UK[2] over the last 25 years, and which has exacerbated the extent of abuse and discrimination while at the same time concealing this in an ideology of individualism and identity politics. Indeed, I am profoundly sceptical about whether I will see progress in intercultural psychotherapy during my working life. Some reasons for this relate to contemporary politics, but others more clearly to a disquiet about the direction of travel in my own professional field. It is to this I now turn. I am a systemic psychotherapist (also sometimes referred to as a family therapist) and I shall first provide a brief description of the problems in relation to intercultural psychotherapy in the field of systemic psychotherapy as I see these, and then go on to a piece of clinical work. I will highlight the cross-cultural tensions and difficulties bearing in mind the processes and developments in social science and in society generally outlined above. In conclusion I shall provide some general reflections.

Cross-cultural systemic psychotherapy

At first glance it would seem that the situation with respect to race relations in the institution in which I work has improved since I began working there just after the implementation of the Race Relations (Amendment) Act of 2000. There are more clinicians from minority backgrounds employed and the groups of students we teach are more culturally and racially diverse. This snapshot is deceptive. For example, as is generally the case in the NHS, no senior managers from Black or minority backgrounds have been appointed (Kline 2014). While this may seem to be a concern, little new thinking or understanding has emerged to address the complexity of this situation. Similarly, while some clients from minority backgrounds are being treated, the client population is overwhelmingly white, British or European, and often metropolitan middle class from the locality surrounding the clinic, and treatments offered generally make few concessions to alternative outlooks and worldviews. The communication with persons from poor, immigrant or refugee ethnic minority populations takes place very much from the premise of particular frames of reference used by UK mental health and psychotherapy professionals, their theoretical frameworks, their training and guidelines such as those provided by NICE as evidence-based practice issued by government. In this context it is virtually impossible to judge the extent of 'symbolic violence' (Bourdieu and Passeron 1990) enacted through the structures and values of UK mental health services, about which individual clients or patients may have little awareness and consequently little ability to protest against (Maitra and Krause 2015).

Systemic psychotherapy is a comparatively new discipline in psychotherapy. It derives from the pioneering work of Bateson as an anthropologist and his subsequent involvement with cybernetics (Krause 2007) as well as from clinicians, psychiatrist and psychologist, during the 1960s and before, finding working with individuals by themselves limiting and instead beginning to work with families including individual family members in the consulting room. In brief, the idea was that communication and behaviour in families contribute to and in some instances maintain the symptoms experienced by individual members. By aiming to help family members know new things about each other or understand each other in new ways and by working with them on how to communicate differently the problem may become more bearable and in some instances disappear. There are overtones of the social functionalism so well known to social anthropologists,[3] and the view from the therapy room or rather from the observation room (systemic psychotherapists are well known for working with one-way mirrors through which supervision is live or members of a team actively participates in the therapy process) generally was one of the 'here and now'. If families could be helped to experience something which was different from the usual pattern in the therapy room this may encourage a change, and a new pattern may give rise to new communications and different ways of relating at home.[4] This also meant that in this first phase of the discipline, while therapists might have been interested in the history and development of individual persons in relationship with others and in the history of symptoms, the wider context and the social ideologies and processes which were the contexts of the lives of persons and families were not of primary interest.[5] This had normative implications and alternative cultural outlooks and theories rarely entered the therapist's thinking, except in those instances, which were few and far between, when the therapist him or herself came from a minority background.

With the postmodern and textual turn in social science and in therapies generally the position of the systemic psychotherapist also shifted. The therapist now considered herself to be part of rather than outside the system and the processes in the therapy room and meaning, which previously had been less contested, now came to be seen to be generated in language through conversations which were seen as intersubjectively constructed or co-constructed (Anderson and Goolishan 1986). This placed the emphasis on an agreement between persons that they are experiencing the same event in the same way or at least in enough of the same way that this can be mutually understood. 'Social organisation is the product of social communication, rather than social communication being a product of social organisation', so wrote Anderson and Goolishan in 1988 (278). Apart from the problem of emphasising linguistic aspects of meaning, this position ignored the problem of clients and therapists speaking different languages and how this might be negotiated (Krause 2012). This shift has opened the way for several approaches in systemic psychotherapy, such as constructionist, narrative and dialogical ones to emerge (McNamee 1992; White 1997; Seikulla et al. 2003; Rober 2005; Pearce 2007), all of which one way or another build on how persons (including the therapist) together make meaning. While persons and individuals are subjects of their actions, of their communications and of their words, and while an emphasis on this points to important aspects of the therapeutic process and the therapists' responsibilities, there are other aspects to meaning making and subjectivity. I am thinking of what has emerged from patterns and meanings in the past, from history and from the longstanding social structures and ideological outlooks, which influence and have influenced, although not determined, persons and their relationships and their interactions. Some of these dimensions are outside the awareness of individuals influenced by them and if the possibility that alternative dimensions, histories, dispositions and meanings cannot be held in mind by the therapist, they will disappear from view. This, it seems to me, is the central challenge of all psychotherapy, but particularly of cross-cultural psychotherapy.

The social ggrraaacceeesss

In the UK, the manner in which cross-cultural and race relations are approached in systemic psychotherapy has been enormously influenced by what has come to be referred to as the social ggrraaacceeesss[6] (Burnham 1992, 1993, 2012; Roper-Hall 1998; Burnham and Harris 2002). This idea began as a mnemonic called 'DISGRRACCE' (Disability, I, Sexuality, Gender, Race, Religion, Age, Class, Culture, Ethnicity) and Burnham describes how the aim was to remind himself of processes of discrimination: 'In a teaching session, I might put the mnemonic across the top of the board as a visual context/guideword for myself and the participants' (Burnham 2012: 140).

Given the emphasis in systemic psychotherapy on individuals in their relationships, their choices and the co-construction in the moments of therapeutic encounter and the aversion towards the weight of unconscious dispositions, it is easy to understand why in systemic psychotherapy the addressing of difference and diversity has taken place within the frame of identity politics. In order to take a distance from the negative overtones of the mnemonic, the idea later became associated with 'gracefulness' and the term 'social' was added to emphasise the social construction of these aspects of experience. New items were also added to the list, the last one, I believe, being 'spirituality', and a distinction has also been introduced between *social* and *personal* ggrraaacceeesss (Burnham 2012: 140) in order to draw attention to social contexts as well as to the way individual experiences are shaped in those contexts. From the point of view of the relationship between institutional racism and identity politics, this distinction is of interest and I shall return to it below. In a recent publication Burnham himself has further developed a more subtle approach by looking at the mnemonic from the positions of four quadrants constructed by two axes, a horizontal one from voiced to unvoiced and a vertical one from visible to invisible (Burnham 2012: 146). For example, from the visible/unvoiced position visible aspects in the room such as a religious symbol worn by a person may not be mentioned or talked about. As

Burnham suggests the most difficult quadrant is the invisible/unvoiced quadrant, and he suggests that perhaps there are some issues in the 'taken-for-granted' experience of clients, about which therapists best refrain from enquiring (Burnham 2012).

The mnemonic was an aid memoire to Burnham himself and is generally used as a tool to flag up or remind us of the dimensions of the differences listed. While this may seem reasonable enough, the mnemonic conceals other more thorny problems for cross-cultural psychotherapy practice. For example, the very idea of a list begs the question of the relationship between the different items on the list, between the different members of the category – in this case, the 'list of differences'. There is a well-known and oft quoted maxim in systemic psychotherapy derived from Bateson's interest in Russell's Theory of Logical Types, which states that

> the class cannot be a member of itself nor can one of the members *be* the class, since the term used for the class is of a *different level of abstraction* – a different Logical Type – from terms used for its members.
>
> *(Bateson 1972: 202)*

Unless we think of all the items in the list as being of the same order, this list presents us with a muddle. Is 'culture' really of the same order as 'age' and 'gender'? What does the idea of a list of social ggrraaacceeesss tell us about how 'culture' and 'ethnicity' are conceptualised? What are 'culture' and 'ethnicity' in this list? Rattansi commented that the categories of 'race' and 'ethnicity' have been based on the 'misleading assumption that it is possible to produce a singular, uncontestable, objective and accurate representation of reality' (1992: 34) and the problem with using ethnicity as a variable at the same level as 'age' and 'gender' in quantitative cross-cultural psychiatric research is well recognised (Bhopal 2001). A Google group of systemic psychotherapists debated this issue a couple of years ago, but as far as I know there was no consensus, although some of us thought that 'culture' is the list or the class referred to and 'culture' therefore cannot be an item in it (Google group, Maitra and Krause 2015; Pocock 2012). Burnham clearly thinks that there is a relationship between the different items on the list, when he suggests that the mnemonic may also be conceptualised as a 'collide-scope', which conveys 'non-symmetrical, sometimes colliding visions of relations between socially produced differences' (2012: 144). If this refers to intersectionality (hooks 2014; Butler 2015), that is to say the way different processes of domination intersect at particular points in time for particular individuals and at particular locations, then this is a starting point which the social ggrraaacceeesss do not overtly encourage us to interrogate. To do this we will have to go 'beyond or behind' the list to the processes behind the items on it and the way these intersect in particular contexts and at particular points in time. This seems to be exactly what Burnham discourages in his latest comments on the mnemonic.

The approach indicated in the use of the social ggrraaacceeesss appears to accord well with Foucault's 'therapeutic government'. The list demonstrates and encourages interest and care in the individual psychological make-up and identity of clients and patients, but does not encourage interest in the processes behind them, processes which in part have constituted the background to the way that identity has emerged. The list may encourage some awareness of discriminatory processes in the present, but does not pay attention to the past. Leaving out the past excludes both a history of oppressive practices (implicating colonisation) and a history of traditions, outlooks and worldviews, which may be very different from those therapists expect. Neither of these aspects of identity and subjectivity may be consciously available, or available in full, to patients and clients. Of course, the details may not be available to therapists either, but excluding these dimensions suggests that we do not know or even acknowledge that they exist. Perhaps this could not be different, since this mnemonic has emerged out of a neoliberal context and therapists are no more immune than are other persons from the influence of dominant ideologies. However, if we are serious about working towards an equitable and just mental health service such as was pioneered at Nafsiyat, *we* cannot afford to ignore what these dominant ideologies leave out.

I now turn to describe and consider two examples from a piece of work of such processes. These processes are not on the surface and therefore persons might have difficulty in speaking about them directly. They nevertheless point to the potential institutionalised discrimination inherent in our own ideologies and in particular embedded in an uncritical acceptance of identity politics.

A Bangladeshi family

Khadija (aged 11) was referred to the child and adolescent mental health service (CAMHS) in which I work as a family therapist (Afuape and Krause 2016) by the head teacher at her primary school because she was withdrawn, distracted and not learning. She was also reported to sleepwalk. She lived with her father, Mr Islam, and her elder brother, Ahmed (14). Mr Islam was born in Bangladesh and his parents had arranged a marriage for him with a British Bangladeshi woman after which he had come to live in the UK where he first worked in a restaurant. He was now out of work and his wife, Khadija's and Ahmed's mother, had left the family two years earlier. Mr Islam's own parents had passed away, but two of his siblings lived in the UK and the children's maternal grandparents were living in the north of England. The children's mother had at first disappeared, but eventually her whereabouts became vaguely known, although she had had no contact with Khadija and had only spoken to Ahmed a few times on the phone. Much effort was made by the professionals in helping, encouraging and facilitating Khadija to make contact with her mother, but Khadija was adamant that she did not want to see her mother because she felt betrayed by her and thought that her father felt the same way. It had been difficult for the previous therapists to accept this and several sessions had been set up for Khadija and her mother. The mother met once with a therapist on her own but did not manage to attend any sessions with Khadija. Mr Islam said that he did not want to stop his children from seeing their mother, but he also did not hide his anger with his ex-wife and spoke about her with disdain in front of the children, whom he found difficult to look after. For example, he complained that being a Muslim he could not touch Khadija or her clothes because he never knew if she had been menstruating. Khadija mostly looked after herself and her clothes, and she also cooked and cleaned for her father and brother as well as for herself. Her father frequently slept on the floor next to Khadija, partly because he was worried about her sleepwalking but also because he himself felt worried and anxious. The professionals strongly disapproved of Mr Islam's attitudes and actions expecting him to show more restraint towards his ex-wife and more competence as a carer and, although they did not tell them so to their faces, he said that he felt they were questioning his way of life. In school both children were chided by other Bangladeshi children, referring to the inability of their father to keep his wife. Although therapeutic work with the mother was not possible, therapeutic work with the children was aimed at helping them speak about her in their individual sessions. This was in some contrast to what the adults around the two children said they wanted. After the family was passed to me, I met with Khadija fortnightly in her secondary school for over a year and although she was sometimes sad and sometimes angry with her mother, she generally did not want to talk about her. I also visited Khadija's father and brother in the home of her paternal uncle and his wife, where this aunt, who now was the nearest adult female relative to Khadija, pressed upon me the need for the family to leave the flat in which their mother's spirit still reigned. On the same occasion Mr Islam took me to one side to tell me about the physical ailments from which he was suffering, wondering whether this was sorcery practised by his ex-wife.

It became very difficult for Mr Islam when he announced that he was getting married in Bangladesh and that he would bring his new wife to live with him in London. Financially this put him in a difficult position, although eventually his brother and the extended family helped raise the sum needed in order to be able to apply for a visa and sponsor the new wife. Once Mr Islam had made this announcement the professionals involved with the children became worried that he was seeking to erase the children's biological mother from their lives, and this concern was again being perceived by Mr Islam as a questioning of his reasons for his actions and of his identity as a Bangladeshi man. After some time, Khadija's new stepmother arrived in the UK and in our sessions Khadija and I talked about the changes in her life which this event had brought about. Khadija explained that she addressed her father's wife as *mai* [7] while she referred to her own mother as *amma* and she was pleased that she could distinguish her stepmother from her biological mother in this way. She also spoke in our sessions about the relief of not having to cook and clean and no longer being the only one who worried about her father. Eventually, she began to talk about other things such as her friendships in school, music and the pressure of school tests. She was particularly keen to find ways of being Bangladeshi and Muslim in a way that suited her contemporary context. She said that she did not want to be a woman who only cooks and cleans, and she talked about friendships she had made with Christian girls. She also began to be interested in contacting her mother. At the same time Ahmed, who was still arguing with his father, had re-established occasional contact with his mother and was a bit more settled in school.

The processes behind identity

Mr Islam's outlook clashed with the opinions and ideas of the professionals involved in several ways to such an extent that the identities to which he referred as a 'father', 'husband', Bangladeshi man, 'brother', 'Muslim' at several stages of the therapy were on the verge of becoming points of misunderstanding and discrimination. The professional expectations of care and parenting (that ideas referring to purity and pollution should not interfere with a parenting function) and of attending to the needs of one's children (that children should be helped to process the loss of their mother) are not difficult to understand, because these expectations are implicit in modern mental health and social care systems. However, in this clash of outlooks, the rationale for Mr Islam's position could only be explained by a reference to a mistaken psychological outlook, which may in the end be portrayed as his views or the views of his community against those of mainstream UK professionals. It might be that there is a feeling that 'any view or outlook must be respected' while in reality this cannot be upheld against the institutional structures, theoretical frameworks and professional duties of the professionals involved in the case. I myself supported Mr Islam's desire for a remarriage to a Bangladeshi woman from Bangladesh, firstly, because of my view that wider social processes or chains become fixed at particular points and that these are articulated in specific ways in the lives of the persons in specific social contexts, and, secondly, from a position of bringing forth an appreciation of the constraints and possibilities inherent at these points (Das 1990) in order to facilitate the emergence of something new. In this case this meant understanding postcolonial political and economic relations not in an abstract way, but understanding the way these processes have impacted on the lives of this specific family, something about which the family may not be fully aware. It also meant taking seriously the 'theory' of relationships articulated by Mr Islam and the adults in the family.

I needed to understand the way labour from ex-colonies was recruited, the way Bangladeshi kinship networks have connected localities in the UK with specific localities in Bangladesh, in this case Sylhet, and the way these conditions have impacted on Mr Islam's family. Such marriages between spouses from Bangladesh and the UK have a long history dating back to the 1950s and 1960s when Bangladeshi men began to come to the UK to seek employment. Labourers tended to find work in restaurants and factories and this was of benefit both to the UK economy and to those men and families who were looking to improve their financial situation in Bangladesh. Workers sent money back to Bangladesh enabling families to buy land and build bigger houses (Gardner 2008). However, since the 1980s and 1990s the immigration pattern from Bangladesh into the UK has changed. This followed changes in the labour market as well as restrictions in UK immigration laws, which stipulated that only persons married to a British citizen should be granted residency in the UK. Whereas earlier in the immigration history of the Bangladeshi community in the UK it tended to be women and children who immigrated, the pattern now has changed to involve many more men. Because the Bangladeshi community had previously sent remittances back to Bangladesh, those families associated with the UK had become richer and it was, and still is, the dream of many Bangladeshi men to come to the UK. For many the only way of doing this is to marry a British Bangladeshi woman. The 'Londoni' (Gardner 2008) villages which have been built in Sylhet with remittances from overseas are manifestations of the desirability for some of being connected with the UK and for these connections to be thickened and consolidated by repeated chains of marriage and kinship relations. However, such marriages may pose a challenge to the parties concerned if they, as they often do, position each spouse structurally against the normative expectations of Bangladeshi patrilineal kinship (Gardner 2008; Callan, 2012). In patriliny, bodily substances from the father's side tend to be considered more important than those from the mother's, and fathers tend to be expected to have more power and control over family members than mothers (Krause 1998). This means that when men from Bangladesh marry British Bangladeshi women and settle in the UK, the expectations of how family life will develop may be, and often are, at odds with the social and political processes which have given rise to these events. The men expect to be the head of the family and in charge, their children belonging to their side and their families, whereas the women often speak fluent English and know much more about functioning in a cross-cultural context. This was the situation in which Mr Islam and his children found themselves. He did not consider that he and his ex-wife had equal rights to their children and possibly neither did she. It was therefore not surprising that the children in the family were orientated towards their father and his side of the family and were not encouraged to connect with their mother.

With respect to processes of identity formation there were, in this case, other suggestions indicating different outlooks from the way these processes may have been understood by mental health professionals in the UK. In South Asia generally ideas of personhood are considered to be created through exchanges of human substances such as semen, breast milk and blood as well as through non-human substances such as objects and food. This is one reason why Mr Islam was reluctant to touch his daughter's clothes, fearing that coming into contact with her menstrual blood would pollute him (Callan 2007). Within this outlook a person tends to be considered to be dividual (constituted of many different elements) rather than individual (a singular entity) (Marriott 1976; Daniel 1984; Busby 1997) with social processes, such as exchanges of things, food or emotions, taking place outside the body directly affecting the emotional and psychological processes inside (Krause 1989; Good 1977; Callan 2007, 2012). In keeping with these ideas Mr Islam expected that the mother of his children or her relatives could be practising sorcery against him either by burying things, in this case a *tabiz* (an amulet, a magic spell) in the ground near his house where he would pass by or by using some other physical substance as a medium through which she or they could pass evil wishes

(Callan 2012). If this was Mr Islam's outlook I would also expect that these ideas played a role in Khadija's and her brother's disposition towards their mother, even though they may not share these outlooks completely.

Concluding remarks

I do not myself share Mr Islam's point of view. Nor did I support Mr Islam out of respect for his identity, for his race, religion, culture, ethnicity and gender, etc. Nor from a conviction that he had a right to choose, since such a conviction would be naïve in the face of both the overt and hidden institutionalised discrimination against him currently and in the past on the basis of his way of life. I was also not naïve in thinking that I should rescue Khadija or that the best thing for Khadija was to follow her father's way of life, although I did think that there may be difficult conflicts about this. I was much more preoccupied with the stuckness of the situation and with how in this stuckness Mr Islam (and the children) could only lose out. In view of the longstanding colonial political and economic processes which have influenced and still constrain Mr Islam and his family and in view of the local (both in Bangladesh and in Bangladeshi communities in the UK) orientation and theories about (family) relationships, this stuckness I felt was articulated at this point with the involvement of CAMHS, where unthinkingly we could have (and maybe did in some ways) reproduced the institutionalised discrimination of which Mr Islam and his family had been victim so many times before. I could not avoid taking a position and I felt that the decision to support Mr Islam in arranging to remarry a Bangladeshi woman from Bangladesh could provide new conditions for new processes. This was because this position recognised the social and psychological constraints which he and his children were subject to as a result of both the contemporary patterns through which the colonial history was articulated and of an alternative psychological outlook, which again cannot have been unaffected by this same history (Callan 2007). In practical terms, this also provided a solution to a situation in which the children were placed in an impossible position. It provided more help and support for Mr Islam at home and a female companion for Khadija in the house and, it would also I hoped, allow both Ahmed and Khadija to be less preoccupied with their father's problems. Did this also provide a solution for Mr Islam's second wife and for Khadija's mother? I do not know, but I know that each of these women are positioned in the UK currently by processes which go beyond their identity and back to the institutionalised processes which have facilitated their current positions to emerge, and that these positions accordingly afford both constraints and possibilities for their personal lives. Perhaps there are some hints to what else might emerge in the way Khadija thought about her two mothers and the way she was able to engage with issues closer to the outlooks of other adolescents in her school.

The social ggrraaacceeesss may be a starting point, but do not in themselves help therapists gain an understanding of the complex intersections of social and institutional processes behind identity formation. Indeed, in the climate of cross-cultural identity politics, if they are thought about at all, these processes before and behind are often shamed or demonised, perhaps causing 'identity' to be set apart from the institutional processes which it implicates. No wonder it is easier now to address discrimination in the language of 'identity' rather than in terms of 'institutionalisation'. Without grasping the whole picture, or at least seeking to grasp this picture, in and out of awareness, systemic and other psychotherapists, working with families and social systems, cannot hope to contribute to the emergence of a better crosscultural world. I fear that, despite the legacy of Nafsiyat, as far as intercultural psychotherapy is concerned we have a long way to go.

Notes

1 My own post in the Tavistock and Portman NHS Foundation Trust was established in order to comply with this requirement. I, a white European social anthropologist/systemic psychotherapist was employed together with a Black Afro-Caribbean social worker as training and development consultants for race and equity.
2 The Commission for Racial Equality was abolished in 2004 and replaced by the Equality and Human Rights Commission. This has now been superseded by the Equalities Act of 2010.
3 Bateson's supervisor in social anthropology at Cambridge was Radcliffe-Brown, a well-known follower of Durkheim (Harries-Jones 1995).
4 These ideas are particularly associated with the structural approach to family therapy (Minuchin 1974).
5 There were exceptions. See for example the work of Boyd-Franklin (1989), Falicov (1995) and Minuchin's work with Black families in New York (Minuchin et al. 1967).
6 This stands for: Gender, Geography, Race, Religion, Age, Ability, Appearance, Class, Culture, Ethnicity, Education, Employment, Sexuality, Sexual orientation, Spirituality.
7 *Mai* means 'mother' and is commonly used among Hindus (in northern India, from Sanskrit *matri*/Hindi *mata*), although *ma* is also common among modern urban Bengali Hindus but may suggest class and rural/urban differences. *Amma* is more common among Muslims in Bangladesh, but is also the 'norm' among Hindus all over southern India. Khadija clearly pointed out to me that she used these two terms as a way of differentiating her two mothers. She also thought that she was not expected to make such differentiation.

References

Afuape, T. and Krause, I.-B. (2016) *Urban Child and Adolescent Mental Health Services: A Responsive Approach*. London: Routledge.
Anderson, H. and Goolishan, H. (1986) Problem Determined Systems: Towards Transformation in Family Therapy. *Journal of Strategic and Systemic Therapies*, 5: 1–13.
Anderson, H. and Goolishan, H. (1988) Human Systems as Linguistic Systems: Preliminary and Evolving Ideas about the Implications for Clinical Theory. *Family Process*, 27: 371–393.
Bateson, G. (1972) *Steps to an Ecology of Mind: Collected Essays in Anthropology, Psychiatry, and Epistemology*. London: Jason Aronson.
Bhopal, R. (2001) Racism in Medicine. *British Medical Journal*, 7301: 1503–1504.
Bourdieu, P. and Passeron, J.C. (1990) *Reproduction in Education, Society and Culture*. London: SAGE.

Boyd-Franklin, N. (1989) *Black Families in Therapy: A Multisystemic Approach*. New York: Guilford Press.
Burnett, J. (2012) After Lawrence: Racial Violence and Policing in the UK. *Race and Class*, 54(1): 91–98.
Burnett, J. (2013) Britain: Racial Violence and the Politics of Hate. *Race and Class*, 54(4): 5–21.
Burnham, J. (1992) Approach-Method-Technique: Making Distinction and Creating Connections. *Human Systems*, 3: 3–26.
Burnham, J. (1993) Systemic Supervision: The Evolution of Reflexivity in the Context of the Supervisory Relationship. *Human Systems*, 4: 349–381.
Burnham, J. (2012) Developments in Social ggrraaacceeesss: Visible-Invisible and Voiced-Unvoiced. In I.-B. Krause (ed.), *Culture and Reflexivity in Systemic Psychotherapy: Mutual Perspectives*, 139–162. London: Karnac.
Burnham, J. and Harris, Q. (2002) Cultural Perspectives in Supervision. In D. Campbell and B. Mason (eds), *Perspectives on Supervision*, 21–41. London: Karnac.
Busby, C. (1997) Permeable and Partible Persons: A Comparative Analysis of Gender and Body in South India and Melanesia. *Journal of Royal Anthropological Institute*, 3: 261–278.
Butler, C. (2015) Intersectionality in Family Therapy Training: Inviting Students to Embrace the Complexities of Lived Experience. *Journal of Family Therapy*, 37(4): 583–589.
Callan, A. (2007) What Else Do We Bengalis Do? Sorcery, Overseas Migration and the New Inequality in Sylhet, Bangladesh. *Journal of the Royal Anthropological Institute*, 13(2): 331–343.
Callan, A. (2012) *Patients and Agents: Mental Illness, Modernity and Islam in Sylhet, Bangladesh*. Oxford: Berghan Books.
Clifford, J. and Marcus, G.E. (1986) *Writing Culture: The Poetics and Politics of Ethnography*. Berkeley, CA: University of California Press.
Daniel, D.E. (1984) *Fluid Signs: Being a Person in the Tamil Way*. Berkeley, CA: University of California Press.
Das, V. (1990) Our Work to Cry: Your Work to Listen. In V. Das (ed.), *Mirrors of Violence. Communities, Riots and Survivors in South Asia*, 345–398. Delhi: Oxford University Press.
Falicov, C. (1995) Training to Think Culturally: A Multidimensional Comparative Framework. *Family Process*, 34: 389–399.
Foucault, M. (2008) *The Birth of Biopolitics: Lectures at the Collège de France 1973–1974*. New York: Picador.
Gardner, K. (2008) Keeping Connected: Security, Place and Social Capital in a 'Londoni' Village in Sylhet. *Journal of the Royal Anthropological Institute*, 14(3): 477–495.
Giddens, A. (1991) *Modernity and Self-Identity: Self and Society in the Late Modern Age*. Cambridge: Polity Press.
Giddens, A. (1992) *The Transformation of Intimacy: Sexuality, Love and Eroticism in Modern Society*. Cambridge: Polity Press.
Gilroy, P. (1987) *There Ain't No Black in the Union Jack: The Cultural Politics of Race and Nation*. Chicago, IL: Chicago University Press.
Giroux, H.A. (2004) *Terror of Neo-liberalism: Authoritarianism and the Eclipse of Democracy*. Boulder, CO: Paradigm Publishers.
Good, B. (1977) The Heart of What's the Matter: The Semantics of Illness in Iran. *Culture, Medicine and Psychiatry*, 1: 25–58.
Hall, S. (1996) Who Needs Identity? In S. Hall and P. du Gay (eds), *Questions of Identity*, 1–17. London: SAGE.
Harries-Jones, P. (1995) *A Recursive Vision: Ecological Understanding and Gregory Bateson*. Toronto: University of Toronto Press.
hooks, b. (2014 [1984]) *Feminist Theory: From Margin to Centre*. New York: Routledge.

Kareem, J. (1992) The Nafsiyat Intercultural Therapy Centre: Ideas and Experience in Intercultural Therapy. In J. Kareem and R. Littlewood (eds), *Intercultural Therapy: Themes, Interpretation and Practice*, 14–37. Oxford: Blackwell Scientific.

Kline, R. (2014) *The 'Snowy White Peaks' of the NHS: A Survey of Discrimination in Governance and Leadership and the Potential Impact on Patient Care in London and England*. London: Middlesex University.

Krause, I.-B. (1989) The Sinking Heart: A Punjabi Communication of Distress. *Social Science and Medicine*, 29: 563–575.

Krause, I.-B. (1998) *Therapy across Culture*. London: SAGE.

Krause, I.-B. (2007) Reading Naven: Towards the Integration of Culture in Systemic Psychotherapy. *Human Systems*, 18: 112–125.

Krause, I.-B. (2012) Culture and the Reflexive Subject in Systemic Psychotherapy. In I.-B. Krause (ed.), *Culture and Reflexivity in Systemic Psychotherapy: Mutual Perspectives*. London: Karnac Books.

Littlewood, R. (1991) Against Pathology: The New Psychiatry and Its Critics. *British Journal of Psychiatry*, 159: 696–702.

Macpherson, Sir William (1999) *The Stephen Lawrence Enquiry*. London: HMSO.

Maitra, B. and Krause, I.-B. (2015) *Culture and Madness: A Training Resource, Film and Commentary for Mental Health Professionals*. London: Jessica Kingsley.

Marriott, M. (1976) Hindu Transactions: Diversity without Dualism. In B. Kapferer (ed.), *Transaction and Meaning*, 109–142. Philadelphia, PA: Institute for the Study of Human Issues.

McFalls, L. and Pandolfi, M. (2014) Parrhesia and Therapeusis: Foucault on and in the World of Contemporary Neoliberalism. In J. Faubion (ed.), *Foucault Now: Current Perspectives on Foucault Studies*, 168–187. Cambridge: Polity Press.

McNamee, S. (1992) Reconstructing Identity: The Communal Construction of Crisis. In M. Gergen and S. McNamee (eds), *Therapy as Social Construction*, 186–199. London: SAGE.

Minuchin, S. (1974) *Families and Family Therapy*. London: Tavistock.

Minuchin, S., Montalvo, B., Guerny, B.G., Rossman, B.L. and Schumer, F. (1967) *Families of the Slums*. New York: Basic Books.

Pearce, Barnett W. (2007) *Making Social Worlds: A Communication Perspective*. Oxford: Blackwell.

Pocock, D. (2012) Objectification, Recognition and the Intersubjective Continuum. In I.-B. Krause (ed.), *Culture and Reflexivity in Systemic Psychotherapy: Mutual Perspectives*, 71–90. London: Karnac.

Race Relations (Amendment) Act (2000). London: Home Office Communication Directorate.

Rattansi, A. (1992) Changing the Subject? Racism, Culture and Education. In J. Donald and A. Rattansi (eds), *Race, Culture and Difference*. London: SAGE.

Rober, P. (2005) The Therapist's Self in Dialogical Family Therapy: Some Ideas about the Not-Knowing and the Therapist's Inner Conversation. *Family Process*, 44: 477–495.

Rober-Hall, A. (1998) Working Systemically with Older People and Their Families who Have 'Come to Grief'. In P. Sutcliffe, G. Tufnell and U. Cornish (eds), *Working with the Dying and Bereaved: Systemic Approaches to Therapeutic Work*, 177–206. London: Macmillan.

Seikulla, J., Arnkil, T. and Erikson, E. (2003) Postmodern Society and Social Networks: Open and Anticipation Dialogue in Network Meetings. *Family Process*, 42: 185–203.

Thomas, L. (1992) Racism and Psychotherapy: Working with Racism in the Consulting Room – an Analytic View. In J. Kareem and R. Littlewood (eds), *Intercultural Therapy: Themes, Interpretation and Practice*, 133–145. Oxford: Blackwell Scientific.

White, M. (1997) *Narratives of Therapists' Lives*. Adelaide: Dulwich Centre.

2

WHO'S BEING ASSESSED?

Post-modernism and intercultural therapy assessments: a synergetic process

Oye Agoro

The first meeting between client and therapist generally involves a meeting of different cultural values and belief systems. This can include different gender identities, sexualities, classes, age sets and religious beliefs. Counselling and psychotherapy have been identified as having their values and theoretical roots in Western, intellectual traditions (Fanon 1965; Kareem and Littlewood 1992; Moodley and Palmer 2006; Mckenzie-Mavinga 2016), with Western epistemology being seen as phallocentric, patriarchal and masculinist, viewing the world from hierarchical, binary, oppositional (Derrida 1967; Irigaray 1985) and white supremacist lenses (Akbar 1996; Hill Collins 1990; hooks 1995; McClaurin 2001).

As a Black diasporic woman of Yoruba heritage, I know that the ethnic diversity in Britain today is the legacy of an imperial history. A history that included the emergence of capitalism from trans-Atlantic slavery and the colonisation of North America, along with the economic plunder, exploitation and genocide of peoples from Australasia, Africa, Asia and the Americas.

The struggle to resolve the contradiction between my commitment to social justice and my work as a therapist and supervisor has been an ongoing process. Integrating my awareness of how racism still affects the lives of Black/Asian/Minority/Ethnic/Refugee (BAMER) communities, in overt and subtle ways, and the underlying value biases at the root of counselling and psychotherapy, has been a complex process. The focus on social justice within counselling and psychotherapy is now more than just a preferred value system but a professional and ethical responsibility (British Association for Counselling and Psychotherapy 2016).

First meetings with clients are pivotal points, determining which clients gain access to counselling and psychotherapy services and the direction that future therapeutic work will take. Traditionally, initial consultations have primarily been seen as an opportunity for practitioners to make assessments about a client's pathology; devising case formulations within the wider framework of medical classifications as outlined by the Diagnostic and Statistical Manual of Mental Disorders; making clinical interpretations based on meta-narratives, such as personality archetypes, attachment or object relations theories, etc. However, when a client and therapist meet for the first time, it is a multifaceted process. With clients making their own assessments about our values as practitioners, based on our physical appearance, gender presentation, observable cultural markers, and the way we use language and conceptualise their narrative.

Postmodernism

Postmodernism can very broadly be described as a questioning of ideas, and a challenging of meta-narratives, with a focus on the deconstruction of power and the recognition of the importance of subjective experience (Foucault 2002; Lyotard 1979). Viewing counselling and psychotherapy through a postmodernist lens can help us to hold a critical awareness of how therapeutic theories are not objective or value free, but have emerged from Western philosophical thought, which holds very particular assumptions about the purpose of counselling and psychotherapy, and that beliefs about health and wellbeing are socially constructed (Freedman and Combs 1996; Gergen 2001; White 2011).

At the heart of a postmodernist therapeutic positioning is the importance of allowing clients to create and establish their own narrative, and an awareness of the position of power we hold as therapists. It can be argued that giving clients the opportunity to determine the direction of their own counselling and psychotherapy is the central foundation of any therapeutic alliance. In reality, this position requires a high level of personal awareness, and can be especially challenging when working with clients who hold different beliefs and values to our own. Significantly, an absence of this critical awareness will inevitably lead to a form of cultural imperialism despite our best intentions.

As clinical practitioners, we generally aim to create therapeutic spaces where we work collaboratively, using our therapeutic skills and knowledge in supporting clients to find their voice and narrative (White and Epston 1990). This is essentially the starting place of all good therapeutic practice. However, within the context of social justice, counselling and psychotherapy can be seen as being diminished without an active acknowledgement of the world we live in, and the way it shapes all our internal worlds.

Hearing a client's narrative in conjunction with having a critical awareness of the way socio- political and economic factors may be impacting on the client's life can help to provide a more holistic understanding of a client's experience and psyche, greatly enhancing the development of a therapeutic alliance.

Socio-political and economic framework

Socio-political and economic realities provide the backdrop to the narratives of our clients' lives, with inequalities being pervasive and manifesting in panoptic and intricate ways. Social inequalities such as ableism, ageism, classism, heteronormality, racism and sexism have become institutionalised and oppressive. Oppression has serious pathological consequences for our emotional, physical, spiritual and psychological wellbeing, with oppressive structures interacting with each other, creating complex dynamics and realities (David 2014; Hill Collins 1990; hooks 1984; Lorde 1984; Mckenzie-Mavinga 2016).

The brutal effects of inequalities are prevalent across the earth:

- The wealthiest 85 people in the world have more money than the poorest 3.5 billion people, with the poorest half of the earth's population owning 1 percent of the earth's wealth, and the richest 1 percent of the earth's population owning 45 percent of the earth's wealth (World Bank 2014).
- In 2015 65.3 million people around the world were forcibly displaced as a result of conflict and persecution (UNHCR 2015).
- In 2011, the UN reported that homophobic and transphobic violence has been recorded in every region of the world and ranges from murder, kidnappings, assaults and rapes, to psychological threats and arbitrary deprivations of liberty (United Nations 2011).
- In developing countries 80–90 percent of people with disabilities are unemployed, in industrialised countries the figure is between 50 and 70 percent (United Nations 2007). In the UK, an estimated 75 percent of those of working age with a mental health illness are unemployed (International Labour Organisation 2007).
- The World Health Organisation states: 'The world's most ruthless killer and the greatest cause of suffering on earth is extreme poverty' (1995).

An analysis of the causes of social inequality is a central theme in Marxist theory. Marxism outlines how the accumulation of capital in the hands of a few and the unequal distribution of the planet's resources have their roots in the capitalist mode of production. Marxists also contend that the control and exploitation of women for their reproductive value (Engels 1972), extreme social inequalities and a propensity towards conflict and warfare are deeply rooted in the dialectical forces within capitalism (Marx 1867).

Ignoring the socio-political and economic realities of our clients' lives leaves us vulnerable to reinforcing inequalities and oppression in society, by locating the consequences of structural inequalities within the individual rather than in the power structures which uphold dominant cultural hegemony.

Gramsci, a Marxist philosopher, described cultural hegemony as the invisible way in which those with wealth and privilege manipulate culture so that their worldviews and beliefs are imposed on the rest of society and become the dominant norm that functions to protect the interests of the privileged (Gramsci 1999; Hall 1983).

Internalised oppression

No understanding of inequalities and oppression from a therapeutic perspective can be complete without an understanding of internalised oppression. Internalised oppression is the process where we internalise and act out negative stereotypes and myths about ourselves which are promoted by dominant cultural hegemony (Fanon 1967; Lipsky 1997; David 2014). This process results in feelings of self-hatred, low self-esteem and false negative stereotypes becoming self-fulfilling prophecy. The way we consciously and subconsciously act out dominant discourses around ableism, ageism, class, heteronormality, patriarchy and racism are complex and diverse. Examples of internalised oppression include the following.

Shadism/colourism

The acceptance and acting out of white–racial skin colour hierarchies in BAMER communities, where lighter skin tones are admired and coveted – consciously or unconsciously – because they symbolise the colour of colonial rulers, with lighter skin tones seen as more beautiful, and embodying ruling hegemony, and stereotypical associations around whiteness assuming inherent qualities: purity, intelligence and civilisation, etc. In comparison, darker skin tones are seen as being negative, inferior, a marker of being primitive, dirty, uncivilised and sexually provocative, etc. One of the manifestations of shadism and colourism throughout the world can be seen in the use of skin-whitening products. Seventy-seven percent of Nigerian women, 59 percent in Togo, 50 percent in the Philippines and 45 percent in Hong Kong use skin-whitening products (Mercury Project 2010). The World Health Organization has linked skin-whitening products to skin scarring, skin rashes, kidney failure, anxiety and depression (David 2014).

Black on Black violence

In 2010, Scotland Yard statistics show that in the UK Black men are twice as likely to be victims of inner-city violent crime, with police identifying the majority of inner-city crime as being committed by Black men (Camber 2010). The significant levels of Black on Black male violence in the UK and US have been linked to the internalisation and glorification of Black male stereotypes, often characterised as criminal, violent, aggressive and masculinist (hooks 1995; Bryant 2011; Mckenzie-Mavinga 2016; Wallace 1979). As a result of fellow group members being seen as inferior, anger and rage are directed horizontally at other group members as opposed to the dominant group (David 2014; Bailey et al. 2014; Freire 1970; Lipsky 1997).

Overworking

Marginalised group members overworking to be better or to gain acceptance from the dominant group.

Contempt for one's own group

'Slut shaming' – denigrating women who feel sexually empowered by being sexually free or liberal with their bodies. People of Black African heritage feeling disgust and revulsion about natural afro hair.

Rigid gender identity and sexuality – suppression of sexuality

Intimate sexual relationships being consciously and unconsciously determined by the enactment of white patriarchal bourgeois family values. Typically embracing heterosexual gender stereotypes characterised by binary dynamics around dominant/submissive and masculine/feminine. People of all sexualities feeling unable to have emotionally intimate or sexual relationships even though they desire it.

Uncritical acceptance of capitalism

Being enslaved to consumerism, and the accumulation of money and material goods being seen as the primary marker of self-worth – 'bling culture', 'ballerism'.

Passing

The denial or hiding of disability, sexuality, age or class to avoid discrimination. Examples of passing include light-skinned African Americans passing for white during segregation to gain access to jobs and other opportunities, people with mental health difficulties hiding their experiences due to fear of stigmatisation, LGBT people remaining in the closet due to fear of being marginalised and persecuted, working-class people adopting middle-class accents to disguise their class origins to avoid negative class stereotyping.

Withdrawal from learning

The withdrawal from learning and education due to the internalisation of dominant intellectual stereotypes about one's own group's educational and learning ability due to wider disability, class, ethnic and gender biases, such as 'chav' cultural stereotypes (Jones 2016).

Passive acquiescence

Being passive in response to inequality, living lives of unrealised potential (Watermeyer and Gorgens 2014), reflecting the subjugation and disempowerment that can occur under oppression.

Internalised domination

Internalised oppression is inextricably linked with internalised domination – the reverse process. Internalised domination describes how members of dominant privileged groups adopt and accept the denigration, subjugation and marginalisation of groups as natural and inevitable (Hitchcock 2002; Memmi 1957; Routhenberg 2002; Tappan 2006). More recently, microaggressions (Pierce 1974; Sue 2010) have emerged as a term to describe the subtle way dominant groups repeatedly affirm stereotypes without meaning to cause offence. For example, on many occasions I have been told that 'you don't act like a normal Black person' and, when I was younger, 'you're pretty for a dark-skinned girl'. I believe these statements were intended to be compliments. I experienced these comments as hurtful. Generally, if I express my feelings of upset and anger about these types of comments, I am invariably told that I am being hostile, oversensitive about race and being a woman.

The interconnected nature of institutional oppression and internalised oppressions can result in most of us unconsciously and or consciously moving in and out of re-enacting positions of internalised domination and oppression in dynamic and complex ways.

Internalised dominance survival strategies

Vanissar Tarakali outlines how there are identifiable strategies adopted by those in privileged positions and those experiencing oppression. Internalised dominance strategies include denial, dissociation, numbness, being unaware of oppression, defensiveness, attacking and blaming marginalised groups, refusal to take responsibility for oppression, self-absorption and avoidance of marginalised groups.

Internalised oppression survival strategies

Internalised oppression survival strategies can often include the following: appeasing, caretaking of dominant members, staying silent or attempting invisibility, withdrawal and isolation from dominant group members, isolation, spacing out, disassociating, numbing, hypervigilant scanning and interpreting everything in the social environment as a threat (Tarakali 2010).

The consequences of oppression are increasingly being understood as a trauma (Alleyne 2005; Duran and Duran 1995; McKenzie-Mavinga 2016; Sue and Sue 2003), and in some cases the trauma is intergenerational and historical. Oppression trauma is a social trauma that deeply impacts on the psyche of the individual and affects the wellbeing of whole communities. Internalised historical traumas have been linked to turning victims of oppression into perpetrators of aggression and violence, as a pathological survival strategy (hooks 2001; Duran and Duran 1995). Illustrations of this include female genital mutilation, Black on Black violence and misogyny in male rap/hip-hop music – misogynoir (Bailey, 2010).

A lack of a historical analysis of the roots of oppression being located in wider societal structures will inevitably lead to victim blaming, further traumatisation for the client and an exacerbation of internalised oppression and collusion with the perpetuation of structural inequalities.

Bringing an understanding of oppression and internalised oppression into therapeutic work and first encounters with clients can have a significant impact on the way we conceptualise a client's distress. Controvertibly, many presentations of distress, such as depression and self-harming within marginalised populations, can be viewed as an unambiguous expression of oppression.

Intersectionality

Thinking about structural social inequalities within a fluid and dynamic framework, allowing for an understanding of the interconnectedness of power structures, instead of seeing them as binary or hierarchical, can be paramount in gaining a deeper understanding of our clients' lives and experiences. Having critical awareness of the interconnection of institutional, interpersonal and internalised oppression can enable us to deconstruct these mechanisms in our clinical practice. This is illustrated in the following case study.

Shazia and Siobhan

Shazia, a 17-year-old British Pakistani woman, is referred for counselling by her GP. Shazia has a history of insomnia, depression, anxiety, self-harming by cutting and has recently been diagnosed with polycystic ovary syndrome (PCOS). PCOS is a health condition that can cause a range of symptoms connected to elevated hormonal levels. Counselling has been offered as a treatment option to support the management of her PCOS symptoms, depression and self-harming.

During Shazia's first meeting with her counsellor – Siobhan, a 30-year-old white Irish female counsellor – Shazia describes the hopelessness and despair she feels about her appearance. Shazia is wearing a beautiful turquoise shalwar kameez, is dark skinned and has heavy hair growth on her cheeks, upper lip and chin. She has experienced relentless bullying and harassment at school, which has led to frequent absences and poor GCSE results. Shazia attends a prestigious ethnically diverse school in a predominantly middle-class area in an inner city. She previously loved school and had aspirations of becoming a lawyer. Shazia tells Siobhan that the support of her family, especially her mother, sisters and grandmother, has helped her to cope with her situation. Nevertheless, Shazia talked about having no hope for her future, and how at times is only able to release her overwhelming feelings by cutting her arms. Shazia expressed guilt and shame about her family's fear that her appearance will make it difficult to find a husband. Shazia lives with her mother, father and grandmother and is the youngest daughter, with two older sisters and brothers. Shazia comes from a Muslim family, her great grandparents having migrated to the UK via Pakistan in the late 1960s as a result of being displaced by the Partition of India.

Siobhan's initial thoughts about Shazia's difficulties centred around how therapy could support Shazia to stabilise her symptoms, along with increasing her self-esteem, with the aim of empowering her to take more responsibility in managing the PCOS by shaving or using hair-removal products. In thinking about the underlying causes of Shazia's distress, Siobhan reflects further about Shazia's appearance as a woman and wonders if her appearance may be symbolic of a deeper gender pathology about her identity as a woman. Siobhan also thinks about Shazia's mother and sisters, and starts to hypothesise that there may be a deficit or dysfunction within the family given that her mother and sisters are not supporting Shazia to remove her facial hair, which Siobhan feels is the cause of her difficulties.

Siobhan stops and checks herself. She thinks about Western stereotypes around femininity. Siobhan feels uncomfortable but consciously acknowledges the way she has internalised the dominant stereotypes about being a woman, and the personal pressure she herself feels to shave her legs – despite having fine blonde hair – in order to gain acceptance as a woman from her friends and family.

Siobhan begins to wonder if the bullying that Shazia has experienced at school may have its roots in sexism, racism and Islamophobia. Siobhan revises her initial case formulation and decides a more holistic and emphatic approach to understanding Shazia's difficulties would be therapeutically beneficial. Rather than solely focusing on ways that Shazia can better manage her symptoms by replacing negative thoughts and using relaxation techniques to reduce anxiety and improve sleep, Siobhan starts by tentatively initiating a conversation with Shazia – which allows for an exploration of how Shazia feels about being a young woman of Pakistani descent in Britain with coarse facial hair – within a wider context of acknowledging how sexism, racism and Islamophobia could be impacting on Shazia's life. This positioning allows Shazia the opportunity to establish a narrative that may be in opposition to stereotypes about being an Asian woman in Britain; along with providing a space to name how interconnected inequalities in society may be causing or contributing to Shazia's distress.

By moving away from a conceptualisation of Shazia's difficulties being located within her internal world and caused by a medical condition, Siobhan's revised formulation facilitates the externalisation of anger and rage related to injustice, rather than internalisation of anger, which allows for a collaborative discussion about the purpose of therapy. Siobhan's initial case formulation implicitly assumed hair removal as the desirable therapeutic outcome. Acknowledging the possible social inequalities impacting on Shazia's life also moves Siobhan away from a deficit- and pathology-focused interpretation of the relationship that Shazia has with her family.

Cultural competence

Cultural competence (Pederson 2000; Sue and Sue 1990, 2003) has been identified as a key skill when working cross-culturally. The key elements of cultural competence are seen as self-awareness, empathic knowledge and understanding of other cultures and conceptualisation of identity formation (Sue and Sue 1990, 2003). Our values and identities as practitioners can have a significant impact on how we see and understand client narratives. Awareness of the dominant cultural values within white Western ruling hegemony can be essential to ensuring that these values are not imposed on our clients without a conscious awareness or explicit agreement.

White cultural values

Having a conscious awareness of dominant cultural values can also facilitate an understanding that white cultural values are not normative or universal, and may help to ensure that these values are not automatically transmitted on clients, but negotiated. Although, there are inherent dangers in making broad generalisations about different cultures, as they can perpetuate mythical stereotypes. White western culture has been identified as having the following markers (Katz 1985):

- Rugged individualism – independence and autonomy are seen as desirable states and the individual seen as being in control of their own lives and environment.
- Competition – winning is everything: a win/lose dichotomy.
- Action orientation – emphasis on the mastering and control of nature, and an expectation that something must always be done in a situation.
- Communication – standard English, the importance of the written word, direct eye contact, limited physical contact and control of emotions.
- Time – adherence to rigid time; time being viewed as a commodity.
- Holidays – based on Christian religion, white history and male leaders.
- Protestant work ethic – working hard to bring success.
- Progress and future orientation – planning for the future and delayed gratification; value placed on continual improvement and progress.
- Emphasis on scientific method – objective rational linear thinking, cause and effect relationships, quantitative emphasis.
- Status and power – measured by economic possessions, credentials, titles and positions; the importance of owning goods, space and property.
- Family structure – the nuclear family is seen as the ideal unit, the male is breadwinner and head of the household, the female is the homemaker and subordinate to husband; patriarchal structure.
- Aesthetics – music and arts based on European cultures; women's beauty based on blonde, blue-eyed, thin and young; men's attractiveness based on athletic ability, power, economic status.
- Religion – belief in Christianity, no tolerance for deviation from single God.

Identity models

The racial identity models developed in America (Adler 1986; Atkinson et al. 1993; Bennett 1986; Cross 1991; Helms 1995; Rowe et al. 1994; Sue and Sue 2003) are a useful starting place for not only thinking about racial identity in the UK, but that also have relevance when thinking about the multifaceted nature of identity within an intersectional understanding of society.

White identity model

Sue and Sue (2003) have developed a five-stage white identity model influenced by the work of Hardiman (1982), Helms (1995) and Carter (1990), which outlines a model for white identity formation under white supremacy. The model can be used as an important professional aid in developing awareness and self-reflective capabilities around identity and values. The model can also be used as a matrix or entrance into understanding identity issues when working with clients. I have adapted Sue and Sue's model to ensure greater relevance to the UK, as follows.

Conformity phase

At this phase of awareness white counsellors and clients are unlikely to see themselves in a racial or cultural way, but hold a belief that white British culture is superior and that other cultures are inferior. Typically, there is little awareness of their own beliefs and an assumption that their values are normal and universal. A common philosophy is that people are people and that difference is not important – 'colour blindness'. White counsellors generally deny BAMER clients' experiences of racism, and consciously or unconsciously act out racial dynamics based on white supremacy. White clients are likely to hold a preference for seeing white counsellors.

Dissonance: conflict phase

There is an increasing realisation of one's own cultural bias and recognition that white cultural values play an important part in oppressing minorities. Rationalisation is often used to exonerate personal inactivity in combating racism and discrimination. White counsellors and clients are likely to experience conflict between appreciation for white British culture and awareness of discrimination. White counsellors may have difficulty in responding consistently to BAMER clients' experiences of discrimination, and may be vulnerable to using the therapeutic process with clients to work through feelings about their own white identity.

Resistance and immersion: 'white liberal'

There is a questioning of one's own racism and an increasing awareness of how racism operates and its pervasiveness in white British culture, along with a growing social political consciousness and acknowledgement of past personal collusion with racism. There is likely to be a tendency towards racial and cultural self-hatred and feeling ashamed of whiteness. White counsellors at this phase are prone to over-identify with BAMER clients and be preoccupied with issues relating to race and culture at the expense of everything else. The counselling relationship is likely to be paternalistic; counsellors may experience difficulties in setting appropriate boundaries as a result of anxiety about their own identity.

Introspection phase

There is a rethinking of what it means to be white and an acknowledgement of past participation in racism and the benefits gained from white privilege. White counsellors will have an awareness that racism is an integral part of British society along with an acceptance of whiteness and a desire to combat oppression. White counsellors at this phase are able to create a therapeutic environment where BAMER clients' experiences of racism are heard and acknowledged. They are also likely to have a high level of self-awareness about their own cultural identity, but experience a high level of anxiety and loss, 'existential anxiety'.

Integrative awareness: 'freedom' phase

White counsellors and clients have an understanding of 'self' as a cultural and racial being, along with an awareness of the political and social nature of racism. White counsellors at this phase are likely to have an appreciation of racial and cultural diversity and commitment to the eradication of racism within counselling and wider society. During this stage, a non-racist, white, British identity and an ease around members of different groups emerges.

BAMER identity model

I have adapted here the minority identity models outlined by Cross (1995) and Atkinson et al. (1993) in order to relay a model of BAMER identity formation in Britain, as follows.

Conformity phase

BAMER counsellors and clients are unlikely to see themselves in a cultural or racial way, but are likely to have a preference for white British values. This phase is characterised by downplaying one's own cultural and racial heritage, combined with a strong desire to emulate and assimilate white British culture and institutions, along with depreciating attitudes towards self and other in the same cultural and racial group. BAMER counsellors may prefer to work with white clients and can be punitive to BAMER clients. BAMER clients at this phase are likely to hold a preference to work with white counsellors.

Dissonance: conflict phase

There is increasing acknowledgement of one's own racial and cultural ancestry and an awakening of socio-political consciousness. There is a questioning of previous white identifications and the beginnings of viewing one's own cultural racial group positively. BAMER counsellors and clients may experience conflict between appreciation for their own cultural and racial heritage and a desire to confirm to white norms. BAMER counsellors may be vulnerable to using the therapeutic process with clients in a voyeuristic way to explore and work through their own feelings about cultural and racial identity.

Realisation and immersion phase

There is a complete surrender to the values of one's own cultural and racial group and a rejection of white dominant values. BAMER counsellors and clients are likely to have a negative attitude towards white culture and be inclined to romanticise their own cultural group. Typically, there may be a discomfort with cultural and racial difference and a difficulty in seeing or understanding other oppressions. At this phase shadism may be expressed consciously by a preference or attraction to dark skin tones. BAMER counsellors may experience difficulty in forming therapeutic alliances with white clients. BAMER clients are likely to prefer to see BAMER counsellors.

Introjection phase

There is comfort and security in one's own cultural and racial identity and the emergence of an assured BAMER identity. There is a questioning of previous hostility to white culture, white British culture is increasingly understood within the context of an historical past and present, and there is likely to be an appreciation and acceptance of some aspects of white culture. BAMER counsellors and clients are likely to use their anger about racial and cultural discrimination positively within their own social group.

Synergetic articulation and awareness: 'freedom' phase

BAMER counsellors and clients have a sense of fulfilment with their own cultural and racial identity, and have a positive regard towards themselves and their own cultural and racial group. Cultural and racial identity are likely to be seen as just one important aspect of one's life. There is likely to be a high level of personal autonomy along with an appreciation and respect for other cultural/racial groups. Characteristically, BAMER counsellors and clients will have a desire to eliminate all forms of oppression and be inclined to make alliances with members of dominant cultures who are committed to ending oppressions.

White and BAMER identity models can provide a starting place to facilitate reflection on the labyrinthian amalgamation of identities and dynamics that can take place between clients and counsellors from different age sets, classes, differing abilities, genders, sexualities and racial/cultural backgrounds.

Safeguarding

A significant part of many clinical assessment processes is an assessment of risk and safeguarding issues. Safeguarding and risk is often viewed from the perspective of clients being at risk to themselves or others, or clients being at risk from other people outside of the therapeutic setting. Safeguarding also includes the importance of having an awareness of institutional abuses in professional practice. This can be an important reference point in helping us to maintain ongoing vigilance in our own practice to ensure that we are not abusing clients by imposing inappropriate clinical assessments or cultural biases into our work.

Conclusion

This chapter advocates that first meetings with clients and the therapeutic process can be greatly enhanced by taking a 'postmodernist' position within a broader historical and structural understating of inequalities in society. I have also outlined the value of integrating an understanding of oppression, internalised oppression and domination along with intersectionality within therapeutic practice. Awareness of white cultural values and white/BAMER identity models have also been identified as key competencies when working cross-culturally and conducting first meetings with clients.

Aspiring to integrative and synergetic awareness in relation to identity across ableism, ageism, class, heteronormality, sexism and ethnicity/culture is a challenge and ongoing journey for all of us. My lived experience as a Black British African woman, intercultural therapist and clinical supervisor tells me that practitioners who are at a place of synergetic articulation and integrative awareness are more likely to work ethically across cultures. I believe we have a professional responsibility to ensure that the work we do does not uphold or collude with dominant cultural hegemony, and the social inequalities embedded in it. We can make a choice to work collaboratively and synergistically with our clients, proactively using our therapeutic skills and knowledge to deconstruct and help dismantle oppressive structures.

References

Adler, N.J. (1986) Cultural Synergy: Managing the Impact of Cultural Diversity. In *The 1986 Annual: Developing Human Resources*. San Diego, CA: University Associates.
Akbar, N. (1996) *Breaking the Chains of Psychological Slavery*. Tallahassee, FL: Mind Productions.
Alleyne, A. (2005) The Internal Oppressor: The Veiled Companion of External Racial Oppression. *Psychotherapist*, 26, Spring.
Atkinson, D.R., Thompson, C.E. and Grant, S.K. (1993) A Three-Dimensional Model for Counselling Racial/Ethnic Minorities. *Counselling Psychologist*, 21: 257–277.
Bailey, M. (2010) They Aren't Talking about Me. *The Crunk Feminist Collective. Where Crunk Meets Conscious and Feminism Meets Cool*, 14, March.
Bailey, T.-K.M., Williams W.S. and Favors, B. (2014) Internalized Oppression in the African American Community. In E.J.R. David (ed.), *Internalised Oppression: The Psychology of Marginalized Groups*. New York: Spencer Publishing.
Bennett, M.J. (1986) A Development Approach to Training for Intercultural Sensitivity. *International Journal of Intercultural Relations*, 10: 179–196.

British Association for Counselling and Psychotherapy (2016) *Ethical Framework for the Counselling Professions*. Lutterworth: BACP.
Bryant, W.W. (2011) Internalised Racism's Association with African American Male Youth's Propensity for Violence. *Journal of Black Studies*, 42(4): 690–707.
Camber, R. (2010) Black Men 'to Blame for Most Violent City Crime' ... but They're Also Victims. *Daily Mail*, 27 June.
Carter, R.T. (1990) The Relationship between Racism and Racial Identity among White Americans: An Exploratory Investigation. *Journal of Counselling and Development*, 69: 46–50.
Cross, W.E. (1991) *Shades of Black: Diversity in African American Identity*. Philadelphia, PA: Temple University Press.
Cross, W.E. (1995) The Psychology of Nigrescence: Revising the Cross Model. In J.G. Ponterotto, J.M. Casas, L.A. Suzuki, and C.M. Alexander (eds), *Handbook of Multicultural Counselling*. Thousand Oaks, CA: SAGE.
David, E.J.R. (ed.) (2014) *Internalised Oppression: The Psychology of Marginalized Groups*. New York: Springer.
Derrida, J. (1967) *Of Grammatology*. Baltimore, MD: Johns Hopkins University Press.
Duran, E. and Duran, B. (1995) *Native American Post-Colonial Psychology*. Albany, NY: State University of New York.
Engels, F. (1972) *The Origin of the Family, Private Property and the State*. New York: Pathfinder Press.
Fanon, F. (1967) *Black Skin, White Masks*. New York: Grove Press.
Foucault, M. (2002) *Archaeology of Knowledge*. London: Routledge.
Freedman, J. and Combs, G. (1996) *Narrative Therapy*. New York: W.W. Norton & Company.
Freire, P. (1970) *Cultural Action for Freedom*. Cambridge, MA: Harvard Educational Review Press.
Gergen, K. (2001) *Social Construction in Context*. London: SAGE.
Gramsci, A. (1999) *Prison Notebooks*. Edited and translated by Quentin Hoare and Geoffrey Nowell Smith. London: Elecbook.
Hall, S. (1983) *Cultural Studies 1983: A Theoretical History*. Durham, NC: Duke University Press.
Hardiman, R. (1982) White Identity Development: A Process Orientated Model for Describing the Racial Consciousness of White Americans. *Dissertation Abstracts International*, 43: 104A.
Helms, J.E. (1995) An Update of Helms's White and People of Colour Racial Identity Models. In J.G. Ponterotto, J.M. Casas, L.A. Suzuki, and C.M. Alexander (eds), *Handbook of Multicultural Counselling*. Thousand Oaks, CA: SAGE.
Hill Collins, P. (1990) *Black Feminist Thought: Knowledge, Consciousness, and the Politics of Empowerment*. New York: Routledge.
Hitchcock, J. (2002) *Lifting the White Veil: An Exploration of White American Culture in a Multicultural Context*. Roselle, NJ: Crandall, Dostie, and Douglass.
hooks, b. (1984) *Feminist Theory from Margin to Center*. New York: South End Press.
hooks, b. (1995) *Killing Rage: Ending Racism*. Harmondsworth: Penguin.
hooks, b. (2001) *Salvation*. London: Women's Press.
International Labour Organisation (2007) *Facts on Disability in the World of Work: The Right to Decent Work of persons with Disability*. Geneva: ILO.
Irigaray, L. (1985) *This Sex Which Is Not One*. New York: Cornell University Press.
Jones, O. (2016) *Chavs: The Demonisation of the Working Class*. London: Verso.

Kareem, J. and Littlewood, R. (1992) *Intercultural Therapy: Themes, Interpretations and Practice.* Oxford: Blackwell.

Katz, J. (1985) The Socio-Political Nature of Counselling. *Counselling Psychologist*, 13: 615–624.

Lipsky, S. (1997) *Internalized Racism*. Seattle, WA: Rational Island.

Lorde, A. (1984) *Sister Outsider: Essays and Speeches.* Trumansburg, NY: Crossing Press.

Lyotard, J.F. (1979) *The Post-Modern Condition.* Manchester: Manchester University Press.

Marx, K. (1867) *Capital: A Critique of Political Economy. Volume 1. Book One: The Process of Production of Capital.* Moscow: Progress.

McClaurin, I. (2001) *Black Feminist Anthropology.* New Brunswick, NJ: Rutgers State University.

Mckenzie-Mavinga, I. (2016) *The Challenge of Racism in Therapeutic Practice.* London: Palgrave.

Memmi, A. (1957) *The Colonizer and the Colonized.* Boston, MA: Beacon.

Mercury Project (2010) *Factsheet: Mercury in Skin Lightening Cosmetics.* Montpelier, VT: Author. Retrieved from: http://mercurypolicy.org/wp.content/uploads/2010/06skin creamfactsheet_may31_final.pdf

Moodley, R. and Palmer, S. (2006) Race, Culture and Other Multiple Constructions: An Absent Presence in Psychotherapy. In R. Moodley and S. Palmer (Eds), *Race, Culture and Psychotherapy: Critical Perspectives in Multicultural Practice.* London: Routledge.

Pederson, P.B. (2000) *A Handbooks for Developing Multi Cultural Competencies.* Alexandria, VA: American Counselling Association.

Pierce, C. (1974) Psychiatric Problems of the Black Minority. In S. Arieti (ed.), *American Handbook of Psychiatry*, 512–523. New York: Basic Books.

Routhenberg, P. (2002) *White Privilege: Essential Readings on the Other Side of Racism.* New York: Worth.

Rowe, W., Bennett, S. and Atkinson, D.R. (1994) White Racial Identity Models: Critique and Alternative Proposal. *Counselling Psychologist*, 22: 120–146.

Sue, D.W. (2010) *Microaggressions in Everyday Life. Race, Gender and Sexual Orientation.* New York: John Wiley.

Sue, D.W. and Sue, D. (1990) *Counselling the Culturally Different: Theory and Practice.* New York: Wiley.

Sue, D.W. and Sue, D. (2003) *Counselling the Culturally Diverse: Theory and Practice.* New York: John Wiley.

Tappan, M. (2006) Reframing Internalised Oppression and Internalised Domination: From the Psychology to the Sociocultural. *Teachers College Record*, 10, October:2115–2144.

Tarakali, V. (2010) Exploring the Places Where Body and Spirit, Healing and Social Justice Intersect. Vanissar Tarakali Blog, June.

UNHCR (2015) Global Trends: Forced Displacement in 2015. Geneva: UNHCR.

United Nations (2007) Enable: Fact Sheet 1, November: Employment of Person's with Disabilities. New York: United Nations.

United Nations (2011) Discriminatory Laws and Practices and Acts of Violence against Individuals Based on Their Sexual Orientation and Gender Identity. New York: United Nations.

Wallace, M. (1979) *Black Macho and the Myth of Superwomen.* New York: Dial.

Watermeyer, B. and Gorgens, T. (2014) Disability and Internalised Oppression. In E.J.K. David (ed.), *Internalised Oppression: The Psychology of Marginalised Groups.* New York: Springer.

White, M. (2011) *Maps of Narrative Practice.* New York: W.W. Norton & Company.

White, M. and Epston, D. (1990) *Narrative Means to Therapeutic Ends*. New York: W.W. Norton & Company.
WHO (1995) The World Health Report: Bridging the Gaps. Washington, DC: World Health Organization.
World Bank and International Monetary Fund (2014) Ending Poverty and Sharing Prosperity: Global Monitoring Report. 2014/15. Washington, DC: World Bank and IMF.

3

NOT YET AT HOME

An exploration of aural and verbal passing amongst African migrants in Britain

Baffour Ababio

In the novel *Things Fall Apart*, Chinua Achebe writes about tensions in the village of Umuofia upon the arrival of the 'White man'. The protagonist, Okonkwo, was deeply grieved and it was not just a personal grief – he mourns for the clan, which he sees fragmenting and breaking down (Achebe 1986: 129). After being exiled from his home village of Umuofia for a traditional infraction, Okonkwo returns to find that it has changed. With the arrival of the Western presence, it is no longer the home he knew. This intersection of cultures ultimately drives him to his tragic end of committing suicide. The manner of his death cemented the irreconcilable gulf of his alienation from his own culture – suicide is taboo in Umuofia. Okonkwo is aware of the legacy his suicide will have but chooses it nonetheless. Observing the swaying body of Okonkwo, Obierika, his friend, enraged turns to the white district commissioner also present and blames him for pushing an exceptional Umuofia man to kill himself, and for the ignoble burial reserved for Okonkwo's manner of death (Achebe 1986: 147).

The forces of imperialism and colonialism heightened tensions and introduced new divisions among ethnic groups in large tracts of West Africa. These conflicts, as we will later see, lodged in the psyches of the conquered peoples, unleashing a sense of shame and a negative evaluation of their traditional cultures (Wa Thiong'o 1994: 16).

Existence at the juncture of differing cultures can evoke dynamics of adaptation, integration and resistance. The newly arrived immigrant in a host culture learns to interpret different modes of dress, speech and accent and encounters myriad new and nuanced ways of interacting. These experiences can be overwhelming in the rapidity of their onset, leaving the individual with a sense that their centre no longer holds. The cultural markers that had hitherto provided some cohesion and sense of belonging now act as barriers, perceived as being somewhat alien, foreign and not prized. The subject in this maelstrom of change is forced to re-examine aspects of his or her identity, potentially introducing some degree of doubt about the self. This sets in train examinations of different strategies to deploy in the new terrain with the concomitant mounting pressure to internalise the denigration of their original, cultural traits. One of the strategies deployed is what is known as 'passing' and this chapter examines this phenomenon particularly amongst some West African migrants to Britain.

Flight and arrival

We see how people from some parts of West Africa are catapulted out of their countries by war, persecution on grounds of religion and political persuasion. Others decide to leave their homes because they feel economically disadvantaged or feel impelled by their postcolonial connection with the 'motherland' to move beyond the stories they have heard to the centre of colonial power. The factors which lead one to migrate to another country are complex and have historical antecedents, as fractionally evinced by the set of reactions in Okonkwo's community to the Western presence in the novel. Whether historic or recent, these factors are intertwined and affect the expectation and actual experience of immigrants on setting foot in the new territory.

The arrival of immigrants from Africa is affected by various factors – some individuals or groups may have arrival parties (extended or nuclear family, or friends) waiting to receive them in Britain, perhaps mitigating the harshness of the arrival. Others navigate their arrival through various organs of the state such as social services and the Home Office, through community or faith groups and, in some cases, through international charities or after surviving maltreatment at the hands of criminal entities such as human traffickers. As aptly put by Falicov, these experiences present the immigrant with the challenge of engaging 'in creating a new life in the midst of multiple uncertainties and cultural dissonance while facing economic stresses and racist or prejudicial treatment in the host countries' (Falicov 2002: xvi).

If problems do emerge upon arrival, the immigrant's uprooting from known and relatively established ways of living in the world has an impact on attachment systems and consequently diminishes help-seeking behaviour. Bowlby (1988: 26–7) understood attachment as:

> any form of behaviour that results in a person attaining or maintaining proximity to some clearly identified individual who is conceived as better able to cope with the world. It is most obvious whenever the person is frightened, fatigued, or sick, and is assuaged by comforting and care giving.

Drawing from Bowlby, Gomez posits:

> [T]he propulsion towards this *clearly identified individual* arises through autonomous biological systems. Hence it is a system that points to the fact that human beings were not designed to live alone and the species' survival is firmly based on the successful forging of strong and permanent bonds. The individual being discussed thrives because of their continual engagement in real experiences with other people.
>
> *(Gomez 1997: 155)*

Gomez further intimates that:

> [T]he ensuing result of this dynamic is what Bowlby termed the *internal working model*, a representation of the world which includes cognitive, emotional and behavioural representations of self and other and of the relationship which mediates their connection. Temporary or permanent separation from those people felt to be essential to survival is, by definition, a crisis.
>
> *(ibid)*

A crisis which is noteworthy when the 'individual self' is defined or allied with the fate of the communal/wider group – as in most African societies, where 'cultural' attributes contrast quite sharply with characteristics in European societies (Kareem 2006: 19).

Populations from various parts of the globe (largely the Commonwealth; former territories of the British Empire) have experienced separation (uprootedness) from their known familiar environments and contributed to successive waves of immigration to the UK. The largest group in the context of Black migration – which appears to have settled and made some success of adapting – would be the 'Windrush'[1] and successive generations from the Caribbean. This group created what has become largely known as a Black urban culture, specifically in the English cities. The newly arrived African immigrant can have pressure exerted on them to conform to this established Black culture formed within the crucible of the wider host white culture.

A client I saw described the bullying she experienced at the age of 12 when she arrived in London from West Africa. The tormenting, she said, targeted her accent and hair and she generally felt denigrated for being different, for being African. This client lived with parents who were themselves in the throes of trying to survive, constantly at work, and as she said, they had no emotional and thinking space left to listen to her. She worked hard to shed her accent and to adopt the Black urban cadences in her speech. She was 'urban' when out of the house and West African when at home with her family. She described inhabiting a split existence. It seemed the blows of derision, which were the hardest for her to deal with, were the ones from people who looked like her – black like her but a different black. She said being called 'African' felt painful, an insult – she no longer wanted to be African. As her psychotherapist – myself of African origin – it stirred up memories of the issues I had processed to some degree in my own therapy. I recalled the camaraderie I thought I enjoyed with work colleagues in a part-time job I held. My experience of calling my Black colleagues by their names and then later within earshot being referred to as 'that African' did hurt; it erected a barrier and I wondered why they could not mention my name. It seemed ironic how the different sections in the Black community were somehow caught up in enacting internalised colonial behaviours.

Colonial roots

The educational structures in West Africa were taken over and shaped extensively by their various colonial powers. In the late 1950s onwards (leading into the postcolonial period), the educational system (a legacy of the colonial regime) in West Africa, notably in Ghana, saw the growth of private, international and preparatory schools at the primary level. This set up a divide between the existing government schools and these private schools. The children who attended these private institutions were coached and prepared to access secondary boarding schools and higher educational establishments, which had huge implications for social mobility. The subsequent introduction of high tuition fees further straitened access to these institutions for children of working-class parents and reinforced these places of learning as the domain of the middle and affluent classes. English had forcibly become the lingua franca of Ghana following its colonisation by Britain. The private and government schools both provided their tuition in English, however, private schools placed a greater emphasis on the acquisition of and fluency in the English language. Children were encouraged to report to their teachers any pupil heard speaking their own local languages, who were then punished. This has been likened to the unleashing of a 'cultural bomb' by Wa Thiong'o (1994: 3): 'The effect of a cultural bomb is to annihilate a people's belief in their names, in their languages, in their environment, in their heritage of struggle, in their unity, in their capacities and ultimately in themselves'.

This initiated a process where the children began to identify with a culture and a language which were far removed from them. Wa Thiong'o describes how children from these private schools read books by English writers such as abridged versions of books by Charles Dickens, Robert Louis Stevenson and Enid Blyton. Children engaged with and prized the English language whilst denigrating their own languages which they spoke every day at home. Civilisation and being cultured became synonymous with one's fluency in English. Children who were not fluent were considered backward, from the 'bush', and were generally scorned and teased. This encouraged and reinforced an alienation from the true selves of these Ghanaian children. Projecting the disavowed parts of themselves into the less fluent in English was frequently practised and entrenched a disassociation from traditionally Ghanaian elements. It also produced people who were literate in a foreign language (in this case English) and semi-literate (unable to read and write) in their mother tongues.

These, to a large extent, were the children who progressed to the boarding schools and universities and migrated abroad, often to the UK. The denigration of their country, its culture and language could be thought of as an attack on the true self, which brings together all the feelings of 'aliveness' (Winnicott 1960 cited in Goldman 1993: 158) and the introjection of an idealised colonial object, which in effect is an illusory shortcut approach to understanding what it means to be British. Consequently, it was assumed that adapting to life in Britain would not be unduly difficult. The process of alienation did not end at fluency in a foreign language. It extended to the mastery and appreciation of foreign foods, clothes, socio-historical trends and generally feigning knowledgeability and familiarity with the unfamiliar. My client, Adama, described his humiliation when he went to the canteen of his college, reached the serving table and chose pizza, lasagne and rice. He recalled sitting down to his meal with a bottle of soft drink and, becoming aware of stares between mouthfuls, he realised he had misjudged things. However, the wound was not as smarting then as in later years when he became accustomed to British food;

he would look back on this with some horror. This is an example of a painful realisation of the perceived inadequacy of one's upbringing in Ghana but can also be the beginning of some insight about the truth about oneself and of Ghana. However, often this is followed with disappointment and disillusionment about life in Britain, which confronts the Ghanaian middle-class individual who has been raised in alienation from themselves.

The acquisition of and fluency in English which had been privileged and was a source of esteem and self-worth had become a badge of humiliation and exposure. It was now seen as not good enough. It was Ghanaian English. Adama recollects occasions when he had to repeat certain words, only to see after several attempts the look of confusion on the face of the listener change to one of amused understanding with the word then 'correctly' pronounced back to him. There was also the time when he recorded his first and only message on the office's answerphone and, whilst it played back, he sat and endured the embarrassment of his colleagues laughing at and mimicking his accent. These experiences dealt blows to his confidence, furthering a shame about himself and intensifying his envy of the Black British.

Envy of the Black British

The newly arrived immigrant has an accent, one that he cannot easily mask. He then looks around to people who resemble him, second-generation Black people, who appear to him to have all that he wants. This evokes envy from the immigrant, who redoubles his effort to assimilate. The situation he finds himself in now is the reverse of where he was in his own country. He is now the one derided, mocked for the very thing that he had spent most of his life honing. His English language is no longer up to par, he is now the 'bush' Black he had projected onto others from outside his immediate social circle in Ghana. He now plunges himself into becoming an instant first- or second-generation Black Briton; another phase in reinforcing his alienation and disavowing his true self further. This denigration is propelled to an abysmal new nadir when he is confronted by his invisibility. It is as if he is a spectre who lacks reflection when he stares in a mirror. That plane of reflection – the disconcerting mirror that is Black Britishness – not only excises him from its frame but denies him the chance of being a constituent of the broader British social narrative by regarding his Africanness as an implement for smear and ridicule (DaCosta 2013). A process of marginalisation that induces the immigrant to buckle under the seemingly unattainable Black British project, thus confirming his invisibility.

Nii Adama

Nii Adama, who I will refer to as Adama, is 48 years old and spent the first 19 years of his life in Ghana. His parents were both middle-class professionals from different Ghanaian ethnic groups, who divorced when he was 14 years old. He was the product of a preparatory school in Ghana and had been educated to prize English as a badge of achievement. When Adama was 8 years old, a young family friend from England spent a few months with them in Ghana. Adama became an ardent student of this boy's English and accent. When the boy returned to England, Adama adopted the boy's accent when outside the house and pretended he had just arrived from England himself. This won the admiration of those he was able to hoodwink. He remembered his father's friend excitedly rushing to Adama's father, urging him to come hear him speak English with a British accent. Adama's father arrived and asked him to 'perform'; he realised there were rewards to this style of speaking. However, he recounted his dismay on the occasion when he came home to find an electrician to whom he had been passing as Black British with his 'acquired' accent. He was found out when the electrician realised that Adama could speak Ga and that he had been masquerading.

Adama had spent 29 years of his life in the UK and had expended a great deal of his energy passing and had, in his mind, made some 'progress' but always with a nagging consciousness of being deficient. He presented for treatment describing feeling depressed and anxious and had difficulty maintaining relationships. He was the father of a 13-year-old son from a relationship which had failed after two and a half years of living together. He lived on his own and worked in public transport. He was feeling dissatisfied with his life, sleeping badly and not eating properly and had been secretly drinking rather heavily most nights. He had become a Rastaman and attended most of the services but said his contact with this faith was fairly superficial.

During the initial phase of the therapy, Adama and I established a trusting working relationship. He had placed me in a Ghanaian social class much like his own and attempted to draw me into a friendship. I observed moments when he appeared low in mood, lost in thought and fumbling for words. This would then change to fluency and self-assurance. This alternation revealed a pattern and, as we wondered about this, it became evident how those low moments facilitated disclosure and increased his capacity to reflect on material he had compartmentalised and deemed as shameful. A corollary was a growing ability to acknowledge the excessive amount of psychic energy he was expending on "passing" maintenance.

Rastafari and identity

Becoming a Rastafarian was an aspect of Adama's attempt to reconnect with himself, because Rastafari, since its inception in the 1930s in Jamaica, has espoused a rejection of Jamaica as a place of exile and a movement and repatriation to Zion, which is Ethiopia in Africa (Chevannes 1994: 1). The return to 'Zion' was therefore a pathway to reclaiming what had been lost through slavery. Adama was apparently reclaiming his identity, an African identity. However, within the Rasta community he seemed unable to deeply connect as he felt stuck in the dynamic of mimicking, which had its roots in the colonial system he had inhabited and been socialised into in Ghana. The link between those emotional shifts in the therapy, his history and his association with Rasta, enabled him to begin to disclose more of what lay below the surface and to uncover the roots of his own attempts to reconnect via Rastafarianism.[2] Adama remembered how he had worked using a different name (using a friend's identity papers); for years, he would go to work and was somebody else, responding to a different name. Adama, through the framework of Rastafari, said he had given his name away under the Babylon system, as per the system which had operated during slavery, where the slave took the name of his or her owner. He felt he had been in exile, away from himself and going further away. He said even during the period when he had not yet left Ghana, where he was supposedly at home, he was in truth far away from himself. Kwame Dawes describes how the reggae singer, Bob Marley, during his period of exile in England following the assassination attempt on his life, wrote the song, 'Running Away' on the Kaya album, which was a response to the rumour that 'Marley was abandoning the ways of Rasta and becoming far too deeply inscribed in the Babylon system of the rock and roll world' (Dawes 2002: 237). Adama in the therapy used the conflicts and turmoil that Marley lyrically intimates in parts of this song to explore his inner landscape. That he had been avoiding 'himself'; which he reflected as being an impossible and gruelling dynamic, he could not, it dawned on him, continue running. He grappled with his sense of guilt and shame, which he said had for a long period been his experience. He wondered, explored and questioned this burden of guilt, what wrong he asked had he done? What was he concealing? Why could he not find his 'own place'? (Marley 1978)

Adama, during this period, was quite dejected. He felt he had lost a significant part of his life (his years in the UK seemed on one hand frozen but spent at the same time) and was in despair as he sensed he could never recover it. He was faced with making something unique of himself (yet continuous with his traditional Ghanaian roots) from what he now, through the therapy, was connecting with. Krause and Miller observe: 'culture ceases to be only a regulating device for how individuals should behave and becomes a flowing body of ideas open for negotiation as well ... for each individual such meanings are constantly confirmed or challenged through interaction with others' (Krause and Miller 1998: 154).

Littlewood in a similar vein states:

> 'culture' cannot be thought of as a bag of memories and survival techniques which individuals carry about with them and of which they have forgotten to divest themselves. Rather it is a dynamic re-creation by each generation, a complex and shifting set of accommodations, identifications, explicit resistances and reworkings.
>
> *(Littlewood 2006: 9)*

It is interesting to note that the language used in the therapy was English but in therapeutic time would change when Adama was seeking to be understood to Ghanaian broken English, and when emotional he would speak Ga. In the main, he spoke in English but used broken English and Ga more often as he engaged with the work and as the therapy progressed. He appeared to vary his use of language(s) to bridge the gap imposed by the English language; to move beyond the limits of translation. He used lyrics from 'Babylon System' even as shame and guilt in the therapy transmuted to anger and latent agency – he was repudiating 'imposed' ways of being, which he had acquiesced to and lived with and was now unveiling a determination to be 'himself' (Marley 1979). Masculinity with its various permutations was present in the therapeutic space and is described as:

> the notion of the strong, black man – interpreted to mean an aversion to talking about emotional problems – results in the accumulation of stress. And the stereotype of the strong black male inevitably seeps into spaces where male interaction often occurs … This could mask or inhibit vulnerability and further discourage men from opening up.
>
> *(Ababio 2017)*

The work with Adama around masculinity was, in part, enabled by Adama originating from the same country as myself and being also a male, but it was this sameness which could potentially have stagnated the process. Although our common 'Ghanaianness and maleness' was one of the reasons Adama gave for choosing to work with me, it also seemed to render him vulnerable and exposed. My not knowing and yet knowing of the Ghanaianness and maleness stance facilitated the working through of that initial rupture (my awareness of the allure of collusion and the decision to stick to exploring the shame which was being avoided) in the alliance. My awareness of Rastafari and its associated music genre was also usefully held within the therapeutic stance of not knowing and knowing. This meant I had to be vigilant about the dangers inherent in making assumptions based on shared experience. I felt I had to hold our shared knowledge and experience of Ghana loosely in a way which could enable Adama to creatively shape and occupy his own space in the therapy. He, in the therapy, uncovered a pathway which linked his parents' different ethnicities, their choice of English as the family language and their acrimonious divorce to the problems he later developed. He admitted his simmering anger towards them. Of feeling let down by them.

Passing

Irene, a character in Nella Larsen's 1929 book, *Passing*, eloquently and painfully describes the strategies deployed by light-skinned 'Blacks' in 1920s America to pass as white and the constant inhabiting of a tense space filled with the fear of being found out. A space where the shifting perceptions of Irene's identity (which she took on) morphed from Italian, Spanish to Mexican. Perceptions or projections which conveniently cloaked her as she continued to dread and to evade attempts to categorise her as a Black woman (Larsen 2004: 8). Adama attempted to pass and be the kind of Black who could move under the radar undetected but, like Larsen's light-skinned Blacks, he knew that this was a precarious survival strategy. For him, the ephemeral reward of the feeling of belonging, of being accepted, was worth the risk but he found the process taxing, energy sapping and depleting. His engagement and request for therapy was perhaps his way of communicating that the scheme was getting too difficult to sustain. Towards the end of our two years of work, he began speaking Ga on his mobile phone in public with growing ease; previously he would generally ignore answering phone calls in public places but especially from people he knew would converse with him in a Ghanaian language. It was, in his words, too awkward. His voice and accent (he had also become sensitised and aware of the instinct of some Black British people to ascertain which person was Black or white by the way they sounded on the radio, it was a game he detested) were like an internal alien entity, perpetually poised to unmask him. He reasoned that if he was quiet nobody could tell who he 'really' was. Once he spoke in public places, he felt it shattered the perception of being 'one of them'. Opening his mouth now and speaking his own language (and also an accented Ghanaian English) in public nurtured the life within which he had compartmentalised and denigrated and also expedited his connection with his wider Ghanaian community (he reported attending a Ga 'Homowo' festival celebration in London and adhering to visiting arrangements with his son). It was in part an indication of the loosening hold of English on Adama and of it being shifted into a space akin to that occupied by a second language and a growing realisation of it as a tool – to bend and use the way Chinua Achebe did in his writing.

Our case of Adama traces the foreign psychological structures which were seeded in the ex-colonies – in this case, Ghana – and transmitted to Adama through various social systems. We see a continuation of this determining dynamic during his time in the UK. The illusion of control which he deployed via projections onto his 'bush' counterparts in Ghana was turned upside down in the UK. He became the 'bush Black' – and was now the container of the projections of other Blacks, who themselves were also caught up in the dynamics of their own internalised racist structures. Adama's difficulties brought him to therapy and, in the end, he was left to choose what hybrid he made of himself. Would he be like Ngugi Wa Thiong'o, charting a path to metaphorically relinquish writing in English to writing in Gikuyu? Or like Achebe, as quoted by Wa Thiong'o, who said,

> Is it right that a man should abandon his mother tongue for someone else's? It looks like a dreadful betrayal and produces a guilty feeling. But for me there is no other choice. I have been given this language and I intend to use it.
> *(Wa Thiong'o 1994: 7)*

Achebe arguably felt he could bend the language he had been 'given' to circumvent the pitfalls of being 'lost in translation'.

Ayodele

Ayodele Kargbo (whom I refer to as Ayodele) grew up in West Africa during years of civil war. Her father had left the country when she was 18 months old for the UK and she lived in West Africa with her mother. She described her mother as a woman who was quite conflicted and suffered from episodes of depression – her mother, she said, was not available emotionally. During the periods when her mother was unwell, Ayodele would spend time with her grand aunt in a nearby small town. Her grand aunt appeared to vacillate in her relationship with Ayodele. She was on one hand attentive and seemingly caring, while on the other hand would severely punish Ayodele for minor transgressions. She recalled having empty cans tied around her waist and being ordered to walk around her neighbourhood with her grand aunt behind her shouting insults. Ayodele sold fried foods for her grand aunt in the market – which she balanced on a big platter on her head whilst walking and hawking her wares for long periods. When she was 13 years old, Ayodele was sent to the UK to join her father. He had by then remarried and had two children. When Ayodele came for therapy she was 41 years old, had experienced depression on and off from the age of 19 and said she has always felt 'unreal', a fraud, that she has had to masquerade through life. She described confusion and uncertainty in interpersonal interactions. Ayodele said she constantly monitored other people's perception and expectation of her with a view to reacting to it. Du Bois has termed this as 'double-consciousness', this 'looking at oneself through the eyes of others, of measuring one's soul by the tape of a world that looks on in amused contempt and pity' (Du Bois and Edwards 2007: 12). Elaborating this double consciousness, Ayodele disclosed an absence of any solidity and an enduring sense of her life as not being worth living, but said she held on to a hope of the possibility for change. She reflected on some achievements, such as raising her two children, who lived with her. She has also produced works of art, was a singer and had secured a postgraduate degree. Ayodele struggled to enjoy any of these achievements and conveyed her difficulty in taking in 'goodness' or connecting with sources of psychic nurturing. Dalal comments how acts of splitting and projection can get stuck 'sometimes because the weakened ego cannot take in the evacuated aspect without being completely overwhelmed by it, so it remains outside, ominous and threatening. If the object cannot be taken in, then life and love are not taken in either' (Dalal 2010: 46).

My work with Ayodele identified areas where she felt most disconnected. She explored her schism from her country of origin, shame about her life with her mother (who was now deceased), her grand aunt, who she felt had failed her, and alienation from her father. She had often thought about him, but on meeting him, experienced his disappointment and reported physical abuse from him. She was caught up in yearning for and resenting him. Ayodele had concluded that becoming acceptable would always elude her.

Ayodele also disclosed a connection with a church which was predominantly African Caribbean and Pentecostal. She participated in the services but kept her personal life separate from the church members. Ayodele recalled being at a gathering in her father's house of extended family who had met to discuss clan matters. Ayodele said it was an unusually tense situation – she was 38 years old then. However, she stood up when it was her turn and spoke to her father about his rejection of her and the life she had had to endure during her early years in West

Africa whilst he was in the UK with his new family. Ayodele said it was an extremely frightening occasion but cathartic. Ayodele's experience echoes and references elements of sections of Victor Turner's paper, 'An Ndembu Doctor in Practice' (1964), during which the healer Ihembi conducts a family/village gathering to resolve tensions which were condensed in a character called Kamahasanyi and affected him adversely. The result was 'a general sense of what we might call "catharsis" – a collective release of tension and general reconciliation' (Littlewood 2006: 51). This meeting was a condensation of Ayodele's years of anger and estrangement from her father and her country of origin, allowing her to seize the opportunity to vent and to confront. The therapeutic work we did around this piece of 'group therapy' she had engaged in allowed her to further embed the experience. The African Caribbean church was one which foregrounded a pride in Caribbean culture and referenced Africa as its source. She described her time and place within this church as being part of her 'cocoon' process. This allowed her some degree of safety and distance to explore her West African culture and identity, about which she was conflicted. Ayodele and I rehearsed these pockets of alienation and shame whilst simultaneously examining her church experience and the 'confrontation' at the family gathering. A capacity to engage and stay with thoughts about her family and culture was emerging. Alongside this was a softening and a developing capability to take in goodness and some appreciation of her agency, which appeared to surprise her. I had, she said, a balance of masculine and feminine qualities. This signalled her transferential experience. It evoked in me a mixture of confusion and of being immobilised, in sections of our work which I processed as a

> temporary tolerance of the patient's attempts to bring the analyst under his omnipotent control. This will enable the analyst to reconstruct the original traumata and their developmental vicissitudes and then attempt to interpret them in regard to their repetition in the analytic situation.
>
> *(Rayner 1996: 231)*

Her experience of my masculinity and femininity also enabled and elaborated the exploration of the experience of an unavailable mother and a father who had abandoned her. It recalled her mother's conflicted relationship with the absent father; of yearning and resentment. As a child, her gaze was fixed in the direction of the UK, a superior place, she felt, inhabited by special people, including her father. Her life as a child in her country had been supplanted and, in a way, halted by a vision of a new life in the UK with her father. She had been groomed for 'real' life in the UK but, in spite of this, dared not entertain the hope of a future in the UK, even after the years of putting her life on pause in West Africa for Britain. A life of conflicts and contradictions.

Ayodele's travel arrangements to the UK were made hurriedly, without her knowledge and participation, but she said this was what she had been waiting for. The relocation abroad occurred after the death of her mother and she found herself in the UK with her father; a superior father, wife and children. She was perplexed, bereft of the materiality of time and real memory upon which to build a relationship with her father. She only had expectations. Her confusion gave way to anger and envy (the source of goodness had been projected onto her father and his family and she wanted it as much as she wished to destroy it) (Dalal 2010: 44). These were not permissible feelings. She could not express them; a dialectic of shame countering envy. She saw constant disapproval in her father's eyes, he deplored her speech, how she spoke English, how she sat and ate her food. Ayodele felt inferior. At school, she said she had initially experienced some 'refuge', as the family then lived in an area of the UK which was quite homogenous in terms of its ethnic mix. It was predominantly white and she was the only Black student; her half-siblings attended a different school. She described being treated as 'special' by the white teachers and her white peers. Ayodele said this changed when the family moved to a more diverse city – in her new school every characteristic was under scrutiny by her Black peers. She was teased for her natural hair plaits and 'African' accent, which reinforced shame and a resurgence of a desire to 'whiten' and 'erase' those maligned characteristics.

Ayodele spoke English with a kind of 'received accent' – linked to the perception of Englishness aspired to in her country of origin as well as to the expectations of her father. A perception which was partly expressed through her experience of me as a nurturing 'proper gentleman' but which also had an underbelly; this was my potential capacity as a man to oppress and hurt her. This allowed anger into the work and connected again with the anger which had emerged during the family meeting. My being a gentleman also had lodged in it notions of class, education and a certain kind of 'Black African' which she felt we shared. To facilitate some movement, I emphasised our differences (which she explored; of gender, of accent, of different ethnic and national backgrounds, as she perceived it), thereby increasing the volume of her own voice, identity and sense of agency. Facilitating this movement was useful in breaking what was, potentially, becoming a mutual enactment and its continuation would not have done much for Ayodele's difficulties. This has been termed 'effort fullness', which refers to participations by the analyst characterised by consciousness (Hirsch 2008: 58).

History and background

> History (as cultural therapy and) as a recapitulation and interpretation of our past, has the power to release our energies and direct our initiatives.
> *(Chinweizu 1987: 74)*

The year 1884 signified the partition of Africa which put its history on a new trajectory and profoundly altered African life and culture. No sooner was the 1884 Berlin conference of European powers over, than European soldiers set out to conquer Africa for their respective countries. By 1914, the result of that scramble was a quilt work of colonial boundaries upon which present day African states are still attempting to build modern nation-states (Chinweizu 1987: 97).

The conference was preceded by centuries of imperial contact, domination and control, a period which belies the actual nature of African development prior to encountering Europeans. Rodney rehearses that precolonial stage of Africa stating that 'the first Europeans to reach West and East Africa by sea were the ones who indicated that in most respects African development was comparable to that which they knew' (Rodney 1982: 69). The first Western contact recorded with what is now Ghana was in January 1471 by the Portuguese. For nearly a century, the Portuguese controlled the trade, mainly in gold and spices, in this part of West Africa, then known as the Guinea Coast. Chinweizu introduces a note of caution that any narrative which has an anti-Western slant could attract coalitions and can have the effect of imposing a homogenous gloss over those coalitions. He points to the pre-existing Arab imperialism and of slave trading on the African continent dating back to the 7th century (Chinweizu 1987: 143). Let us, however, stick to the British and West African interaction. The English made their first contact with the Guinea (Gold) Coast in the mid-16th century. 'Wyndham was followed by other English visits to the Guinea coast, including those of John Hawkins in 1562, 1564, and 1567, who took home slaves, and that of Francis Drake' (Buah 1998: 68). The Portuguese had initiated trade in human beings prior to the English engagement. This trade became the trans-Atlantic slave trade. By the time of its abolition in 1807, it has been estimated that about 20 million West Africans had been traded (Buah 1998: 71). By 1884, Britain had gained considerable toeholds on different parts of the Guinea coast, through trade and treaties with an inevitable assault on the integrity of the experience of Africanness. The 1884 conference and partition of Africa was a consolidation of the preceding centuries of exploitation of the continent, its peoples and resources. A desecration that separated a significant number of Africans in the New World as captives with different environments and subject to processes entirely different from the experience of the Africans left on the continent. The processes to which the two Black populations were subjected occurred within an overarching white Western oppressive framework. In Ghana, we see the introduction of foreign goods, cultures, language: the slave trade exacerbated existing tensions and induced wars to feed the demand for slaves. We see boys being taken abroad and educated and returned home in the service of British interests.

> Another lasting result ... are the numerous place names, such as Cape Coast, Saltpond and personal names such as Bannerman, Robertson, as well as anglicized native names such as Quayson (Kwesi), Yawson (Yaw). Equally important are a number of names of articles which the Europeans introduced into the country.
>
> *(Buah 1998: 75)*

The next section will reference the fate and experience of the second population transported to the Americas and the Caribbean. Both experiences, slavery and colonialism, inextricably link these two populations in terms of how they are perceived by 'others'. Each population's fate is projected onto the other which to a degree regulates how both groups are generally understood and treated.

In the play, *The Blinkards*, Kobina Sekyi satirises the anglicised ways of some sections of his ethnic group: the Fanti. Kobina was born (in the then Gold Coast, now Ghana) in the late 19th century into an upper middle-class family and educated in a secondary school in Cape Coast modelled on the English public school system. He read philosophy and law at the University of London and it was during his time in England that we begin to see his questioning of his own 'Anglomania', as he described it. His disillusionment with his 'borrowed clothes' led to the writing of the play. A character called Mr Borofo (Mr English) utters the following:

> The worst of it is that some of us got into these foreign ways through no fault of our own. We were born into a world of imitators, worse luck ... and blind imitators at that. They could not and cannot distinguish cause from effect, so they have not been able to trace effect to cause, as yet. They see a thing done in England, or by somebody white, then they say we must do the same thing in Africa.
>
> *(Sekyi 1974: 7)*

In another section, his wife, Mrs Borofo (Mrs English), in an exchange with him, says: "'I like you to sing like that. It is like a white man's voice." Mr. Borofo (testily), "my voice is my own. I am not an ass'" (Sekyi 1974: 15). When this 'mimicking' interacts with other aspects of colonial forceful impositions, it prepares the ground for a class of Africans and Ghanaians to potentially engage in the process of passing.

Diaspora meets Africa

On the other side of the world, where the African human captives had been taken, we see the impact of centuries of systematic brutal dehumanisation. Barbara Fletchmann Smith writes:

> The people sent away were never heard from again, and for those Africans made slaves in the plantations of the Caribbean, or in North and South America, a permanent severance of their connections with their families lay before them. Their past, their family name, history and home, were systematically erased from history.
>
> *(Fletchmann Smith 2003: postscript)*

The Africans left on the continent had to wrestle with the pain and memories of loved ones who were never to be seen again and those complicit in the trade of humans were left to grapple with the guilt of their acts of betrayal. I propose these are memories (oral tradition/written sources and art forms act as vehicles) which are transmitted and held by successive generations.

It is against this backdrop that the Caribbean migration to Britain and their interaction with Africans who had not undergone the 'middle passage' but had also migrated to Britain, occurs. In an observation on the West Indian perception of the 'African' during the 1930s to 1940s, Fanon notes:

> we may say that the West Indian, not satisfied to be superior to the African, despised him, and while the white man could allow himself certain liberties with the native, the West Indian absolutely could not. This was because, between whites and Africans, there was no need of a reminder; the difference stared one in the face. But what a catastrophe if the West Indian should suddenly be taken for an African.
>
> *(Fanon 1988: 20)*

In 'Encounter on the Seine: Black Meets Brown', James Baldwin writes about this interaction and even though it references the dynamic between an African American and an African in Europe, it is my view that it is apropos, in part, to the Caribbean-African interrelationship.

> They face each other, the Negro and the African, over a gulf of three hundred years – an alienation too vast to be conquered in an evening's good-will, too heavy and too double-edged ever to be trapped in speech. This alienation causes the Negro to recognize that he is a hybrid. Not a physical hybrid merely: in every aspect of his living he betrays the memory of the auction block and the impact of the happy ending. In white America, he finds himself reflected – repeated, as it were, in a higher key – his tensions, his terrors, his tenderness. Dimly and for the first time, there begins to fall into perspective the nature of the roles they have played in the lives and history of each other ... that this depthless alienation from oneself and one's people is, in sum, the American experience.
>
> *(Baldwin 1985: 39)*

The West African who arrives in the UK operating under the sway of colonial introjects and projections attempts to deal with his growing awareness of his difference. He initially moves to deny any experience of the pain evoked by an ever increasing sense of his vulnerability by taking on elements of Black Britishness and identifying with it. The Black British to him appear to have mastered and synthesised something which is not just white and not entirely African but somewhat Black. The attempt on the part of the African to manage his pain by this identification is sometimes rebuffed by hostility and hurt by the Black (Caribbean) British individual; this depends on which memories are evoked. For sections of the UK-settled Black Caribbean population who still unconsciously/consciously retain ancestral memories of having been captured and sold by other Africans, this manoeuvre of identification by the African might trigger feelings of being again the target of capture and exploitation. The African individual who endeavours to pass as Black British can be perceived as sidestepping the ancestral pain that he is perceived as bearing some responsibility for but which he is seen as unable to acknowledge or perhaps in denial about. The African operates with internalised powerful colonial objects, exerting a push towards an identification with Black Britishness – the ultimate aim being identification with white Englishness. Aspects of this system of 'passing' are sustained when elements of the mutation are isolated for praise and attention, and this praise is especially privileged if offered by a white English person. The praise targets areas such as a mastery of English language, food, dress and mannerism – these indices of alienation attracting praise metaphorically pour further fuel on the fire of the dynamic of the disavowal of the true self.

Passing has occurred amongst other minorities who have sought to cross lines of exclusion to access benefits denied them. The history of the oppression of Jews has had the impact of some Jewish people resorting to passing as Gentile as a strategy; this affords the Jewish person some acceptance and acts to ward off the aggression inherent in anti-Semitism. The price paid for this passing is a denial of aspects of Jewish identity, a psychic cost being the sacrifice for fitting in. Aideen Lucey (2014) explores the Irish history of being colonised and Irish people's experience of living in England. Using ideas from Frantz Fanon's *Black Skin White Masks* (1952) to translate a uniquely Irish experience, Lucey says

> in order to deal with that unbearable state of affairs, they end up wanting to be not like themselves but like their superior – that is the oppressor. In other words, by adopting a superior position, the colonizer projects feelings of inferiority into the colonized and the colonized comes to experience themselves as inferior. You can see then why there is a need to get rid of this through identifying with the oppressor and why, consciously or unconsciously, one may play down or hide one's identity.
>
> *(Lucey 2014: 170)*

Goldman (1993), with reference to Winnicott, says that 'living from the True Self enables an individual to "feel real" which means to "exist as oneself"' (Winnicott 1967, cited in Goldman 1993: 158). He goes on to describe the development of the False Self as that which interacts with the external environment and serves as a shield for the True Self. A problem occurs when these facets of the self split off from each other, with the effect of the individual experiencing life as futile (Winnicott 1988, cited in Goldman 1993: 160–1). Thomas posits a 'proxy self' which he comments is used by Black children as a strategy for surviving as a minority in a white society (Thomas 1998: 186). The Proxy Self serves as a diagnostic tool to enable the Black child to ascertain which white adult or therapist to trust and to what extent the child can allow her or his True Self to be seen. I utilise Thomas' model in advancing the case that the adult African migrant (operating a 'double consciousness'), in their unfamiliar territory, mobilises a proxy self to decipher their new world. Over time, excessive transactions between the Proxy Self and its uncertain external world become reinforced and installed through a reward system (aimed at selective behaviours) to the proxy self, supplied by others (Black or white British adults). The eventual hijacking or grooming of the proxy self by this reward system has the following consequence: it mutates into a 'passing proxy self' in service and in capitulation to the operating apparatus of passing.

Conclusion

Passing, as a term, has been associated with the phenomenon of light-skinned Blacks of mixed ancestry assimilating into the dominant white population in the United States. It has been known to exact a high psychic cost on the individual engaged in the process. Passing operates under various guises and with the occasional humorous application – the LinkedIn profile article of Ahuma Bosco Ocansey (2016) tells the story of a Ghanaian music presenter in Kumasi, Ghana, announcing a fire outbreak at a public venue in Jamaican patois (an English based language with West African influences). Eventually he had to drop his 'locally acquired foreign accent (LAFA)' to get the attention of the emergency services. Humorous or not, this points to the enduring nature of the basic contours of culture and language (West African influences) and its capacity to weather adversity over the centuries and, as in this anecdote, then reflected back to its spatial origin: Ghana (West Africa). Passing in this chapter has been examined within the context of its activity within and between some sections of the 'Black community' in Britain, operating in the aural and verbal sphere of interaction. A process which involves a denigration of self and adopting the characteristics of another, the seeds were sown during colonisation, preceding migration to Britain. Much of the dynamics between Africans and the African Caribbean (a term signalling an attempt to bridge both populations) community in Britain has had some airing with references to existing tensions. Overshadowing, to some extent the history and ongoing collaborative ventures between the populations (African and Caribbean) on micro-everyday ordinary settings to macro-political shifts, such as the activism behind the waves of independence in African countries facilitated in the mid-20th century. The first prime minister of Ghana, Kwame Nkrumah, worked politically in London within a coalition of African, Caribbean and African American activists which included George Padmore and W.E.B. Du Bois; both highly influential on the Pan-African scene (Rooney 1988: 21–2). What has also been lacking is perhaps a deeper exploration of the toll on mental health and the roots of the tensions (between African and African-Caribbean communities) glimpsed, only in part, in attempts to pass as Caribbean/Black British by some Africans. Further conversations could usefully prod the proverbial elephant in the room, acknowledging (and working through the impact of) the degree of complicity of African compatriots in the holocausts that were the Trans-Atlantic and Arabian slave trade. Advancing this exploration could for example also unearth the collusion of West Indian, local

West African soldiers in the service of British troops arrayed against the Ashanti during the Anglo-Ashanti war in the late 19th century. We again see from this how the theatre and arena of this psychological drama of 'passing' is enacted and powered, largely, by internalised colonial objects, within an overarching oppressive white Western framework. The Caribbean and African 'actors' involved, wrestle, it appears, with the process of engaging from their true selves. The individual experiences guilt and shame for his betrayal of himself and of his values; the cost of passing is repressed and denied. The psychotherapist in the therapeutic space offers the client an arena to facilitate a re-examination and a recalibration of this colonial structure. The therapist holds and contains. Caroline Garland references Wilfred Bion in describing containment as

> linking what the mother can do for the baby with what the therapist can do for the patient: help transform the unbearable into something that can eventually be thought about, held in the mind and considered, rather than responded to as an overwhelming experience that causes a further breakdown.
> *(Bion 1967 cited in Garland 2007: 110)*

An area for further thought and exploration (within a post-Brexit context) might be the experience of second- and third-generation British Africans having to contend with the rejection of not being embraced as Ghanaian or real Africans after expectantly visiting Africa. Anecdotally, this experience has potentially been known to release energy towards deconstructing the intergenerationally transmitted structures of aural and verbal passing, and to embrace their definition of Africanness by fashioning a hybrid; uniquely theirs (whilst retaining an awareness of and engaging with the wider Black communities, their historical roots and narratives as well as with useful contributions from other cultures), ameliorating the perniciousness of the disavowal of self (histories and communities). Psychotherapy could further engage and facilitate this process.

Notes

1 The events of spring 2018 in the UK dubbed the 'Windrush scandal' led to the resignation of the then home secretary Amber Rudd and the appointment of the first ethnic minority home secretary, Sajid Javid. It was a 'scandal' which calls into question the 'settled' status of this population (*Al-Jazeera News*, The UK's Windrush Generation: What's the Scandal About?, 10 April 2018).
2 Rastafarianism and its musical genre, reggae, steeped in Pan-African lyrical content, have enjoyed wide coverage and been embraced particularly by the youth in many African countries. Consequently, it has forged coalitions and identificatory pathways via Rastafari between these two Black populations.

References

Ababio, B. (2017) *Strong Black Male: Barbershop Chronicles*. West Yorkshire Playhouse, National Theatre and Fuel co-production.

Achebe, C. (1986) *Things Fall Apart*. Reading: Heinemann.

Baldwin, J. (1985) *The Price of The Ticket (Collected Non-Fiction 1948–1985)*. London: Michael Joseph.
Bosco Ocansey, Ahuma (2016) LinkedIn profile.
Bowlby, J. (1988) *A Secure Base: Clinical Applications of Attachment Theory*. London: Routledge.
Buah, F.K. (1998) *A History of Ghana*. London: Macmillan.
Chevannes, B. (1994) *Rastafari Roots and Ideology*. New York: Syracuse University Press.
Chinweizu (1987) *Decolonising the African Mind*. Lagos: Pero Press.
DaCosta, C. (2013) Animating Homeland: Toward a Definition of the Notion of Home and Place. Unpublished paper delivered at the 2013 Society of Animation Studies Conference, University of Southern California, Los Angeles.
Dalal, F. (2010) *Race, Colour and the Processes of Racialization*. London: Routledge.
Dawes, K. (2002) *Bob Marley, Lyrical Genius*. London: Sanctuary.
Du Bois, W.E.B. and Edwards, B.H. (2007) *The Souls of Black Folk*. Oxford: Oxford University Press.
Falicov, C. (2002) Foreword. In R. Papadopoulos (ed.), *Therapeutic Care for Refugees: No Place Like Home*, xvi. London: Karnac.
Fanon, F. (1988) *Toward the African Revolution*. New York: Grove Press.
Fletchmann Smith, B. (2003) *Mental Slavery: Psychoanalytic Studies of Caribbean People*. London: Karnac.
Garland, C. (2007) Issues in Treatment: A Case of Rape. In C. Garland (ed.), *Understanding Trauma: A Psychoanalytical Approach*, 2nd edition. London: Karnac.
Goldman, D. (1993) *In Search of the Real: The Origins and Originality of D.W. Winnicott*. Lanham, MD: Jason Aronson.
Gomez, L. (1997) *An Introduction to Object Relations*. London: Free Association Press.
Hirsch, I. (2008) *Coasting in the Countertransference*, 1st edition. New York: Analytic Press.
Kareem, J. (2006) The Nafsiyat Intercultural Therapy Centre: Ideas and Experience in Intercultural Therapy. In J. Kareem and R. Littlewood (eds), *Intercultural Therapy*, 2nd edition. Oxford: Blackwell.
Krause, I. and Miller, A. (1998) Culture and Family Therapy. In S. Fernando (ed.), *Culture and Family Therapy*. London: Routledge.
Larsen, N. (2004) *Passing*. New York: Dover.
Littlewood, R. (2006) Towards an Intercultural Therapy. In J. Kareem and R. Littlewood (eds), *Intercultural Therapy*, 2nd edition. Oxford: Blackwell Publishing.
Lucey, A. (2014) Paradoxes and Blind Spots: An Exploration of Irish Identity in British Organizations and Society. In F. Lowe (ed.), *Thinking Space: Promoting Thinking about Race, Culture, and Diversity in Psychotherapy and Beyond*, 1st edition. London: Karnac.
Marley, R. (1978) *Running Away, Kaya*. London: Island Records.
Marley, R. (1979) *Babylon System, Survival*. London: Island Records.
Rayner, E. (1996) *The Independent Mind in British Psychoanalysis*. London: Free Association.
Reggae Music in Ghana (2016) LinkedIn, May 3.
Rodney, W. (1982) *How Europe Underdeveloped Africa*. Washington, DC: Howard University Press.
Rooney, D. (1988) *Kwame Nkrumah: The Political Kingdom in the Third World*. London: I.B. Tauris & Co.
Sekyi, K. (1994) *The Blinkards: A Comedy and the Anglo-Fanti – a Short Story*. Oxford: Heinemann.
Thomas, L. (1998) Psychotherapy in the Context of Race and Culture: An Intercultural Therapeutic Approach. In S. Fernando, ed., *Mental Health in a Multi-Ethnic Society: A Multi-Disciplinary Handbook*. London: Routledge.

Turner, V. (1964) An Ndembu Doctor in Practice. In A. Kiev (ed.), *Magic, Faith and Healing*. London: Collier-Macmillan.

Wa Thiong'o, N. (1994) *Decolonising the Mind: The Politics of Language in African Literature*. Portsmouth: Heinemann.

Wambu, O. (1999) *Empire Windrush: Fifty Years of Writing about Black Britain*. London: Phoenix.

4

GROUP PSYCHOTHERAPY WITH TURKISH-SPEAKING WOMEN AT NAFSIYAT

Migration, gender and ethnic difference as catalysts to growth in the psychodynamic group

Dilek Güngör

This chapter is about my clinical work as a conductor in the early 1990s with a group of Turkish, Kurdish, Armenian, Bulgarian and Bosnian women who all come from particularly rural areas in Turkey. Thus, the name of the group was: Turkish-speaking women's group.

I would like to dedicate this chapter to the memory of my ex-client, dear Mrs AX, who was brutally murdered in the UK by her husband at an early age. I must mention that she was not a participant in the group which I will describe below.

I would like to say thank you to all my clients who took part in the group sharing their deepest, most painful, intimate feelings. I would also like to thank Mine Aslan, my colleague and my friend, for all her support during the process of writing this chapter.

What kind of group therapy and why?

When they were referred by general practitioners, or other health and social care professionals, I saw the women on an individual basis for two sessions. In this way, I felt I was able to help them to explore their feelings and expectations, i.e. how they felt about attending the group and what they wanted from the treatment process. Whilst deciding whether to join the group, these women were confronted with the difficulty of crossing a boundary in their families and communities. They were practically breaking the silence and asking for help. They felt shame and guilt and thought that they were 'mad'. They were preoccupied with what others would say. In Turkish, there is a saying: '*El alem ne der?*' meaning: 'what would everybody else say?' They all sustained some form of fear of being caught by others.

The women seemed emotionally absent and lost at the beginning of the therapeutic process and were full of judgements about themselves and others. The main themes were quite strong feelings of all good or bad, guilt, shame and fear.

They felt that they had to defend their family honour and they had no right to challenge the family.

Both shame and guilt are highly important mechanisms to ensure socialisation of the individual. Guilt transfers the demands of the society through early primitive parental images. Social conformity achieved through guilt will be essentially one of the identifications. A highly patriarchal, feudal and hierarchical society such as Turkey puts a high emphasis on guilt and shame (Piers and Singer 1953: 53).

These women were all affected by racial discrimination either because of their ethnicity or because they are seen or see themselves as 'bloody foreigners', as expressed by this popular, racist remark in the UK. I feel it very important to allow them the space to mourn about the racism, discrimination, talk about their feelings, thoughts, perceptions and experiences about living in a racist society before they work on their personalities through their individual stories. How they expressed their stories was a therapeutic tool for me to understand their personalities and help them to explore their internal world (Kareem and Littlewood 1992: 14).

They were all refugees, either living in temporary accommodation or with friends. They were illiterate, with low-paid manual jobs, experiencing poverty, domestic violence and racism, with cultural and language barriers. Some women had lived in the UK for many years but were only now beginning to address their painful experiences. Some were single mothers. For these women, the group was a way out of isolation and loneliness; a place where they could experience some warmth, cohesion and power over their personal situation. A place where they could be themselves without getting punished for expressing their real feelings.

I explained that they were free to talk about whatever came to mind, any of their feelings, especially anything they found troubling. They understood that group psychotherapy offered a clear sense of boundaries with awareness of links between behaviours and unconscious motivations. I never promised a cure or magic remedy (which seemed to be what they were looking for), however, I helped them to feel more hopeful about the whole process. The contract for the members comprised the following points: regular weekly attendance for 44 weeks, confidentiality, no social contact between members outside the group, and the significance of remaining in the group particularly when they were anxious or having to deal with difficult or painful matters in the group. In a way, I had to educate these women during the individual sessions because they had no idea what therapy was. There were nine women in the group aged between 21 and 67. The most common symptoms were intense anxiety accompanied by heart or chest pain, stomach ulcers, insomnia, sexual problems, backaches, bereavement, low self- esteem, self-harm and suicidal thoughts. The duration of stay in the UK was between three to 18 years.

Themes and processes in the development of the group

Everybody attended the first session. There was a long period of silence at the beginning. I decided to break the silence by beginning with a question. 'I wonder what this silence might be about.' They all sighed with relief. S, a 67-year-old woman with a history of bereavement responded suddenly by saying, 'I think a baby girl has just been born!'

In Turkey, the custom is that after the birth of a baby girl there is a lot of sadness and silent moments but when the baby is a boy there is a lot of celebration, joy and noise. As soon as S made her comment the women were able to connect with each other positively. They began to examine their births in their families and their parents' disappointment because they were girls. The sadness of being born girls and families became the main theme. They expressed their feelings of loss that they were unwanted children. Nevertheless, this feeling helped them to relate to, and communicate directly with, one another enabling them to explore their births at the Nafsiyat Centre and in the group with me.

AX, a 28-year-old Kurdish woman who was three months pregnant and had five daughters, was desperate for a boy. Once she bore a son, she assumed that her status would increase and it would reach its peak when the son grew up and brought in his bride, the cycle thus repeating. She said, 'If I don't have a son, my marriage will end! My mother-in-law is looking for another bride for my husband because I am hopeless at bearing a son. Please pray for me so I have a son. I will love my baby son and protect him; my life will change for better!'

In some, a secret wish to produce a baby boy might be associated with feelings of accomplishment, because their mother did not give birth to one (Welldon 1988: 51). When a son is so highly valued and brings so much to his mother, it is only natural that he is given much love, protection and indulgence by the women. This experience was very different and interesting for me because my personal experience was the opposite. My birth was a joy for the family. This is why my name is Dilek. When feelings of envy and frustration were stirred up in the group, my name (which means in Turkish 'a wish or something wished for') was used as a theme that I must have been a wanted daughter as opposed to themselves who were all rejected by their mothers.

From the beginning, it seemed as though the group had been running for a long time. I immediately became their wise, educated 'sister who knows a lot, cares a lot'. I was regarded as a role model by the group. Transference was present from the start. Several themes were discussed in the first session such as ethnic differences, culture, racism, refugee issues, depression and group boundaries and commitment. The issue of confidentiality was also raised.

I did not wish them to feel suddenly vulnerable, exposed, frightened and ignored. I wanted the women to feel safe and secure enough to be able to continue with group therapy. Also, to realise that group therapy was different to other social groups; to understand the positive aspects and what they could get from it. In essence, the group offered the potential for change; here, too, were safe boundaries (Kennard et al. 1993).

I felt that it was a powerful group with all its unique characteristics and wealth of experience in its own way of being together. During the next few sessions, the group discussed the subject of health, recognising how a whole range of issues could affect a person's health. Social environment, stress levels and emotional wellbeing were some of the other points raised by the group.

Feelings of inferiority were internalised by all of them. At the beginning, they did not seem to listen to each other and constantly avoided facing painful feelings. During the life of the group, the members went through cycles of loss and depression and there was some scapegoating and idealising going on. They looked to me to provide answers to all of their problems and when I could not do this, they felt punished and wanted to leave the group. During those days they thought all was hopeless and the group was making them worse physically and emotionally and it would be better to go to an English psychiatrist or a GP and to get the right treatment with pharmaceutical drugs. Whereas on other occasions they expressed more positive feelings: 'We are better. Talking means freedom and our therapist is brilliant.'

I became aware of the factors influencing my work in a positive way, such as my life experiences, culture and ethnicity: I was born to immigrant parents. My mother, being Turk/Mongol and my father's family root as Kurd/Kirmanji, have been two of the most important factors which enabled me to work interculturally with this particular 'hurt' women's group. The richness and power of the group in which women found themselves regressing alarmingly, yet supported by the group itself, were enormous.

Gradually, they realised that they had to look at themselves rather than try to change their husbands, fathers and others in order for their lives to change for the better. In the beginning, they were negative and reactive. As time went on they came to realise the extent to which they had internalised the negativity, oppression and violence. I encouraged them to look at their own experiences when examining how society creates norms, rules and makes judgements which control, devalue and undermine individuals as well as the group.

One day, B, a 28-year-old woman with a history of depression said, 'for the first time, I am talking about myself and saying, "I am", not "we are", and I don't feel guilty about it!'

Turkish aphorisms quite naturally came into the conversation but now they questioned and analysed the meaning of these sayings. It was important for the women to share the folk sayings, expressions and talk about delicious Turkish food, which was an enriching experience as a reflection of their identity but which also added to the group identity. The women felt more empowered when they had the opportunity to question and challenge the customs, especially where gender issues were concerned. Here are some examples to give a flavour of the kind of common beliefs reflected in these sayings:

An enemy of the spoon (Women are a burden to the family)
Long hair with a small brain (Women are incapable of thinking and deciding for themselves)
Feed the rook, it will dig out your eye (Women are disloyal)
She is a woman like a man (complimenting a woman using masculinity)

The female bird is the one that makes the nest (The woman is responsible for looking after the family)

One who does not beat their daughter will one day beat their knee (One must not allow their daughter to become a free-thinking, independent individual)

If a man has an affair, it is dirt on his hands. Wash up and it disappears, but when a woman has an affair, it is a stain on her face (which she cannot clean away during her life).

These commonly used expressions caused a stirring amongst these women, they expressed a great deal of anger towards their mothers and other relatives who had brought them up.

Towards the end of group therapy, they became able to play with these Turkish sayings and with the male-dominated culture. By exploring their thoughts and feelings they could see just how much they had been affected and how they had internalised a 'second-class gender identity'.

They found it very strange and different not to be given any directions by me. The group members expressed their surprise at not being criticised and blamed by me. They were listened to and respected for who they were, even if they thought they were 'in a mess'. There was a strong sense of intimacy and solidarity between them. They were able to become individuals as well as being part of the group and contributed creatively into the group life. I found that the less intellectually sophisticated ones provided the group with valuable emotions, feelings and deep insight. Foulkes states, 'In his role as a conductor the therapist supports this group-centred integration directly. Gradually, as the group becomes stronger and can integrate better on its own, it is less in need of borrowing strength' (Foulkes 1984: 63).

They felt valued to have a Turkish-speaking therapist which meant that they did not have to use an interpreter in order to be understood. However, in this group, there was cultural diversity and many regional as well as class differences, but shared language was important to them. They were all aware that switching to another language could widen the gap between the social and family language, causing worry and anxiety as well as affecting them and their family's educational achievement.

When the theme was loss and separation from their homeland, the group felt that there was 'good enough care' in the group (Winnicott 1985). They felt safe to mourn their losses and separation. I, too, felt homesick after some intense sessions, which made me realise that I needed to work through my own losses.

Honour, marriage and women's sexuality

Quite basic to sex role segregation and the subordination of women is the concept of 'honour', particularly in relation to the sexual modesty of a woman. The implication is that men control the sexuality of their women and, thus, have honour. Their control is socially recognised and legitimised. Honour reflects the other social relations within the community, the great significance of other evaluations and 'shame' orientation. So the reaction to an insult to honour should also be public; fights or even blood feuds are communal, not private affairs (Dogramaci 1984). 'Marriage is for life. Only the woman's funeral cask can leave the house.' Divorce is rare in rural Turkey. Even though under the civil code women have inheritance rights equal to men's, in some traditional areas women still get either nothing or half of what men get and these issues are resolved informally within the family, community or the village (Stirling 1953). Women, especially young brides, are expected to serve all the adults within the patriarchal household (Meeker 1976: 383–423).

S said: 'When I was 19, I was in love with a guy. One day I kissed him. I could hear my mother's voice shouting at me, that if any man touches you before marriage you are dirty. You have to be a virgin. If a man has an affair it doesn't matter, it even gives him more power, but if a woman has an affair with a man before marriage then she will always carry the stain on her face. It will be forever visible and she cannot wash it away.'

She continued to tell the group how she had never enjoyed that kiss because of the guilt, shame and fear. She never saw him again. She also said that she never enjoyed sex with her husband and still feels guilty about that first kiss. S has been married for seven years and has three children. She mentioned that she works in the house like a slave because of these feelings of guilt.

One of the women asked what an orgasm was. She said that she heard about it at the Women's Centre. She has been married for four years and has a child. TR, a 50-year-old Armenian woman asked the same question and she is married with seven children.

The group reacted to this issue with tears, laughter and embarrassment. They were able to share most of the secrets in their lives with the group, from politics to sexual relationships and how they felt about them. The more of their lives they shared, the stronger the commitment to each other as a group. Every session was unique. Tears, laughter, joy were present as well as loss. It has been an emotional, stimulating, interesting and unique experience for everyone in the group.

One woman said that they 'lack of skirt', which means that as women, they were vulnerable and needed to be protected and looked after by men. However, later, they all laughed at the irony of this saying it was they, the women, who actually looked after everybody else. It was a pleasure to witness the women celebrating their womanhood, sexuality and being able to accept themselves and each other as they are.

S, a 23-year-old Bosnian woman, said in a late session, 'I am very happy that I am a woman. Otherwise, how would I know all these wonderful women? What a big loss it would be to not know this group. It is a privilege to be here in this group at Nafsiyat.' After this comment, they all cried. It was deeply moving. Every positive feedback released tension and tears which had been trapped within them for so many years.

During the therapeutic process, they were shocked to find out how strongly they could express feelings of anger, envy, jealousy and competitiveness towards each other and me. They also expressed their admiration towards me and said, 'You are all right.'

In the group, they noticed that I sometimes wore the traditional blue amulet which helped them to explore the fear of envy as well as the fear of being envied. They teased me about it supposing that I might possibly wear the blue stone because I have a fear of envy. The meaning of this superstition is that the stone is supposed to send away/protect against any evil or envious eyes. In a way, they found it a relief to think that I too have insecurities about these things and this made it easier for them to admit their fears and insecurities.

Being asylum seekers, the women had to put up with a great deal of uncertainty in their lives because they did not know whether they would be able to stay in the UK or be deported, which could happen at any time. From time to time, their anxiety levels would shoot up when cases regarding refugees and asylum seekers were reported in the media or if they were visiting solicitors about their immigration problems. It was very difficult to hold on to these concerns. I wrote letters for the women to the Home Office to support their applications for residency. The group was worried about having to leave the country without saying goodbye, which was what they had experienced when they left their country. In the group, none of the women ever mentioned leaving the group before the designated time, which was very different from the other groups I ran. They started together and wanted to finish together. We had to work on the ending from an early stage of group life. They mourned the fact that others would be deciding whether they could stay in the UK and therefore whether they could remain in the group.

With the ending of this group, they felt like 'asylum seekers' in the group, and as therapists, we were almost like the officials from the Home Office who were going to decide what happened to them. Through transference, they came to terms with the fact that mourning for the loss of their homeland and loved ones would continue until they die. This was a very powerful realisation and it was very moving when they cried together in the group.

There was a strong preoccupation with religion which either led to an agreement within the group or resulted in conflict and tension. The group members were predominantly *Sunni* or *Alevi*. Some did not have any faith. For some members and particularly for Armenian women, it brought up some painful and difficult experiences. Through the group experience, they learnt how to express difficult subject matters and respect each other's differences.

In the 19th session, the theme was predominantly guilt and pain. Pain is used as a symbol to express emotional distress amongst the Turkish-speaking people, especially women. This symbol has its roots in the belief system, historical and social structure of the community. As a result of not having enough psychological services for this particular client group in Turkey or in the UK, individual members of the community depend on each other for social support. Hence, bodily complaints are the preferred form of appeal for help from the community because mental illness is seen as the sufferer's own responsibility (Yazar and Littlewood 2001). Bodily complaints may be interpreted as an appeal for attention and support from family members, as a reaction to loss and separation or as a demand to be loved, as illustrated by two group members (Van Moffaert and Vereecken 1991: 298–311): F was saying: 'I don't know why but since I came to the UK I have a severe pain in my shoulders. Whenever I go to my GP, he says that I have nothing wrong! It is all in my head! But please believe me I have an unbearable pain.' T, a 40-year-old Cypriot woman who suffered severe back pain as a result of her husband's violence, claims 'I think I am guilty. If I didn't have back pain all the time, my husband wouldn't have left me.' The group explored deeply why they felt guilty throughout their lives. In T's situation, it was her husband who made her ill and yet the idea of divorce made her feel guilty. In a way, 'they were guilty merely by virtue of being a woman'.

The nurturing which they received in the group seemed to help them in turn to nurture their children, partners and families. Two women were able to convince their partners to have individual therapy. One of them decided to start couple therapy with her husband to change together for a better relationship. Two other women were able to end the abusive relationships they had been in for many years. One woman decided to go to Turkey for a holiday after being absent for 18 years. One woman found a refuge house to separate from her violent husband. The majority of women were no longer homeless.

A Kurdish woman had her sixth daughter. She brought her baby to the group and said: 'I don't want any of my daughters to feel the same way I felt. I learnt to value my motherhood and womanhood. I am glad to have my girls and I love them dearly. Thank you to you all.' She reported that her husband values her too.

A 67-year-old woman said: 'This group provided me to have an emotional recycling. My past can't change but now I have strong emotional muscles to cope with whatever happens in life. I feel if I have just started to enjoy my life.'

They all learnt to live with their past lives accepting what had happened to them. As a result, they were positive and forward-looking and were able to use their difficult and painful experiences as a bridge to move on and integrate. They complained less about physical symptoms and reduced their visits to their GPs. As Freud said, 'Symptoms, as we know, are substitute for something that is held back by repression' (Freud 1991: 339).

The women were surprised when they realised how much power and control they had in their environment as well as in the group. They always expressed interest and excitement towards each other, particularly when they were able to shift and move on for good. They were changing both physically and emotionally in terms of the way they looked, dressed, spoke to each other, listened and responded to each other. They all started to learn English. They were able to get in touch with their own needs without feeling guilt and fear. In summary, they were able to recognise their emotional, psychological, physical and social needs. A respect and tolerance towards others developed alongside these feelings of empowerment. This Turkish-speaking group therapy enabled them to realise what they wanted and gave them an emotional tool and confidence to make real and informed choices in their lives. They started to enjoy life in the present with the people they loved most. They had hopes and plans for the future.

The final session

Everyone attended the last session. As with the first session, there was a long silence. The group had worked through the termination very intensely for the last nine weeks with such difficult issues as envy, competition, separation and loss. Who is better than the other? Who has gained most from the treatment? They expressed strong disappointment towards me that I could have done better. I said that I could have done better but I believe that this group has had 'good enough' treatment here for the last year. This interpretation was like a remedy for them. I acknowledged the sadness of having to say goodbye after 44 weeks. The group was strong enough to stay with the feelings of a depressive position. I did not have to be active in this last session. They all wanted to know if I would miss them. I simply answered 'Yes, I will keep you all in mind.' They cried.

Supervision

I had to work through many feelings that were aroused in me during that time. My feminist views led me to jealously guard the group. I did not want to share my female clients' experiences with my supervisor, who was a white, Jewish male analyst. I wondered if I should continue with him or if I should find a female supervisor. I doubted his ability to be a 'good enough' third eye for my women's group (Behr 1995). I then realised that I still have issues around male dominance as well as anxiety about whether I would be able to remain detached from my own issues and still be able to help this particular group. I also worried that I might identify myself with the group issues which would arise as a result of my own experiences. I raised the issue with my supervisor, voiced my anxiety of my supervisor's ability to be a good enough neutral, third eye for the group. We had a good laugh as well as some heated discussions similar to those we had had in the past about racial issues, but now we are both experienced enough to challenge each other about many issues. We enjoyed working through the issues and learning together.

Eventually, I decided that I would continue to work with him. I have always received a great deal of positive and valuable feedback as well as challenges from him. I recognise the need to be aware of the issues the clients bring to the consulting room as well as taking care of my own emotional needs. I have received ongoing support, inspiration and ideas which helped me with the group. Through these tense discussions, I learned more about others as well as myself.

Conclusion

Before the group started, I was angry and disappointed with the attitudes and beliefs expressed by other professionals, including some Turkish workers, about a Turkish-speaking women's group. They were negative and hopeless. They didn't believe that the women could use therapy but also they didn't believe in talking treatment. However, in time they changed their assumptions and this was promising. There is now a demand for more group therapies at Nafsiyat and other therapy centres.

I would like to raise the issue regarding the availability of this kind of therapy. People from ethnic minorities are least likely to have access either to individual or group therapy, because they do not fit in with the 'ideal' model based on traditional Western practice. They do not fit in the present therapy field, economically, socially or culturally. This appears to be the main reason why minority clients are not accessing mainstream services. The regular services do not provide a long-term, safe and affordable space for them.

I believe that psychotherapists should be able to work across all cultures and be prepared to learn that the 'white' (Western) culture is not universal and English is not the only language in which to speak and to communicate. This group psychotherapy experience shows that people on low income or working-class clients can benefit from an intercultural psychotherapy if it is offered appropriately. Clinicians need to rethink their own stereotypes and biases.

As a group analytic/intercultural psychotherapist, I was 'holding rather than analysing' (Winnicott 1985; Mistry and Brown 1997). Sheila Ernst writes that,

> Winnicott ... is saying that the group analyst, him or herself, must make up early maternal task of holding using the framework of the group as part of the holding environment. Group analysis, like individual analysis, works increasingly with the pre-oedipal. Liesel Hearst writes that the group could not be left alone with the maternal holding function but needed the active and direct participation of the conductor.
>
> *(Ernst 1993: 413)*

The emphasis on the 'here and now' approach worked well and enabled members to express their anger and resentment towards their families and the male-dominant society. They were able to express their sadness and anger towards Nafsiyat and me for the termination of the group as they all felt they required long-term therapy sessions. It was important to ensure that the process continued effectively when the group was stuck. I was particularly careful not to make controlling comments which was the experience they had had in their homeland or families. Sexuality and womanhood were explored in great depth and here I was able, I hope, to use my personal and professional experience as a tool.

As a group conductor, a sense of achievement was felt for the group and myself. I believe that the intercultural approach has played an important part in helping this women's group to integrate into society and the community and has enabled them to develop a positive image of themselves, their culture, ethnicity and gender. This group demonstrated that culture, gender and ethnicity can act as a catalyst to growth in a short-term psychodynamic/intercultural psychotherapy group (Kareem and Littlewood 1992: 14). Seeing the clients feel better, show more motivation and enthusiasm towards the group and each other as well as their external lives has been the most rewarding part of my role.

References

Behr, H. (1995) *The Third Eye, Supervision of Analytic Groups: The Integration of Theory and Practice*. London: Routledge

Dogramaci, E. (1984) *Status of Women in Turkey*, 2nd edition. Ankara: Meteksan.

Ernst, S. (1993) Boundaries and Barriers between Men and Women. In W. Knauss and U. Keller (eds), *9th European Symposium in Group Analysis: 'Boundaries and Barriers'*. Heidelberg, 29 August–4 September. London: Mattes Verlag Heidelberg.

Foulkes, S.H. (1984) *Therapeutic Group Analysis*. London: Karnac.

Freud, S. (1991) *Introductory Lectures on Psychoanalysis*. Harmondsworth: Penguin.

Kareem, J. and Littlewood, R. (eds) (1992) *Intercultural Therapy*. Oxford: Blackwell Scientific.

Kennard, D., Roberts, J. and Winter, D. (1993) *A Workbook of Group Analytic Interventions*. London: Routledge.

Meeker, M.E. (1976) Meaning and Society in the Near East: Examples from the Black Sea Turks and the Levantine Arabs. *International Journal of Middle East Studies*, 7: 383–422.

Mistry, T. and Brown, A. (1997) *Race and Group Work*. London: Whiting and Birch.

Piers, G. and Singer, M.B. (1953) *Shame and Guilt: A Psychoanalytic and a Cultural Study*. Springfield, IL: Charles C. Thomas.

Stirling, P. (1953) Social Ranking in a Turkish Village. *British Journal of Sociology*, 4: 31–44.

Van Moffaert, M. and Vereecken, J.A. (1991) Somatisation of Psychiatric Illness in Mediterranean Migrants in Belgium. *Culture, Medicine and Psychiatry*, 13: 297–313.

Welldon, E. (1988) *Mother, Madonna, Whore*. London: Guilford.

Winnicott, D.W. (1985) *The Maturational Processes and the Facilitating Environment*. London: Institute of Psycho-analysis, Karnac.

Yazar, J. and Littlewood, R. (2001) Against Overinterpretation: The Understanding of Pain amongst Turkish and Kurdish Speakers in London. *International Journal of Social Psychiatry*, 47: 20–33.

5

FINDING OUR VOICE ACROSS THE BLACK/WHITE DIVIDE

Race issues in therapy

Eugene Ellis

In January 2014, the author set about trying to create the type of space that he thought would be perceived as safe enough in order for dialogue around race issues in therapy to take place. Therapists of all backgrounds came together, both Black and white, to look at issues of race in their therapy, supervision and training practice. They brought with them dilemmas they had experienced in their day-to-day practice where race was a feature. The group as a whole engaged in processing these dilemmas and extracting learning from them. There were no teachers.

This chapter explores and expands on some of the issues and processes that arose out of the group space.

Most schools of psychotherapy and counselling are rooted in an ethos and commitment to the common good and to liberating those people who have been burdened by their experiences and circumstances. This ethos is alive and countering such issues in the human condition as depression, sexual abuse and gender bias among all cultures and peoples. The area where there is much less engagement, insight and conversation, however, is the area of 'race', and the hidden impact that race has both on the mental health of individuals and on society in general.

The response to issues of race in the therapeutic space and in the psychotherapy and counselling profession is (whilst there are exceptions) often silence, denial and rage. There may also be a focus on the distress of those who are not in the oppressed group, which results in the person experiencing the oppression being left with their distress having not been met, with a sense that their distress is too much for others to handle. Even for the well intentioned, the race conversation is difficult to begin and maintain. However, for the profession to fulfil our common and good ethos, the first step must be engaging in it within therapeutic practice and in the training of therapists.

In January 2014, I set about creating the type of space that I felt could have potential for a meaningful dialogue to take place around race issues in the therapeutic process and in training. These forums were initially called Trainers' Forums, but they were then differentiated into two different forums, one for trainers and one for therapists, as it became clear while going through the process that there was a need for a similar type of space for clinicians who were not trainers.

The first few groups were initially facilitated by me and Celia Levi, who had previously developed and taught on the Diploma in Practitioner Counselling at London's City Lit, and were hosted by City Lit. Subsequent groups were then hosted by Place2Be and were facilitated by me and my colleague, Arike (several forums were facilitated by me and psychotherapist Kris Black). Both Arike and I have experience in teaching diversity issues on psychotherapy and counselling training courses and both of us identify as Black men. Arike and I also felt some measure of ability and confidence in holding issues that might come up for individual members of the group and for the group as a whole. At the same time, we declared that we were not experts but fellow participants on a journey towards becoming more competent in working therapeutically with these issues.

The forums were attended by therapists and trainers of all backgrounds, both Black and white, to look at issues of race in their therapy, supervision and training practice. During the initial groups, the participants' expectations and what they experienced as the blocks to working with race were explored, and from there the basic outline of the group was established.

This chapter will reflect on the process of setting up the structure of the forums, taking into account those things that were identified by participants in the early stages and also our thinking around what would constitute significant dialogue. This chapter will also reflect on the forum participants' process as race issues came into the foreground, from both sides of the race divide, with a view to identifying what would encourage and maintain an ability to stay at what Perls calls the Contact Boundary (1992) of the race dialogue, and to identify the processes individuals go through to find their voice in this area.

It should be noted that participants in these forums had chosen to be there, were well-intentioned and thoughtful people, and felt a need to heal the hurts of racism and empower themselves in order to move past the trauma they see internalised in themselves and in others. This is not of course how the typical group within training institutions and elsewhere is constituted, but it was hoped that what eventually emerged out of this space would contribute towards the growing body of knowledge and experience that others were also engaged in exploring.

The first trainers' forum took place in January 2014. Twenty-eight tutors, trainers and supervisors from a range of ethnicities and theoretical orientations met to begin the process of envisioning the forums to come. Not everyone in this session was a trainer and there was a lot of uncertainty about what the group was about, including on the part of the facilitators. It was, however, emphasised by the latter that the focus of the forum would be about addressing the specifics of Black/white issues in psychotherapy and counselling practice. This would not be to the exclusion of other oppressed groups, as it was acknowledged that it would be hard to talk about specific oppressions without other oppressed groups being evoked, but the focus of the forum would always return to the issue of race as a way to stay focused and to achieve an adequate depth of exploration in one area.

What arose from this first forum was that participants wanted to increase their self-awareness and knowledge about Black and minority ethnic (BME) issues. Participants were looking for a space to share real experiences and scenarios in small discussion groups. Some participants had expected the forum to be a training session, however, they did feel that they received what they needed from observing the group process and listening to other participants sharing their experiences around race. The general feeling after the first forum was that this was a rare opportunity to think with others about their own identity and feelings about their differences in relation to others.

The second forum was held in March 2014. On this occasion, there were 15 participants: two Black men, seven Black and Asian women, one white man and six white women. This forum meeting focused on what people would like from the forum in more detail and was facilitated in a more structured way. A presentation on race was given at the beginning of the forum, and participants were asked to observe what was happening to them as they listened and were drawn into the race conversation. We observed the following:

- Being made to feel responsible for racism.
- A feeling of physical constriction in the body.
- A lot of 'left-brain activity' with participants' thinking becoming more rigid.
- A feeling of having to take responsibility along with internal questions such as 'Why do I need to do that?' and then noticing 'I do not want to take responsibility'.
- A recognition of: 'Oh, that's me', 'That's mine' with resultant shock. There was first a 'not recognising' and then a recognising.
- Some participants were reminded that their personal hurt associated with racism is not normally seen.
- Someone noted: 'As we talk and need to talk, it gets harder to talk'.
- There were questions around safety: can it be safe? Can it be taught?
- There were thoughts like 'I want you to tell me what to do'.

Participants were asked about what they held for the future around these issues in the therapy profession. Among some of the responses were that diversity training would become more common; that trainers would become more competent and understand their limits (conscious incompetence); that there should be a diversity of therapists that reflected the community in which they worked; that there could be more environments where listening around race issues happens; that trainers have the capacity to work with the hurt and pain of racism; that the identity of whiteness must be explored within training; and that accrediting bodies should take a lead and be more proactive.

Blocks that were identified by participants around race, and which related to their own personal development, included a lack of safety felt when voicing their shared concerns, managing the fear that then arose and the limitations of the theoretical models that they had been taught.

The facilitators reflected on the experiences of the group as well as their own experiences in similar race conversations and began to structure what the group might look like in the future. Participants in the forum were experiencing real physiological responses that were uncomfortable and they felt fear, shame and anxiety. They also felt that there was no clear map of where we were heading, which generated further fear and unsafety. The forum participants felt an inner compulsion to work on these issues but had doubts about the possibility of any real change in how they responded in the race conversation and doubts that working on these issues would make a difference. What was clearly needed was a roadmap to work through the trauma associated with racism on both sides of the race divide, as well as metaphors and theories that conveyed the landscape into which participants were entering. Trauma can be defined as a series of events, or a set of enduring conditions, in which an individual 'experiences (subjectively) a threat to life, bodily integrity, or sanity' (Saakvitne et al. 2000).

Recognition trauma

Dr Isha McKenzie-Mavinga's doctoral project in 2005 was intended to make a difference to counsellor training. At the beginning of the study, she brought to the surface the shared concerns of students on training courses. These concerns were displayed in different ways by both Black and white trainees:

> White trainees expressed the fear of losing their assumed power in the unconscious schema of institutional racism. Black trainees experience fears associated with their emancipation from the role of the oppressed. I have named the processing of these fears and feelings for both black and white trainees 'recognition trauma', because this term gives meaning to the emotional process of exploring black issues.
>
> *(McKenzie-Mavinga 2009: 1)*

She goes on to say 'trainees' feelings about racism, guilt, history and trust needed to be processed to form a bridge that would enable their progress from fear to transformation' (2009: 2).

McKenzie-Mavinga is suggesting here that despite the considerable challenges in facilitating the journey through the fear associated with the race conversation, there is a process people can go through that moves them from feelings of survival to a place of compassion and empathy for the many points of view and people expressing them within this subject (2009).

When given this idea of recognition trauma, the facilitators of the forum began to think less about the forum being used to give information around race dynamics in the therapeutic process (though this is still important) and instead began to envision the forum as a means by which group members could work through the process of recognition trauma.

Working through recognition trauma may be likened to the working through of Klein's 'depressive position' (Klein 1940). Klein posited that from six months old, a child splits the mother into good and bad, which facilitates the containment of the child's destructive drives and allows the creative development of its self-organisation. If all goes well, good experiences predominate over bad and the child is led to withdraw its projection of destructive urges as it comes to realise, at an unconscious level, that its destructive attacks at the bad mother are also directed at the same person — the good mother. This leads to intense feelings of guilt and sorrow, and is termed by Klein as the 'depressive position'. Once the depressive position is worked through, the child develops the capacity to form emotionally durable relationships, to experience other people as separate, and as having both good and bad human qualities.

If all does not go well and bad experiences dominate over good, the child does not go through the depressive position and continues to split people into good or bad, and that bad people are simply a receptacle for their destructive fantasies. 'Klein's position that therapists can provide a container for repairing destructive urges from the past sits well with the healing process of racism' (McKenzie-Mavinga 2009: 81). The process of working through recognition trauma starts off with the supposition that 'the impact of racism can lay dormant in the psyche through generations or the lifetime of an individual' (2009: 80). She named this 'ancestral baggage'.

Once unconscious material related to race begins to surface, there is then a recognition or an awakening of the hurt related to racism, either as a victim or as a witness. This recognition brings with it powerful and often overwhelming distress and there is often an experience of feeling physiologically unsafe. Defensive strategies of denial, silence and rage can be used as survival strategies to protect ourselves against this distress. These defences can be fixed or they can be used as a way to come to terms with the trauma in our own time.

The unconscious becoming conscious provokes a need to heal the hurts of racism and empower oneself in order to move past the trauma associated with racist provocation, whether that is from others or the internalised self. As we become more aware of the internalisation of the 'race paradigm' in our thinking, feelings and behaviour, the challenge then becomes finding appropriate support where one can work through what comes up and find strategies to help one remain curious and stay in the new paradigm. When working through recognition trauma, there can be a recovery from the trauma where one can be left with the recognition.

Relationship trauma

Along with a psychoanalytical approach to understanding what was happening, the facilitators were also aware of their own and the other participants' physiological responses. There was clearly some activation of traumatic material in all members of the group regardless of race or ethnicity. The physical responses that people were experiencing, such as increased heart rate or tightening of the stomach, needed to be contextualised in terms of trauma theory: an understanding of what was happening on a bodily level might offer the potential to have some mastery over these physiological responses. It may also provide some strategies to help participants remain at the contact boundary of these issues.

The central theme for everyone with regard to opening the race conversation is fear. There is a sense of feeling unsafe, and wondering 'why is this?'. A question then arises – 'Is it possible to feel safe?' Before digging into this question, we need to give some attention to where this feeling of being unsafe comes from and why it overpowers our cognitive functioning.

The research into intergenerational trauma is strongly pointing towards the idea that extreme trauma experienced by social groups has psychological consequences for subsequent generations, and that there is a right-brain-to-right-brain communication between parent and child of disorganised states of mind. This might happen not just between parents and children of survivors, but also parents and children of non-survivors.

Aileen Alleyne (2012) argues that when one thinks of the Jewish experience today, it is hard to separate it from the Holocaust and, in exactly the same way, the Black experience today cannot be separated from the systematic dehumanisation of African slaves. She notes that while there is a feeling that slavery has been dealt with (it happened a long time ago), as we know, along with all kinds of trauma, one still has a dysfunctional relationship with the traumatising other, which gets passed on through the generations.

Barbara Fletchman Smith (2000: 21), in her book 'Mental Slavery', says:

> I think that history has fundamentally influenced the way people of European and African origin treat one another today, and also the way in which each regards themselves. Slavery severely traumatised people – to such an extent that it affected people's capacity to procreate. Terror, perpetual fear, cruel abuse and gruelling work were the order of the day.

She goes on to note that 'By damaging others, people also damage themselves, and I suspect that if I were to focus on the children of former slave owners, then I would discover traumas there too. In the making of empires, it is inevitable that crimes will be committed' (2000: 15).

Given that there is much evidence that points us towards intergenerational trauma in survivors and witnesses, how does it manifest itself in the therapeutic space and in the therapy room?

Often, the suffering of parents is repeated by the children who, on the unconscious level, repeat themes fundamental in the lives of the parents, precisely because the parents have consciously forced themselves to reject that suffering in order to survive, disassociating certain memories or features from the self (Mucci 2013). These themes become what are called implicit memories (Viotti 2016): memories that are not conscious and that can be neither remembered nor verbalised because of the way they are encoded in the brain. Under the trigger of the race conversation, these implicit memories are activated, which dysregulates the autonomic nervous system and leads to the physiological symptoms the people in our forum described.

These implicit memories also carry with them the capacity to activate the shame response. Shame is one of the socialising emotions that permeates the race conversation. If we are to accept that intergenerational trauma shapes unconscious organising principles that get passed on through generations, then it is easy to see that the race conversation can trigger shame without there being an explicit memory to contextualise the experience. Once shame is triggered, we feel – at our core – bad. We are then triggered into one of the four general responses of shame, which are avoidance, withdrawal, attacking oneself or attacking others. In simple terms, the race conversation, when it gets underway, most of the time develops into a 'what you are' or 'what I am' conversation, rather than a 'what was said' or 'what that means' conversation (Smooth 2011). The 'what you are' conversation might look like blaming the person that triggered the uncomfortable feelings (normally a person of colour) or feeling like a bad person for showing racial cognitive biases and becoming overwhelmed by it, or radically defending the 'good person' position.

Along with this, it should not be forgotten that in almost all racial encounters, what is also present is commonly called 'everyday racial microaggressions', which are brief and commonplace daily verbal, behavioural or environmental indignities, whether intentional or unintentional, and which can impair the development of a therapeutic alliance (Sue et al. 2007).

To summarise the theory and thinking that the facilitators were holding as the trainers and therapists' forums progressed, the notion of recognition trauma gives us a sense that there is a paradigm shift still to be made, one where an individual moves from triggered defences to a more flexible and situation-specific engagement with the issues of race, together with a greater capacity to stay at the contact boundary with another when race is evoked. The understanding of how trauma transmits itself intergenerationally was also taken as important, as were the everyday racial microaggressions that made up part of everyday life.

Given that the forums were entering into the landscape of trauma, the facilitators also approached the sessions through the lens of 'relational trauma'. Relational trauma is a type of trauma that is man-made, as opposed to trauma that is accidental or caused by nature. This is a burgeoning field of treatment and research, which focuses on the body as a significant organiser of experience and includes body-focused and mindfulness approaches.

The facilitators now felt they had a framework to make sense of what was happening to the body and the mind. The forums were then organised around these ideas and theories. Attention was paid to people's 'window of stress tolerance' (Siegel 1999), which is the term used to describe the zone of arousal in which a person is able to function most effectively. With an understanding that people's autonomic nervous systems were likely to be in states of active defence, future sessions started with a 'mindfulness body scan', which was usually welcomed. It also gave participants a sense of slowing things down, moving away from negative cognitive narratives and staying in touch with their present selves.

There was then an activity that made a connection between participants' present experience and their imagination. This was usually done through visual images or metaphors, which are powerful mediums in the race paradigm. The mindfulness and visual metaphor activities would allow participants to make a connection with their implicit memories in a way that was regulated and at the same time stayed in contact with what was there.

In the early forums, participants were asking for a space to share real experiences and scenarios in small groups. The facilitators also felt that there were imaginary or fantasy scenarios that were held by individuals that could also be invited into the space. After the initial body tracking and metaphor activities, the forum space would then invite participants to bring scenarios in their work, real or imagined, where race was a feature that could be used as material for processing. The intention was to work on these scenarios and, whilst doing so, receive enthusiastic support, make attempts to cognitively organise the normally unseen and unsaid and to be witnessed and acknowledged in the places that people found themselves.

The following three scenarios and experiences within the forum were chosen to highlight the normal dynamics of the landscape of the race conversation so that others, who might wish to create similar groups, can get a sense of what they could expect. They will also provide some thinking about what is going on underneath the behaviour in order to give the behaviour context and foster understanding.

In my role as director of the Black and Asian Therapist Network, I receive a lot of correspondence from Black students regarding their final dissertation and the difficulties this arises for the students and the institutes they train in. Elucidation of themes of race in the therapeutic space is often chosen for the final dissertation, which can result in both the student and the organisation being caught up in rather confusing race conversation dynamics.

In our forum, a participant who was connected to a training organisation brought an issue about the number of fails in the final dissertation the previous year. A disproportionate number of the failed students were from marginalised communities, mostly BME. The dissertations were challenging and innovative pieces of written work, but did not meet the expected criteria. The dissertations were not critically evaluative, and research, along with ethics, were not fully considered. The question from the institution's point of view was – what is going on here? The students also had to submit a final draft to their dissertation supervisor before actual submission, but in some cases, this did not happen.

There were many ideas, which were shared in small group discussions. What emerged was that students are often in a position of writing the dissertation, not having had many opportunities to work through the race paradigm in the course of training. Coupled with this, there is limited reference material about race and the therapeutic process in the course material. Also, a dissertation submission that is about race puts the training organisation in a race conversation with the student, with all of the complications that this brings. The organisation is then potentially in the unenviable position from the student's point of view of, consciously or unconsciously, retraumatising and invalidating the experience of the Black student once again.

The second scenario from the forum came from a Black participant. This participant was teaching a group of students with various heritages, and two Black students kept themselves separate from the rest of the group: also one of the two was often late. There was no particular question as such, but a sense of wanting to become clearer about what might be going on unconsciously. The forum wanted to explore how any unconscious material might impact on their perceptions of the trainer challenging what was happening, given that both teacher and students identified as Black.

To process this situation, a group of participants took the position of trainer, while another group represented the student position and a third group represented a supervisory position. Each of these groups positioned themselves in the middle of the wider group and spoke to the rest of the group from that position.

Amongst themes relating to the dynamics of oppression and system beating (Batts 1998) and possible splitting towards the trainer in the form of idealisation or devaluation, what emerged was a sense that the students felt they needed to come together to feel safe. The importance of identity emerged as a central theme and how important this is when living one's life.

To have an identity is like life and death. Who is in my tribe? Once our identity is worked out within us we can settle into living our lives with more ease and with less preoccupation with safety. On the one hand, identity gives us an association with a group who will look out for us and at the same time it sets up 'the other' (however that is organised, in this case possibly the Black other who is not us anymore) as a potential threat.

There is also often a threat that people feel when they are faced with contemplating the effect on them of Black people meeting separately in groups. For Black people, it is an opportunity to feel a connection with a group of people who are engaging in a particular way and with a particular focus. At the same time this is happening, the other, who is not part of the group, feels an undercurrent of threat and 'not belonging', which is the other side of identity.

The third scenario we had was from a white participant who noted during one session that they had left the previous group with a lot of shame, and that this shame had stayed with them for four weeks and was clearly a big experience. They were not sure that they wanted to come back but fortunately did. The reason for the shame was explored and what came to light was that this participant imagined that one of the facilitators, who was a Black man, would see her as a bad person. The particular incident that brought this feeling about was then explored. What emerged was that the situation, which felt profoundly significant to the participant, was not one of which the facilitator had any conscious memory.

The shame that this participant had felt could be said to have been activated through some implicit memory and unconscious organising principle, which the facilitator activated unknowingly. This activation of shame moved the participant into a 'what I am' conversation and 'what I am is bad'. The participant then attributed this mental state as something the facilitator must be thinking, too. If this was a normal everyday situation, or if the participant had made another choice and decided not to come back to the forum or had chosen not to verbalise their experience when they did come back, then the opportunity to challenge what was felt to be happening would have been missed. The participant was taking quite a risk as the facilitator could theoretically have said 'Yes, I do think you are a bad person' and that would have been devastating for the participant.

The participant in the previous scenario must have, at some level, sensed that their disclosure would have had a high probability of being met with a compassionate response. Coming back to the theme of feeling unsafe in the race conversation and the question 'Is it possible to feel safe?', it is possible to organise the field so that there are more opportunities for individuals to experience a sense of safety, but this also needs to come with an understanding that there can be no change if it is too safe.

Conclusion

One area of development for the future of the forum would be around working with the rage that is very near the surface for many of the participants. There is something about rage being witnessed and hurt being acknowledged and validated on both sides of the racial divide that makes it a very important part of the healing process. As Laub and Auerhahn (1984) attest, 'the more profound the outer silence, the more pervasive was the inner impact of the events'.

This is probably our biggest hurdle in working with race in the therapeutic process. In my own training as a psychotherapist, my expressions of rage and hurt from racism were expressed through the arts and in the therapeutic setting through the non-verbal. These are powerful modes of working with rage, hurt and grief, and I suspect in future forums that these modes of working, along with others, will need to be explored more fully.

The willingness of the participants who attended the trainer and therapist forums to explore their personal experience of the race paradigm offered an important opportunity to get in touch with what happens at the boundary of the Black/white divide. Evoking this divide triggers a physiological response of not feeling safe, of danger or of life threat. This experience makes sense when you begin to get in touch with the legacy of racism and its many indefensible acts that result in life-threatening inner and outer realities, unconsciously and non-verbally, being transmitted to our children and repeated through the generations for both victims and witnesses.

In our forums, what did encourage staying at the contact boundary of this race conversation was the idea of recognition trauma, which brings with it an understanding that there can indeed be a recovery from intergenerational race trauma. When this is worked through there is both a recognition of the impact of race on people's lives and an inner freedom to respond with more flexibility in the actual moment.

What also contributed to a participant's capacity to stay at the contact boundary was the bringing of mindful awareness to inner body sensation and movement as well as monitoring awareness of the present moment. Bringing this kind of awareness to the race conversation is important because trauma tends to organise current experience towards a preoccupation with past events or future consequences, which then compromises our ability to respond to what lies behind the trauma-activated behaviours, which are within us and within the other.

The question I posed earlier in this chapter 'What constitutes a significant race dialogue?' can be answered as a willingness to recognise and stay in contact with the hurt that race has inflicted on both sides of the Black/white divide. As well as this, there needs to be a willingness to give voice to the parts of us that are in denial or feel silenced or feel either rage or shame, and for others to bear witness to this and to demonstrate acceptance and understanding.

It is rare to have a therapeutic setting where one can engage significantly in the race conversation. It is essential, however, that these types of therapeutic setting become more common if the profession that specialises in working with all aspects of the human condition (and on what impacts on the mental health of individuals) is to fulfil its commitment to the common good and to liberating those that have been burdened by that silence which is part of the race paradigm.

References

Alleyne, A. (2012) Transcending Intergenerational Trauma. Giving Voice to the Silent Impact of Racism: BAATN Conference, London. Retrieved from: http://baatn.podomatic.com/?p=2 (accessed 13 November 2016).
Batts, V. (1998) *Modern Racism: New Melody for the Same Old Tunes*. Cambridge, MA: Episcopal Divinity School.
Fletchman Smith, B. (2000) *Mental Slavery: Psychoanalytical Studies of Caribbean People*. London: Karnac.
Klein, M. (1940) Mourning and Its Relation to Manic-Depressive States. *International Journal Psycho-Analysis*, 21: 125–153.
Laub, D. and Auerhahn, N.C. (1984) Reverberations of Genocide: Its Expression in the Conscious and Unconscious of Post-Holocaust Generations. In: S.S. Luel and P. Marcus (eds), *Psychoanalytic Reflections on the Holocaust*, p. 154. New York: Holocaust Awareness Institute, Center for Judaic Studies, University of Denver, and KTAV Publishing House.
McKenzie-Mavinga, I. (2009) *Black Issues in the Therapeutic Process*. Basingstoke: Palgrave Macmillan.
Mucci, C. (2013) *Beyond Individual and Collective Trauma: Intergenerational transmission, Psychoanalytical treatment, and the Dynamic of Forgiveness*. London: Karnac.
Perls, F. (1992). *Gestalt Therapy Verbatim*. Highland, NY: Gestalt Journal Press.
Saakvitne, K.W., Gamble, S., Pearlman, L. and Lev, B. (2000) *Risking Connection: A Training Curriculum for Working with Survivors of Childhood Abuse*. Lutherville, MD: Sidran Press.

Siegel, D.J. (1999) *The Developing Mind*. New York: Guilford.
Smooth, J. (2011) How I Learned to Stop Worrying and Love Discussing Race. TEDxHampshireCollege. Retrieved from: www.youtube.com/watch?v=MbdxeFcQtaU (accessed 29 March 2017).
Sue, D.W., Capodilupo, C.M., Torino, G.C., Bucceri, J.M., Holder, A.M.B., Nadal, K.L. and Esquilin, M. (2007) Racial Microaggressions in Everyday Life: Implications for Clinical Practice. *American Psychologist*, May–June: 1.
Viotti, G. (2016) Attachment, Implicit Memory, and the Unrepressed Unconscious. In G. Craparo and C. Mucci (eds), *Unrepressed Unconscious, Implicit Memory, and Clinical Work*. London: Karnac.

6

RACISM IN THE ROOM

Internal working model of the 'non-white' introject

Deri Hughes

Introduction

This is an account of my understanding of a psychotherapy treatment I undertook with a male Asian patient suffering with severe anxiety which manifested itself mainly in chronic paranoia. The chapter focuses on the way that projective identification facilitated my understanding of the patient's issues and unconscious distress. It also highlights the way that the therapists' and patients' life experiences may together contribute to an understanding of what is wrong and so enable a lessening of personal distress and allow a more benign and valuable experience of the self. The following insight by Bhui is central to this chapter:

> A common feature of prejudice is its capacity to silence victims and destroy the 'capacity to think'. Confusions arise in the mind of the victim, thinking is disrupted. Attacks on the capacity to think and link thoughts have been described in the psychoanalytic literature as a function of psychotic process, a projection of destructive 'breaks' into someone else's mind in order to paralyse and prevent them making sense of what is being done, not to them as a physical person, but to their mind.
>
> *(Bhui 2002: 58)*

The term 'non-white' in this chapter refers to my particular patient's specific experience of an internal object in the context of a white racist society and I generalise this introjection as relevant particularly to many Black, Asian, Middle Eastern and Latino people in the UK. The terms 'non-Black' and 'non-Asian' and so on could also be substituted in the context of a different society and patient. An African patient of mine recently told me that she had not realised she was Black until she came to the UK. I shared with her my experience of not realising I was white until I went to Africa and the Middle East.

I am white and live and work in the United Kingdom where I grew up, which is a predominately white society and I use the term 'white racist society' to indicate the historical and current institutional and social attitudes, conscious and unconscious, that have and still do oppress persons who do not have what is generally known as white skin colour. This is not to say that every white person in the UK is consciously racist, even though some are. However, unconsciously, I speculate it is a different matter. When I decided to train as an intercultural psychotherapist I arranged to meet the clinical director of the course outside his office in London for an interview. As I was looking down the road, a voice behind me said, 'Deri Hughes?' When I turned around I saw a tall, middle-aged, Black man, not the old, grey-haired white man in a trilby and tweeds that I suddenly realised I had been conditioned by racial stereotyping to expect. In the interview that followed we were then able to think together about how I had become aware of my own unconscious racism in that moment. Unconscious racism is, I believe, endemic in the UK and it is vital that psychotherapists become aware of their own racially prejudiced attitudes if they are to be at all helpful to patients who have been hurt by racism.

In writing this chapter I have a therapeutic audience of psychotherapists, psychologists and patients in mind and have therefore assumed a certain basic familiarity with psychotherapeutic terms. However, I have also deliberately tried not to use dense language and endeavoured to maintain clarity. I hope this is your, the reader's, experience.

My ex-patient GS has given his permission for me to give an account of his psychotherapy treatment with me and has approved the content of this chapter.

Therapist experience

Bhui's statement above describes very well the impact upon me of a public interaction I had a few years ago with a Black speaker at an intercultural psychotherapy conference in London. I am a middle-aged, white, male, Welsh psychotherapist. During questions at the end of his helpful talk I challenged the speaker's use of the term 'non-white' in his discourse and in his writings as a negative identity label given to groups of people and individuals, by a predominately white racist society, either consciously or unconsciously, creating a numbing sense of inferiority in human beings. His response was to angrily dismiss my question as of no relevance in a manner that appeared to me to convey contempt and intolerance. I was shocked into the state of mind that Bhui has conveyed in the quote above. My instinct at the moment of the interaction was that I was being dismissed out of hand because I am a white person. This produced the state of mind in me that Bhui describes so well. After some time reflecting on this incident the thought occurred to me that I was dismissed because I was a 'non-Black/non-Asian'. In the speaker's mind at least, it seemed that at an intercultural gathering where the majority of people attending were from various people groups and of various skin colours, a white person had to know his place, and he does not challenge a Black speaker. At least in retrospect that is what I thought. Sometime later I recognised my experience in what McKenzie-Mavinga (2011) has described as 'recognition trauma' (see below).

Freud (1946) outlines well the vehement indignation by a person at someone else's (perceived) wrongdoing as the precursor of and substitute for guilty feelings on their own account. Their indignation increases automatically when the perception of their own guilt is imminent. This can also be observed as the way someone responds to accusations of racism when they suddenly become aware of their guilt. This is my theory about the Black speaker at the conference and his indignant response to my questioning.

My patient: GS

My patient, the eldest son in a Sikh family now in his late 30s, grew up in Britain as a boy with a top-knot, experiencing regular racist abuse and humiliation from a white community that he perceived as 'better' than him, a concept that was reinforced by a family that had historically migrated from India and had experienced the widespread 'no Blacks' prejudice barring them from jobs and accommodation in the UK. His father had worked very hard to establish a successful family business, despite the odds. GS himself is a successful businessman who has provided very well for his own family through hard work and a sense of never being good enough, never ever doing enough and so striving for perfection and acceptability in everything. He runs the family business inherited from his parents and has been constantly dependent upon their approval to feel acceptable to himself. He is relatively wealthy, his children are in university and he provides for everyone very well. And yet he is unwell due to having internalised both a castrated view of himself as a male person and a racist view of himself as 'non-white'. Non-man, non-white, 'pathetic' and 'useless'. Racism has not traumatised him in the accepted sense of trauma. There are no outward signs of illness. The scars are internal, private and largely unconscious although manifesting outwardly occasionally in paralysing anxiety, paranoia and fear of what others will think of him. His developmental experience of psychological castration and disapproval grew a self-hating view of himself as inadequate and pathetic as a man. This laid the ground for the impact of racism in the wider society to imprint the negative self-view even further and identify himself with the inferior 'other'. He grew up into racism as it were. For GS his ethnic inferiority to the white other was a given that he did not question; an internalised racism conditioned by an abusive family history. The white racist view of him as not good enough was simply a message he had received about himself all his life, he just accepted it along with his anxiety. His presenting issues for therapy were not consciously to do with his ethnicity, they were to do with crippling anxiety about himself as a man in a persecutory Asian family and social context.

Clinical material

Subsequent to my experience with the speaker at the conference (see above) a similar experience of attack on my ability to think happened to me again in a completely different context and manner. I had been treating GS for some time with a combination of psychodynamic and eye movement desensitisation and reprocessing (EMDR) psychotherapies. He had presented with complex post-traumatic stress disorder relating to developmental bullying and denigration by family members during his childhood, adolescence and adulthood who had humiliated and physically abused him privately and in public and who castrated him in a psychological sense to such a degree that he experienced himself as a ridiculous, pathetic person who could not call himself a man. He saw himself as 'a wuss'. It was clear that his early experiences had traumatised him. We decided to address the trauma anxiety with EMDR (Shapiro 2001) work first and this was successful in reducing his distress over a period of time. This work was largely focused on trauma experienced in the Asian context of an extended family and the expectations of the wider Sikh community in his role as the eldest son. During this trauma work, there were times when GS explicitly affirmed his inferiority to me as a white man. Our interactions about this led to a second phase of therapy using a psychodynamic approach to address the wider issues of social anxiety and self-loathing affecting his confidence and identity as a man worthy of respect. He constantly compared himself to other men and found himself lacking. It was a given for him that he was inferior to white people.

In one session, I highlighted the fact that I am a white male therapist and I wondered with him if he imagined I found him pathetic and not much of a man. His response froze my ability to think or make sense of his response temporarily in the context of a 'safe' therapeutic relationship. His replies were matter of fact, unequivocally stated:

THERAPIST: Perhaps you imagine I think you are a pathetic excuse for a man.
PATIENT: I shouldn't really be in the same room as you, a white man.
T: Because?
P (smiling profusely): Well … you are white and better than me.
T: You believe I am better than you because I am a white person?
P: Well, yes.
T: (not able to think momentarily and feelings of huge uncertainty and fear of doing the wrong thing).

I realised later that what had happened to me was an experience of projective identification:

> Projective identification is a concept that addresses the way in which feeling states corresponding to the unconscious fantasies of one person (the projector) are engendered in and processed by another person (the recipient), that is, the way in which one person makes use of another person to experience and contain an aspect of himself. The projector has the primarily unconscious

fantasy of getting rid of an unwanted or endangered part of himself (including internal objects) and of depositing that part in another person in a powerfully controlling way. In other words, the recipient is pressured to engage in an identification with a specific, disowned aspect of the projector.

(Ogden 1992)

In reflecting on my experience with him after the session I understood the interaction as his unconsciously projecting his unbearable experience of racism into me, the recipient therapist, and my identifying with it from my own experience of the incident with the speaker at the conference. GS's belief that I was superior to him because I am white triggered my painful experience of feeling inferior to the Black speaker. It was as though my amygdala had identified an experience similar to a past traumatic experience and brought the paralysing emotions and experience to mind, but my left brain did not identify the specific issue causing the feelings until later when I was able to reflect on the interaction (see McGilchrist 2009). I had felt a 'non'-person at the conference and my patient's comments triggered this emotional memory as he unconsciously projected his experience of being a 'non-white' patient in the presence of a white therapist. He and I had both experienced a kind of racial identity negation which was now being projected by him and identified with by me unconsciously in the therapeutic encounter. He felt that he was not entitled to a voice in the room with me, just as I had experienced 'voicelessness' at the conference. Somehow we had both complied with this oppression of our racial identity, suggesting the presence of what I shall call the 'non-'internal object relationship. In addition, GS's life experience of psychological castration at the hands of his extended family, compounded by the majority white society's racist oppression and outgroup identification (Bhugra and Bhui 2002), had left him convinced of his inferiority to both other, particularly Asian, men and to the white world outside of his own ethnic community. He hated himself and he was unconsciously communicating to me what the impact of the racism he had suffered was and its causal part in his crippling anxiety and paranoia.

GS disclosed at one point that during his childhood he thought of white people as gods. It was, he commented to me, as though they came from a different, better planet. In another session, much later on in his treatment, he was wondering where to take his family on holiday. He mentioned that he had been looking at locations and hotels and had seen some lovely destinations:

PATIENT: Some of the hotels are nice, the 5-star hotels, they are really nice but I couldn't take them there.
THERAPIST: What do you mean by that I wonder?
P: Well ... those hotels are for white people.
T: You want me to know that you don't feel good enough to stay in a 5-star hotel because you are Asian, because your skin is brown.
P: Well yes, of course.
T: Of course?

P: Yes. Those places are not for people like me.
T: I am a white person and you seem to be telling me you know your place.
P: Well yes, I do.
T: You think I am better than you because of my skin colour.
P: Yes.
T: And you assume that is what I believe because I am white. That I won't have a problem with that.
P (smiling nervously as though he had done something wrong): Yes ... is that not what you think then?

My response to this was to feel a deep sense of shock and I found it difficult to think again. I just could not think about what was happening in the session. By 'think' here I refer to what the Kleinian analyst Wilfred Bion understood: 'thinking as a human link – the endeavour to understand, comprehend the reality of, get insight into the nature of oneself or another' (O'Shaughnessy 1988).

Sometime after this interaction I again became aware of the projective identification and a vague awareness of feeling excluded. After the session, I found myself suddenly aware of a self-conscious emotionally traumatic memory of when I was a foreigner in Iran during the revolution of the 1970s, a white Westerner having my life threatened on more than one occasion: terribly anxious, scared and desperate not to be noticed as non-Iranian on the streets of Tehran as Khomeini's anti-Western rhetoric permeated the society. Again I had identified with my patient's unconscious projection onto me of his experience and my mind had been disabled in the therapeutic interaction. I had been frozen by fear.

Oppression is about abuse of power and this introjected abuse is now self-inflicted within my patient by an internal object relationship between 'white' and 'non-white', the 'worth its' and the 'not worth its', the useful and the useless, the powerful and the powerless. The non-white internal object.

This 'non-'identity was inevitable given his developmental years. Everywhere he turned it seemed he was a non-someone. A non-good enough son, a non-man, a non-Sikh who was not good enough to represent his family at the Gurdwara. The non-identity was familiar and internalised as an abusive, persecuting, bullying object. A racist view of himself was just another layer of already familiar denigrating abuse, this time negating him as a person because of his ethnic identity and his skin colour.

GS was so entangled with the non-white internal object that it had become ego syntonic. He was surprised by my questioning his belief that I was superior because of my skin colour. I felt it my responsibility as a therapist to challenge this view in order to facilitate his perception becoming ego dystonic so that we could work on it together therapeutically. It was not long before the trauma of recognising the racism he had experienced became apparent.

McKenzie-Mavinga (2009, 2011) has described how recognising one has been a victim of racism is 'recognition trauma' and the possibility of doing this presented itself quite suddenly as a resistance to treatment due to my challenging his beliefs that I am superior to him in some way because of my ethnicity and skin colour. He was emotionally split off from his distress about this and hit a blank when he tried to understand my interpretations or confrontations about it. Accepting that he had been treated as inferior because of his ethnicity would mean the undoing of his very familiar negative self-perception and the way he experienced himself in the world. It was an alien concept to him, one which threatened to unmake his world and plunge him into an emotional deluge.

> I have introduced the concept of 'recognition trauma'. The concept identifies the process that both black and white people go through when emerging from being silenced about racism. It describes the awakening of hurtful experiences which sometimes evokes feelings of guilt, shame, hurt and anger.
>
> *(McKenzie-Mavinga 2011)*

My understanding now is that the introjection of the non-white internal object had effectively silenced his life experience of racism and all his hurt and humiliation and rage had been isolated away from his thinking self in the defensive manner that Freud (1946) identifies as 'isolation of affect'. The feelings are too devastating and traumatic to be allowed into consciousness.

Linguistic perspectives: language in use and implied meaning

In the English language, it is alarming to realise how prolific the use of the term 'non-white' has become. In my view, it represents a most insidious form of institutional racism: the idea that a majority white society has the right to define a person of any other skin colour or ethnicity a 'non'-person. Even more shocking is the use of the term by Black or Asian people to define themselves. This suggests the successful internalisation of institutional racism and is particularly the case in Black and Asian writings on intercultural/racist issues. Austin (1962), in his seminal work *How to Do Things with Words*, came to the conclusion that all utterances are performative in the sense that they constitute a form of action, rather than simply a matter of saying something about someone or something, and the linguistic discipline of pragmatics has long been concerned with the meanings of language in use (rather than in the way it is grammatically constructed only) and the implicatures (implied meanings) generated. Implicature is the action of implying a meaning beyond the literal sense of what is explicitly stated (Thomas 1995; Huang 2014). *Are you white or non-white?* is probably more a comment on social acceptability or status than just a question of colour. Depending upon the speaker, it could signify disapproval or rejection as well as the opposite, depending on social context.

So, when we speak to or write about someone, we do something to them, often implying deeper meaning than the words of the utterance themselves suggest. We approve or disapprove, criticise or praise, denigrate or idealise, reject or affirm and so on. The linguistic study of pragmatics also demonstrates that utterances have meanings in situations, that language can be used by a speaker/writer in a situation to exert a 'force' or impact upon a listener/reader (Leech 1988; Huang 2014). This can sometimes explain why when we are in conversation with someone, we feel suddenly uncomfortable without knowing why when they have said something which appears quite ordinary. The term 'non-white' used in a white racist society is full of implicature about negation of approval and identity, of not being good enough, of not being like 'us'. Not acceptable, not equal.

That is why I challenged the speaker at the conference. The use of the term 'non-white' damages the integrity and sense of personhood of the other. The utterance meaning can be understood as 'not white' but the pragmatic force of the utterance in a white racist society is 'not acceptable/not as good as "us"'. In a wider social context, this 'force' was 'absorbed' by my Asian patient as an identity label for himself which exacerbated the abuse he had suffered at the hands of his dismissive and invalidating family and left him looking down on himself and emasculated. When my patient told me that I was better than him because of my skin colour, two things happened. The first was that I was aware that he was passing on to me the impact of his own personal experience of racism and the second was that in doing so he was communicating, via 'countertransference', his experience of having his capacity to think attacked, resembling the attack in thinking processes found in psychosis (Bhui 2002). It seemed to me that he had lost touch with the reality of himself. And at that moment in the session so had I. I could not think and was confused, numbed. He had projected onto me and I had identified with unconscious communication from him. This evoked feelings in me of confusion and disorientation. GS was unconsciously defending himself from unbearable feelings by projecting them onto me as a way of defending himself from them. I felt the racist attack that he could not speak.

The view that I suggest here is that this attack is caused by the non-white internal object created by the process of internalising racism in an attack upon the self. In the case of my patient, the non-white internal object confirms and accommodates a history of denigration and humiliation as being what he deserves. The non-white internal object becomes an internal working model (Bowlby 1988) of relationship in which the self is persecuted, oppressed and devalued in line with the overbearing superego requirements based on the cultural forces, expectations and stereotypes operating in the predominantly white society. In short, the racist lives inside, introjected, and becomes part of the way we see ourselves, we experience ourselves as inferior. We enact racism against ourselves. All the good resides in the racially different other, not in us.

The moral defence against bad objects

Fairbairn has described a developmental defence in which a child growing up in an abusive and (emotionally) neglectful family will believe that anything that goes wrong in the relationship with his parents or other family members is his fault (Fairbairn 1952; Celani 2011). He takes the bad into himself, believing that his parents must be right. All the good is in the parent, all the bad in the child. He therefore grows up with an enormous sense of guilt and sense of himself as inadequate. Fairbairn calls this 'the moral defence against bad objects'. I have found this to be an extremely common and present reality in many of my patients. A self-belief that they are bad, they get it all wrong, that they are a problem, a burden and so on. They will try to be a good patient for the therapist so that s/he will 'like' them, just as they tried to be a good boy or girl for mummy and daddy so that they would love her/him. This never worked of course because the problem, the bad, was in Mummy and/or Daddy, not in the patient. In the therapeutic interaction the transference becomes full of manoeuvring in order to please the therapist/parent's perceived agenda.

This sense of self in such a person dovetails into a racist view of themselves as the unacceptable other when institutionally racist messages are absorbed and personal experience confirms it. A psychotic view that labels the other as containing all the bad, the wrong, as being a problem, as being inadequate. This is what was so hard for me to get my head around at the time of interaction in the therapy session: my patient was expressing an unrealistic view of himself and projecting this onto me which disabled my ability to think and gain insight clearly. I liken this to a psychotic attack on my thinking. An unconscious attack upon my thinking which threw my relationship with him into a kind of internal void. But I could also identify with it because of my experience with the speaker at the conference, as well as other experiences of racial intolerance towards me during my time in Iran, where I coloured my hair and skin in order to escape detection as a Westerner (the other) in a kind of psychotic paranoia of inferiority.

Concluding remarks

In presenting my work with GS for consideration I have incorporated what seems to me to be relevant theoretical ideas from psychoanalytic, intercultural and linguistic disciplines to highlight three important issues:

1. The social injustice perpetrated on persons of whatever ethnic origin or colour by referring to them as 'non' anything, particularly by use of the term 'non-white' in a predominantly white racist society.
2. The impact upon persons psychologically and emotionally of internalising the 'non-white' identity as an unconscious internal object which perpetuates the introjected racism against themselves throughout life, causing anxiety and paranoia which they do not understand but assume is how life is for them.
3. The onus on the therapist to raise and confront the impact of unacknowledged racism and place it on the therapeutic agenda, particularly when the non-white internal object makes its abhorrent presence known.

When GS came to me for help he initially doubted that I would see him at all. He expected me to disapprove of him as an Asian man and found it unthinkable that I could consider him equal as a fellow human being. Psychotherapy challenged this negative experience of himself by containing and processing the unconscious distress he projected into my keeping and, when I had been able to emotionally process and think about it enough in the blender of my mind, so to speak, to hand it back to him in hopefully manageable interpretations for him to work through.

As a white therapist working with GS it was apparent that in the transference I almost immediately represented the white other who viewed him as 'non-white' and therefore inferior, and his response to me was as if I were rather disapproving and at times contemptuous of him because of his skin colour and ethnicity: in short a racist. He did not articulate this and was largely unconscious of it in the first few months of therapy. However, my ability to resist transformation into a familiar racist object in GS's inner world was a mutative factor in his psychotherapy. I agree here with Celani (2010: 123) that this was a necessary first step that allowed GS to see me for who I am, a white person who does not consider himself superior because of his skin colour and who respects him as an equal human being. This then facilitated a process whereby me as the white person/therapist began to be internalised as a more benign and equal internal object in GS's internal world, promoting a recalibrating of the developmental process and eventually a resolution of the transference.

As his therapy drew to a close GS had begun to challenge the intimidating and unspoken attitudes of white and Asian people in his social and business network. He was less accepting of being 'walked over', 'a doormat' as he put it. He also reported enjoying, to a small degree, the respect from others that his unwillingness to accept disrespectful treatment brought him. In short, it seemed to me that he was beginning to experience himself as deserving of equality and respect as a human being and his anxiety and paranoia were waning. My hope is that the non-white internal object died, starved of racist nourishment or at least is terminally ill. I guess time will tell.

References

Austin, J.L. (1962) *How to Do Things with Words*, 2nd edition. Oxford: Oxford University Press.
Bhugra, D. and Bhui, K. (2002) Racism in Psychiatry. In K. Bhui (ed.), *Racism and Mental Health: Prejudice and Suffering*. London: Jessica Kingsley.
Bhui, K. (2002) Psycho-Social and Psycho-Political Aspects of Racism. In K. Bhui (ed.), *Racism and Mental Health: Prejudice and Suffering*. London: Jessica Kingsley.
Bowlby, J. (1988) *A Secure Base: Clinical Applications of Attachment Theory*. Oxford: Routledge.
Celani, D.P. (2010) *Fairbairn's Object Relations Theory in the Clinical Setting*. New York: Columbia University Press.
Celani, D.P. (2011) *Leaving Home: The Art of Separating from Your Difficult Family*. New York: Columbia University Press.
Fairbairn, R. (1952) *Psychoanalytic Studies of the Personality*. Hove: Routledge.
Freud, A. (1946) *The Ego and the Mechanisms of Defence*. London: Karnac.
Huang, Y. (2014) *Pragmatics*. Oxford: Oxford University Press.

Leech, G. (1988) *The Principles of Pragmatics*. London: Longman.
McGilchrist, I. (2009) *The Master and His Emissary*. New Haven, CT: Yale University Press.
McKenzie-Mavinga, I. (2009) *Black Issues in the Therapeutic Process*. London: Palgrave Macmillan.
McKenzie-Mavinga, I. (2011) The Concept of Recognition Trauma and Emerging from the Hurt of Racism. Black, African and Asian Therapy Network, September. Retrieved from www.baatn.org.uk/Resources/Documents/Training
O'Shaughnessy, E. (1988) W.R. Bion's Theory of Thinking and New Techniques in Child Analysis. In E.B. Butt-Spillius (ed.), *Melanie Klein Today: Developments in Theory and Practice. Volume 2: Mainly Practice*. Hove: Brunner-Routledge.
Ogden, T.H. (1992) *Projective Identification and Psychotherapeutic Technique*. Northvale, NJ: Jason Aronson.
Shapiro, F. (2001) *Eye Movement Desensitization and Reprocessing (EMDR), 2nd edition: Basic Principles, Protocols and Procedures*. London: Guilford Press.
Thomas, J. (1995) *Meaning in Interaction: An Introduction to Pragmatics*. Harlow: Longman.

7

INTERCULTURAL PSYCHOTHERAPY, INTRACULTURAL PSYCHOTHERAPY, OR JUST GOOD PSYCHOTHERAPY?

Peter Cockersell

Introduction

I think it's important to say something about where I come from because the arguments I put forward here are mine and arise from my professional experience and training, and my life experience. I trained as a psychoanalytic psychotherapist through an intercultural therapy course and clinical training with Nafsiyat/University College London, and have now been practising for over 15 years postqualification. I have used psychotherapy in the NHS and privately, and currently practise privately and supervise psychotherapy in the NHS, the private and third sectors. I have also worked in homelessness for over 20 years in a variety of roles, including as a psychotherapist and supervisor of psychotherapists.

Over these years I have had the privilege to work with men and women from a large number of cultures from every continent of the globe, and I continue to have clients from at least half a dozen different ethnicities/cultures at the moment of writing.

I myself am male white British, born in northwest London to British parents, and was schooled in Britain in the late 1950s and most of the 1960s (I left school at 15). I have travelled a bit and lived in South America and France, and in various parts of Britain, though mainly London. I now live in Hampshire with my partner and children. I dress quite smartly and look middle-aged (at least!) and middle class. It would be very easy to make a lot of assumptions about me, and most people do.

I want to look in this chapter at culture and difference, and cultural differences, and at the individual within cultures and within societies, and the assumptions we make and their implications for what we call (and what we don't call) intercultural therapy, and for psychotherapy in general.

Culture

There are many definitions of culture. Anthropological perspectives of culture generally start from Tylor's 19th-century definition: 'that complex whole which includes knowledge, belief, art, morals, law, custom and any other capabilities and habits acquired by man as a member of society' (Tylor 1871). Northouse's 21st-century definition, taken from a work on business management and leadership (so reflecting the views of the dominant culture's model of culture?), describes culture similarly: 'culture is defined as the learned beliefs, values, rules, norms, symbols, and traditions that are common to a group of people' (Northouse 2007: 302).

Einstein once said that 'common sense is nothing more than a deposit of prejudices laid down in the mind prior to the age of eighteen' (Einstein, quoted in Barnett 1948). The definitions above suggest that something similar could be said of culture – it could be defined as a sort of collective ontology, a set of assumptions shared between a group of people that define their sense of being and determine the specific context(s) into which they place the events of their individual and social histories, which each of us has learned from the dominant social/cultural influences acting upon us in our formative years. We could paraphrase Einstein and say that 'culture is nothing more than a deposit of prejudices laid down in the mind prior to the age of eighteen'.

However, it is not static: the transmission of these 'prejudices' is fallible. Where people from one cultural background are assimilating into life within another cultural context, particularly the second generation (those born within the host culture) will be subject to different, and potentially conflicting, sets of learned 'prejudices'. Where various cultural models are available, dynamism is likely to be increased, and so cultural change itself is likely to be accelerated. As Acharrya puts it 'culture … is dynamic. It is ever-changing and … encompasses all of everyday life from the mundane, such as the type of food eaten, even mealtimes, and clothes, to religious practices and important attitudes to others in terms of age, sex and social roles' (Acharrya 1992: 74).

This is all very well at a social level. Indeed, we use the word 'culture' to denote something socially held and socially shared – if there is a 'culture of bullying' or a 'culture of racism', this is group behaviour; similarly, company bosses try to develop a 'culture of excellence', and sports team managers a 'culture of winning'; and we talk of 'British culture' or 'gang culture'. Of course, what forms part of a specific culture, and what does not, is usually based on a set of cultural assumptions, or prejudices, held by a particular group or subgroup. Many Muslims in 2017, for example, say ISIS/Daesh are not 'real Muslims', and ISIS/Daesh say exactly the same about most other Muslims; in a similar vein, the Grand Mufti of Saudi Arabia recently said that Iranians were not really Muslims at all (Independent 2016) but Zoroastrians, a view not shared in Tehran or most other parts of the Muslim, or indeed non-Muslim, world.

Culture, however, is also a question of perspective. When I lived in France, I was British and the French were French; when I lived in South America, the

French and I were Europeans together. Quite apart from individual differences in the sets of assumptions within any culture, and at the 'macro', social level of what people believe in public and say that they do, there are still great differences – cultural differences – between groups of people who may be classified within the same overarching culture from another perspective, like me and the French man beside me. People talk of Muslim culture, but Muslims are not homogenous; people talk of Scottish culture, and neither are Scottish people all the same. Muslim culture means very different things in Istanbul or Riyadh, Whitechapel or Tehran, and has meant very different things in different historical periods; similarly, the Scottish culture of the central Glasgow terraces and the farms and fisheries of the Hebrides are quite different; and despite a former prime minister's assurance that 'we're all in this together' (Cameron 2008), the culture of the Eton/Oxbridge millionaires of Notting Hill and the unemployed steelworkers of Sheffield are not the same; the culture of 'austerity' is different in Tower Hamlets and in the City of London just a couple of miles away. These differences are often classified as 'intracultural' – the Muslimness or Scottishness or Britishness are seen as overarching cultural categories, with the differences as subcategories. This is perhaps simply an effect of perspective, like the Europeanness of me and the Frenchman – the further away you are (and the less you know?), the more homogenous any cultural grouping appears.

Culture, then, is rather like a fractal – the closer you look, the more subordinate patterns you see. Pinpointing even the culture of a particular group is, then, a complex thing because there are so many variants. The cultural assumptions of London led many politicians to think that a vote for Brexit in 2016 was impossible: the cultural assumptions of much of England meant they were wrong. Indeed, it could be argued that there are only variants once you get up close: the culture of the city centre is different to the culture of the suburbs, the culture of the poor is different to that of the rich even though they may (as they often do in London) live on opposite sides of the same street. The generally accepted set of assumptions and associated behaviours – the standard form of that culture within that group, if you like, the form from which deviation is measured – is often referred to as the 'cultural norm'. An individual set of assumptions about the world, on the other hand, a sort of personal ontology, is called other things: a 'worldview', a 'personal faith', a 'belief system', or if it is a long way from the cultural norm, 'genius' or 'madness'. Personal sets of assumptions are influenced by culture, but they are never identical with it. Anthropology neatly makes the distinction between what people believe in public and say should be done, and what they actually believe and do in the real world. As Bourdieu argues, individual social actions within any culture are 'a long way from the objectivist model of the mechanical interlocking of pre-regulated actions' described by analysts of specific cultures and cultural phenomena; the example Bourdieu uses is gift exchange, but it could be any other (Bourdieu 1977: 8). He goes on to say:

only a virtuoso with a perfect command of his 'art of living' can play on all the resources inherent in the ambiguities and uncertainties of behaviour and situation ... to do that of which people will say, 'There was nothing else to be done'.

(Bourdieu 1977: 8)

People also often set out from quite a different place to that of the culture within which they grew up or now find themselves. Personal sets of assumptions may be antithetical to standard assumptions, and deliberately (as in revolutionary ideologies) or unconsciously (as in anti-social or criminal ideologies) set against the cultural norms: people have an individual agency and use culture and the cultural norms to try to achieve personal and social objectives. Culture in reality, Bourdieu argues, is not a mechanistic enactment of a set of prescribed social rules, but a dynamic of practice: 'We are a long way, too, from norms and rules: doubtless there are slips, mistakes, and moments of clumsiness'; he talks of 'the art of the necessary improvisation', and that 'the generative, organising scheme ... is an often imprecise but systematic principle of selection and realisation, tending, through steadily directed adjustments and corrections, to eliminate accidents when they can be put to use and to conserve even fortuitous successes' (Bourdieu 1977: 8).

If culture and cultural variants are so multiplicitous, then individual representations of culture are as numerous ... well, as individuals. Two people from the same place of the same heritage and of similar ages and genders might give a deeply overlapping account of the culture they were born into and have lived in, though there will still be some differences because of their personal historical experiences; but as we take accounts from people of increasingly different social and demographic features, so the difference in their perception of their cultures will increase. When anthropologists began to ask women what their cultures were like, they got a resoundingly different answer to the one they had received when they asked only men (as they had roughly up until the 1950s and 1960s: Reiter 1975). If you ask people of 70 or people of 20 what the culture of their country is, you are likely to get quite different responses; and many of the cultural norms shared by 20 year olds – social interactions through electronic media, for example – will be more like other 20 year olds, whether they are Egyptian or English, Greek or Chinese, than like 70 year olds of their 'own' cultural heritage. Cultural self-identity, in this fast-changing world of global communications and global commerce that we live in, is changing.

But of course, culture is always changing, and always has. Human social groups adapt and respond to their environments socially, and if culture is the sum of the meaning sets that holds a group together, then culture has to adapt to meet new circumstances if it is to survive (and of course many cultures do not survive; history and archaeology are populated by cultures that have either evolved – changed – or have died out). Culture is influenced by wider economic and environmental determinants, and culture change, both individual and collective, is often spurred by economic or technological change, and by changes in power relations (Nowotny 2006).

Identifying someone's individual cultural self-identity is, then, a hugely complex thing. There are so many potential variants and it depends on personal and social history as well as local cultural variants and overarching cultural norms – it is, indeed, as individual as the individual in front of you.

Psychotherapy

There are many interactions that could be called therapeutic, or healing, and many that have a therapeutic or healing effect on the psyche, or mind. Psychotherapy, though, is generally used to mean a formal 'talking treatment', derived by some process or pathway from Freud's development of psychoanalysis in the early 20th century. It is most commonly practised between two people, a therapist and their client or patient (depending on the setting) – the 'therapeutic dyad'; though, of course, psychotherapy is also commonly practised in groups, especially in the NHS (where it's seen as cheaper, or more 'cost-effective', because more patients are seen per paid professional), usually facilitated by one or two therapists. The therapist is usually a trained and in some way qualified professional; the client or patient may come from any background at all, though the processes of referral in NHS or other institutional settings and the process of self-selection in private therapy settings may narrow or even determine which backgrounds the clients and/or patients actually are from in reality – with young Black men for various reasons the least likely demographic on either side of the dyad.

Since then, of course, and particularly since the 1950s, an enormous number of different psychological therapies have been developed – psychodynamic, behavioural, cognitive, humanistic, mindfulness, mentalisation, various forms of 'body psychotherapy', and lots of variations particularly on psychodynamic and cognitive therapies with three-letter acronyms. Psychology and psychoanalysis have grown distant to each other, though psychotherapy is claimed by both; and all schools are now having to reappraise their understandings and practices in the light of the physiological findings of neuroscience, leading to a whole new range of psychotherapies – to name but a few, neuropsychoanalysis, cognitive neuroscience, interpersonal neurobiology, and so on.

Essentially, though, all these psychotherapies share the common feature of being concerned with, and conducted through, a relationship between two people. The fundamentals of the 'therapeutic relationship' are a commonality between psychoanalytic/psychodynamic, cognitive and humanistic therapeutic approaches, which are seen as central to therapeutic effectiveness by all three. The findings of neuroscientific research confirm this centrality, and explain some of the mechanisms behind it (for example Schore 2013).

Psychotherapy often focuses on the so-called 'pathology' of the individual, and this is perhaps especially so for cognitive approaches which are often based on a disease/condition treatment model very much aligned to the medical model. However, the meta-psychologies do not support this perspective of individualised pathology, and certainly neuroscientific, psychoanalytic, psychodynamic and social cognition theories all hold a perspective that the psyche, and by extension psychotherapy, is shaped by the interaction between an individual's inner world and their experience of intimate relationships, wider relational contexts and other environmental influences. Freud started it off by saying that 'individual psychology … is at the same time social psychology as well' (Freud 1921), and the 'object relations' school of modern psychoanalysis and psychodynamic theory had Winnicott saying 'there is no such thing as a baby … meaning that if you set out to describe a baby, you will find you are describing a baby and someone. A baby cannot exist alone, but is essentially part of a relationship' (Winnicott 1965). This is borne out in the findings of neuroscience on development of the self (Schore 1994) and in the exploration of complex unconscious communication by social psychologists (Bargh and Morsella 2008). I have argued elsewhere that psychotherapy happens in the interface between the social and the individual (Cockersell 2015).

This is an important point. The individual has an 'inner working model' (Holmes 1993), an 'inner world' which forms the core of the self, of self-experience and of experience of the external world, too: it acts as a lens through which perception of all interactions with the environment is focused and/or distorted. It is made up of the person's collated experience, which includes their experience of the activations of their attachment and other primary biological systems (Heard et al. 2009; Panksepp and Biven 2012) by their intimate others, initially led by their emotional experiences and later by their cognitive systems and language (McGilchrist 2010; LeDoux 1998), and of course influenced by social circumstances and cultural modes of expressing emotion, and familially, locally and culturally created meanings, hierarchies and experiences.

With the inner world forming the core of their self and their self-experience, the individual will go about amassing a personal history of interactions with their environment and society – benign interactions and hostile ones, pleasant experiences and traumatic ones, ones that make sense within their meaning systems and ones that don't.

At some stage in their history, for the purposes of this chapter, these experiences become difficult to align within the individual's self-experience and meaning sets, and they experience social and personal distress, and often exhibit associated dysfunction. In various cultural contexts this can be seen as possession by spirits or gods, being bad or evil, being anti-social or revolutionary, or being mad or having mental health problems. In British society and increasingly in British culture, this may lead to the person being referred, or referring themselves, for psychotherapy (though if they are young Black men, or homeless, or otherwise socially excluded, they will probably be diagnosed with a severe mental illness and given heavy-duty drugs instead: Littlewood and Lipsedge 1997).

Intercultural psychotherapy

'Intercultural' is defined as something – an event, an interaction or conversation, some sort of social exchange – that occurs between individuals or groups who come from different cultures. 'Intracultural' is something that takes place within a particular culture or cultures, like campfire singing in the Scouts, or circumcision among Jewish or Muslim groups (amongst others), or celebrating Hogmanay among the Scottish.

'Intercultural psychotherapy' could be used to describe any therapeutic dyad or group where the members are from different cultural backgrounds; however, it is more commonly used to describe an approach to psychotherapy between a therapist and client/patient from different cultures where cultural difference is recognised overtly, and explored as part of the therapy. As Jafar Kareem, the founder of the Nafsiyat Centre, puts it, intercultural therapy is 'a form of dynamic psychotherapy that takes into account the whole being of the patient – not only the individual concepts and constructs as presented to the therapist, but also the patient's communal life experience in the world' (Kareem 1992). The overt recognition of difference enables some of the transferences and power dynamics to be more openly explored than would be the case otherwise: it is arguable that not mentioning the difference actually reinforces the unspoken and often unconscious power imbalances derived from the cultural milieu even where the therapist is not themselves influenced significantly by unconscious 'culturism', racism or xenophobia. Kareem again:

> The very fact of being from another culture involves both conscious and unconscious assumptions, both in the patient and in the therapist. I believe that for the successful outcome of therapy it is essential to address these conscious and unconscious assumptions from the beginning.
> *(1992)*

However, I think the idea of 'intercultural therapy' raises two questions that I want to look at: firstly, how do we know when we are (or are not) in the presence of cultural difference (or sameness)? How clear is 'the very fact of being from another culture'?

And, secondly, even when it is clear that the patient/client and therapist are from other cultures to each other, is the *therapy* for the client/patient really *inter*cultural or is it, at least to a large extent, *intra*cultural? What I am suggesting here is that, if what is being mediated through therapy is the interface between the individual and the social, then the therapeutic endeavour for the patient/client is actually *intra*cultural: it is about how they interact with and within the cultural and social context in which they find themselves.

Let me amplify this a bit with a couple of examples.

Two questions on the intercultural and/or intracultural nature of therapy

Let us look first at the question of how we know whether we are in the presence of cultural difference or sameness. Two clients of mine spring to mind – one was a white British man in his 50s, the other an Egyptian woman in her 20s. OK, so far so easy: I'm a white British man in the same age range as the first client, and I am not a Muslim woman and I'm not 20-something. Straightforward.

Of course, nothing is so straightforward (and even less so in psychotherapy). 'Straightforward' simply means that we are going along with our assumptions, our prejudices or our common sense, however you want to label it. That is not particularly helpful in any field of human interaction, but is certainly always dangerous in psychotherapy: it means we are not looking at and seeing the unique individual in front of us.

In fact, the white British client in his 50s came from a working-class family from northern England, a family that had broken up when he was quite little, and he had experienced abuse, institutionalisation, long-term meandering from homeless place to homeless place, and multiple bereavements and several incarcerations; he had a history of being on the receiving and delivering end of violence, and had been alcoholic (though was not when I met him). This is not my cultural background. I come from a family of professionals, my family had its troubles but it didn't break up, I went to university and got various degrees, I'd recently finished my doctorate, I have my own family and longstanding relationships and settled accommodation pattern. If I had assumed that I knew this client's culture, then I would have been a long way from being able to understand anything of what was happening for him. I had to learn something of his culture from him, and we had to talk about power, and about how he might experience me in my position and role (and, of course, being a psychoanalytic psychotherapist, in his projections and transferences); it was actually quite a long piece of the therapy, for us to be able to form a trusting, working therapeutic alliance because of the degree of our differences and because of the power dynamic often experienced by him from oppressive professionals, including many from the 'caring' professions, which he naturally associated with me through his transferences and cultural assumptions. So was this actually 'intercultural therapy'? It certainly met 'the very fact of being from another culture' criterion.

Interestingly, it was a much easier part of the work to form a therapeutic alliance with the young Egyptian woman. She was modern, worldly, atheistic, educated (she was in the process of completing a doctorate at the time of her therapy) and came from a family of middle-class professionals who had their problems but were still together; she had lived with her parents until going to university, and had essentially led a settled life. We were obviously different, but we found it quite easy to talk because we shared many common reference points, down to books and film characters we could use as examples when discussing behaviour/meaning and experience: she was also familiar with the social, conceptual and intellectual framework within which 'therapy' takes place, unlike the white British man in his 50s, for whom the whole idea of being 'in therapy' was culturally alien. It was also perhaps easier to work through some of the transferences, which were more overt too: I was not far from the age of her father, and it was quite easy within the power dynamics of our relationship to explore some of the power dynamics of that relationship. Of course we were different, but it was easily obvious, so less easy to fall into assumptions – I was clearly not a woman, nor Egyptian, nor a non-believer from a Muslim upbringing (though I am a non-believer from a Christian upbringing). Her atheism was a major factor in her coming for therapy, because it made difficult her relationships with her parents, who remained Muslim; she had recently 'outed' herself by refusing to take part in Ramadan. What this meant to her was something I could perhaps intellectually imagine given my own experiences, but experientially I could not: again, I needed her to teach me something about her culture, and her family culture (and what being Muslim, and their daughter not believing, meant to them). She wanted to be a modern young woman, just like the other modern young women she met at university: she was part of the electronic communication, mobile/tablet-based, create-your-own-identity world of the young – another cultural difference to me! I also therefore needed her to teach me about her self-experience and her experience of the world and how she saw her place and her future in the world that she, not I, inhabited.

In both cases, the 'problems' we ended up working on in the therapy were what you might term psychosocial pathologies, or even psychocultural pathologies – they were about resolving tensions between the clients' inner worlds and their social worlds, their cultures; and working through some of the stresses that had been caused in their inner worlds and their self-experience by the impact of their social and cultural environments. In a very real and significant way, the work we did was intracultural – it was enabling them to feel better and function better within their cultural milieu, and enabling them to make sense of their own self-experience in relation to the social and cultural worlds they had experienced and come from. This is, if you like, part of them finding their own personal interpretation of their cultural self-identity, one which will enable them to live successfully within the social and cultural mainstream, or at least some recognised and safe subsection of it (not a persecuted subsection – a drunk, anti-social rough sleeper in one case, a modern, young, non-practising Muslim professional woman stuck in a set of traditional assumptions, beliefs and roles in the other).

What we were working with in both cases were the inner worlds and self-experience of the clients, and trying to see how they had been formed by their experience of and interactions with their social and cultural environment, and then also at how their inner worlds and self-experience was currently interacting with the social and cultural world they currently found themselves in, including the therapeutic relationship; and finally looking at how their inner world, self-experience, experience of therapy and understanding of the external world and their important relationships might enable them to achieve an effective and fulfilling life. The work was deeply individual with each client, and could only proceed by being so; and in each case it would have been very negative and perhaps fatal to the therapy if I had made an assumption of either cultural difference or sameness.

Conclusion

If intercultural psychotherapy is where the cultural differences between the therapist and the client/patient are overtly acknowledged, and the impact that cultural beliefs and assumptions around those cultural differences is acknowledged, and the power dynamics of cultural difference are acknowledged, and all this becomes part of the therapeutic work – then I would suggest that this is just good psychotherapy. If we make and work on the basis of unquestioned assumptions about cultural difference or cultural similarity, then we are 'missing a trick' and losing some of the unique reality of our particular relationship with that specific client.

Further, I suggest that a large part of the work for the client/patient is actually intracultural – it is about working out how their own individual inner world and self-experience have come to be influenced and moulded by their interactions with their social and cultural environment, and about how they now, being the person they are and with the experiences they have had and the working through they are doing in their therapy, how they use all that to create their own personal meaning system and relationship network within the culture that they are living in: how they develop and/or become conscious of their own personal take on their culture and cultural milieu(x), and how that self-in-relation-to-the-other understanding enables them to function successfully and lead lives that they find fulfilling.

I have said earlier that psychotherapy takes place in the interface between the individual, inner world and the social, cultural, external world; I would go further and say that good psychotherapy follows the example of intercultural therapy and acknowledges and works with the cultural differences and power dynamics between the protagonists of the therapeutic dyad – wherever they both come from. If, as Freud said, ultimately all psychology is social psychology, then so all psychotherapy should be intercultural psychotherapy.

References

Acharrya, S. (1992) *The Doctor's Dilemma: The Practice of Multicultural Psychiatry in Multicultural Britain*, in J. Kareem and R. Littlewood (eds), *Intercultural Therapy*. Oxford: Blackwell.

Bargh, J.A. and Morsella, E. (2008) The Unconscious Mind. *Perspectives on Psychological Science*, 3, 73–79.

Barnett, L. (1948) *The Universe and Dr Einstein*. New York: Mentor.

Bourdieu, P. (1977) *Outline of a Theory of Practice*. Cambridge: Cambridge University Press.

Cameron, D. (2008) We're All in This Together. *BBC*. Retrieved from: http://news.bbc.co.uk/1/hi/uk_politics/7643524.stm

Cockersell, P. (2015) Psychology of Social Exclusion. In *Clinical Psychology Forum, Special Edition: Homelessness – The Extreme of Social Exclusion*. Retrieved from: www.bps.org.uk/system/files/Public%20files/cat-1678.pdf

Freud, S. (1921) Group Psychology and the Analysis of the Ego, cited in P. Gay (ed.) (1995), *The Freud Reader*. London: Vantage.

Heard, D., Lake, B. and McCluskey, U. (2009) *Attachment Therapy with Adolescents and Adults*. London: Karnac.

Holmes, J. (1993) *John Bowlby and Attachment Theory*. London: Routledge.

Independent (2016) 'Iranians Are Not Muslims', Says Saudi Arabia's Grand Mufti. 7 September. Retrieved from: www.independent.co.uk/news/world/middle-east/saudi-arabia-grand-mufti-iran-sunni-muslims-hajj-a7229416.html

Kareem, J. (1992) The Nafsiyat Intercultural Therapy Centre: Ideas and Experience. In J. Kareem and R. Littlewood (eds), *Intercultural Therapy*. Oxford: Blackwell.

LeDoux, J. (1998) *The Emotional Brain*. London: Orion.

Littlewood, R. and Lipsedge, M. (1997) *Aliens and Alienists*, 3rd edition. London: Routledge.

McGilchrist, I. (2010) *The Master and His Emissary*. London: Yale University Press.

Northouse, P.G. (2007) *Leadership*. London: SAGE.

Nowotny, H. (2006) *Cultures of Technology and the Quest for Innovation. Volume 9: Making Sense of History*. Oxford: Berghahn Books.

Panksepp, J. and Biven, L. (2012) *The Archaeology of Mind*. New York: Norton.

Reiter, R. (ed.) (1975) *Toward an Anthropology of Women*. New York: Monthly Review Press.

Schore, A. (1994) *Affect Regulation and the Origin of the Self*. Mahwah, NJ: Laurence Erlbaum.

Schore, A. (2013) *The Science of the Art of Psychotherapy*. London: Norton.

Tylor, E.B. (1871) *Primitive Culture*. London: John Murray.

Winnicott, D.W.W. (1965) *The Child, the Family and the Outside World*. London: Penguin.

8

POSTCOLONIALISM AND COUNTERTRANSFERENCE IN TWO CASES OF THE SEXUAL ABUSE OF WOMEN BY DOCTORS

Roland Littlewood

> I myself should have everything to fear if the spirit of tyranny and the spirit of culture ever went hand in hand.
>
> *(Beccaria 1764/1964: 19)*

The two patients I am describing raised, at least for me, questions of cultural analysis – my own – as well as my personal psychological response.[1] They do perhaps say something about the therapeutic process, especially the White European psychotherapeutic process, and if they say anything about culture, that's also my culture we are talking about (Littlewood 1993). I saw the two about 25 years ago. Neither of them was seen as part of formal psychotherapy and they came to me by chance, as it were. The first one was in his early 40s, about my age then. I'll call him 'Abdul'.

He was from northern Africa, Arab, a Muslim, an only child. His father was a sort of semi-military stationmaster. His mother died of tuberculosis when Abdul was about 12, and his father married again – a much younger woman. Good at school studies, and in conscious grieving for his mother, he decided to become a doctor and to care for sick women.

His father was austere, a practising Muslim especially as he got older but none too enthusiastic, and temperamentally closer to the country's military government of the time than he was to Islam. Abdul recalls him as dour, harsh and ambitious, not very understanding of his son, although he encouraged his education and his choice of medicine. Comparatively wealthy, his father sent him away to a boarding school. On returning for the school holidays when he was about 14, he found his father ill and restricted to bed. He recalls his attractive young stepmother undressing in front of the young boy and, on the pretence of checking Abdul's clothes, she started fingering him. Horrified but excited, he always withdrew but then constantly dreamed about her – her body, him having sex with her, trying to imagine her down below, and comparing his imaginings with the pictures of dissected animals in his biology textbooks. He masturbated to her image.

Nothing further happened with his stepmother and he went away to medical school in the capital. I know little about his student years, but he gained a satisfactory degree and maintained good relations with the other students, drinking local beer and frequenting the prostitutes who lived with their children near the entrance to the university. After passing his final exams, he was sent to an outlying district to practise general hospital medicine. On his visits home he found his father aged and his stepmother no longer attractive to him and now with a family of her own. There were no local prostitutes in the country area and he was sexually frustrated until he realised that by offering free medical services to some of his younger women patients, he could fondle them and even sleep with them. How he managed this, I do not know, but it is perhaps something to do with the power of an educated postcolonial metropolitan elite faced with a much poorer and totally subservient rural tribal group dependent on the powerful for patronage and indeed for basic facilities such as transport, work and housing, as well as medical care. (The area incidentally is now the seat of genocide directed against Black African villagers by Arab mercenaries who are driving them into refugee camps on the other side of the border.)

Abdul's actions now became increasingly disconnected from normative medical ethics. He no longer treated his patients on the promise of future sexual intimacy but he had sex with them immediately prior to treatment. His whole life became compulsively organised around this, and he no longer sought a transfer back to the capital to begin his specialisation. Around this time, his father became terminally ill and, on visiting him, Abdul found the old man's austerity had hardened into a harsh bigotry. The father then died and, in what I take as a confused and rather guilty period, he neglected his inheritance leaving the management of it to his stepbrothers, and joined an Islamic political party which was planning to oust the then military president. Abdul returned to his country hospital and, after a period of sexual abstention, grew back into his old habits and eventually stories circulated among his colleagues. The scandal reached the capital, inflamed by other rivalries and by the local doctors' annoyance at the failure to meet his professed Islamic principles: he was recalled to the capital. He embarrassed his political colleagues in the party and they eventually refused to associate any further with him. He went to work for some years in the Middle East before coming to Britain.

He was referred to me by his GP for 'depression' whilst working in a general hospital medical post. I saw him maybe five times, prescribed him some antidepressants and tried to make sense of his story, which he told me quite readily when we first met. What struck me at the time (and still now) was the complete absence of remorse, merely anger at his father and stepmother, and a sort of sense that he could not settle anywhere; he was motiveless and drank whisky heavily. Given his current job situation, I was not worried that he would repeat his past actions, and I did not feel too concerned even when he told me of his poor relations with senior female colleagues. He contemplated suicide but said Islam forbade this; otherwise he was not very religiously observant, and I formed the opinion that his membership of an Islamicist party had been some sort of ambivalent identification with his father, as well as a rejection of this father whom indeed he frequently compared to the country's dictator. His 'Islamic' convictions seemed to have represented his opposition to this semi-secular figure rather than anything very 'spiritual'. (But that's perhaps a rather Christianised idea of religion, and whether we can anyway separate our religious convictions from our psychodynamics is another question.)

The regime in his home country changed. But Abdul did not go back. After five sessions with me, he failed to turn up, letters were left unanswered and I do not know what happened. I was not interested enough to contact his GP and ask.

The second man was Rama, a 32-year-old doctor who recounted a curiously similar story. He was a middle-caste Hindu, born and brought up in south India. He had an elder brother, and his mother died when he was a baby. In his early teens he was seduced by his brother's wife only a few years older than himself; the affair continued intermittently during his schooldays but ended when he went to medical school where he specialised in gynaecology. His later feelings for his brother's wife were distaste and disgust, and he avoided her on his return home, although she was obviously sad and lonely and clearly wanted to continue the affair. After qualification, like Abdul, Rama was sent to a country area, not as a general doctor but as a gynaecologist-in-training, where he too found he could offer medical treatment to the families of the poor in exchange for sexual access. Not only could he obtain sex but this took increasingly bizarre forms facilitated by a local matrilineal kinship system which allowed women greater autonomy (and less male family control) than in his own home district. Indeed, he described the local women to me in contemptuous terms as 'promiscuous'. In the end Rama was offering to carry out abortions in exchange for intimacy, and described how he would sexually penetrate the woman on the hospital trolley before proceeding to a termination of pregnancy. Indeed, I suspected he actually preferred to do this. Like Abdul, he was fairly unrepentant about all of this, and still perceived it as a perk of his job, almost his reward for having worked hard at medical school, a sign of his superior social and male status. No scandal ensued. Unlike Abdul, he never seemed to have gone through a period of doubt about all this, and proceeded to England in an attempt to practise there, ostensibly as a career move.

I saw him after he referred himself to me for advice and 'cultural counselling' because he was unhappy and had repeatedly failed the qualification exam for foreign medical graduates. As I got to know him, I was amazed as to how he had qualified in medicine as he did not seem to know much at all. Having no money, he was boarding with the elder brother who had immigrated previously and set up a moderately successful import business. His relations with his brother's wife, the ex-lover of his teens, were completely non-emotional and non-confiding. Neither talked of the past, and she seemed to have settled into the role of the older Indian matron, concerned with the marriage of her daughters and the family's own local respectability. Curiously, the arrival of a doctor into the family added to this and she did not seem to resent his presence, on the surface at least. Their father having recently died in India, his brother was now head of the family, and there were frequent recriminations over Rama's continued failure to pass his exam and earn his keep. He went out with a number of white girls, but his relations with them were short-lived. Did they involve physical sex? I'm not sure, but I think not. I suspect the girls found him as boring and tiresome as I did. Like Abdul, he continued to masturbate to images of his earlier exploits, including – I was horrified to realise – the whole postcoital abortion scenario. I developed a strong dislike of Rama. For me he was vain, supercilious, stupid and ingratiating – what a colonial British generation would once have described as oleaginous. He said he felt a bit better, and tried (and failed) the examinations two more times. I gave him revision advice and recommended courses. He gradually faded out of appointments: I cannot recall if we agreed to end them formally, and it is significant that I have both lost his clinical notes and forgotten his correct name.

So why do I now recall these two more than 20 years later? Obviously, both have similar stories and were seen nearly at the same time. Neither requested therapy for what was obviously a continuing issue for them; but both saw the past as incidental, and in neither case did I consider that they presented a future risk. When confronted, Abdul blamed his stepmother, Rama his brother's wife. Neither saw themselves as personally responsible: do we similarly see them both as victims? Obviously we can offer a similar Oedipal interpretation in both cases, with sexualisation preventing fears of abandonment (by their dead mother) and a fear of engulfment (sexual relations with an older woman) in early adolescence. Deprived of masculinity by being seduced, they then reassert it. The internalised biological mother is projected onto some other individual who becomes the target of sexualised aggression because of her perceived failure or vulnerability (Woods 2003). Neither described any other anti-social actions beyond the past abuse of women and the abuse of their medical role: they would have been angry at the suggestion of it. And both vigorously criticised the lax morals of tribal, and matrilineal, and now British society for not 'protecting' women more.

How true were their descriptions of their actions? Is it possible that, as for me, both were feeding into some sort of Gothic horror reminiscent of the Chapman brothers' fantasies of torture and defilement? On the whole, I do credit their accounts, for the accounts of abuse, when described, fitted neatly with the more prosaic events of their personal lives.

Why my own horrid fascination? I had recently dealt with an issue of the sexual abuse of a patient by my own senior house officer (I forced him to resign): I was also writing a lecture on military and para-military rape (Littlewood 1997) and was curious about how isolated individual decisions such as rape, when repeated on a mass scale, became 'a culture'. Were the actions of these two then 'pathological' or perhaps rather becoming 'cultural' (Littlewood 1993)? Or both? Clearly they were rather disturbed and atypical people, yet in a situation of dominance of an illiterate rural population by a metropolitan elite, were their actions so very rare? Or had they been back in the colonial period, God forbid? The idea that they were engaging in a 'cultural practice' did not sound so unlikely when looking at police action in Bihar and Kashmir or now Darfur (Littlewood 1997). We know that abused women will often 'facilitate' the abuse of their own children (Welldone 1988): is this how event may become translated into structure? Is this one way by which abusive cultures become perpetuated?

Both these two themselves certainly favoured 'cultural' rather than moral explanations: 'You are British: you don't understand what it is like there.' Both justified themselves and neither did they see themselves as abnormal. In my work on military sexual abuse, I had continually confronted the issue of cultural norm versus individual perversity. But what of my own perversity (Winnicott 1960)? The idea that this sort of sexual behaviour was a norm in certain situations easily leads into a 'Are you surprised? It's what "they" do.' Now, I'm quite familiar with 'the other' engaging in actions not conversant with Western liberal norms, and this was the period when the British Black community was taking on the issue of sexual abuse in Black families. (My Albanian informants during recent field work still participate in blood feuds and in the course of them may kill young boys: I recall being taken aback five years ago in the northern Albanian village where I worked when, on asking about female adultery, I was told gravely 'Well that is very serious and we take it very seriously. All the elders gather together and we discuss it carefully at length: "What has gone wrong?" Then we shoot the woman.') But what sort of fantasies were the exploits of these two telling me? What sort of colonial imaginings about indiscriminate sexuality and structural violence were they rehearsing? A bit like female circumcision (Latour and Stengers 1997)? At a conscious level, the two accounts filled me with disgust. But at the level of the 'pre-transference', as Lennox Thomas (2000), following Andrew Curry (1964), calls it, at the level of all the cultural baggage that a white patient brings to his initial encounter with the Black psychotherapist – or perhaps I should say here at the level of the 'pre-countertransference' – we cannot avoid the presuppositions which by my being a white and also an anthropologist psychiatrist I necessarily bring to the interracial encounter: what fantasies of Black immorality and subversion of medical ethics might I impose on my two clients? Where culture, where horror? From whence my fascination? An identification with their apparently limitless sexual power (Winnicott 1949)?

Could I have employed my disgust more usefully in assisting these two by subordinating it to the therapeutic task (Heimann 1950)? Neither Abdul nor Rama came for formal psychotherapy; both left rather mysteriously after initially idealising me and my cultural skills. At the end, I am left not only with the politics of systems which allow domination and exploitation of the weak, but my own response to this, perhaps with historical complicity. And a complicity from whose baggage I am never entirely free.

Note

1 R. Littlewood, Colonialism and Countertransference: Two Cases of the Sexual Abuse of Women by Doctors, *Transcultural Psychiatry*, 43(2): 235–42. Copyright © [2006] (Roland Littlewood). Reprinted by permission of SAGE Publications (https://doi.org/10.1177/1363461506064851).

References

Beccaria, C. (1764) *Dei delitle e delle pene*. Reprinted in A. Manzoni (1964), *The Column of Infamy*. London: Oxford University Press.

Curry, A. (1964) Myth, Transference and the Black Psychotherapist. *International Review of Psychoanalysis*, 45: 89–120.

Heimann, P. (1950) On Countertransference. *International Journal of Psycho-Analysis*, 31: 81–84.

Latour, B. and Stengers, I. (1997) Du bon usage de l'ethnopsychiatrie. *Le Monde*, 21 January: 5.

Littlewood, R. (1993) Ideology, Camouflage or Contingency? Racism in British Psychiatry. *Transcultural Psychiatric Research Review*, 30: 243–290.

Littlewood, R. (1997) Military Rape. *Anthropology Today*, 13(7): 7–16. Reprinted in R. Littlewood (2002), *Pathologies of the West*. London: Continuum.

Thomas, L. (2000) Racism and Psychotherapy; Working with Racism in the Consulting Room: An Analytical View. In J. Kareem and R. Littlewood (eds), *Intercultural Therapy*, 2nd edition. Oxford: Blackwell.

Welldone, E.V. (1988) *Mother, Madonna, Whore: The Idealisation and Denigration of Motherhood*. New York: Guilford Press.

Winnicott, D.W. (1949) Hate in the Countertransference. Reprinted in D.W. Winnicott (1947), *Collected Papers: Through Paediatrics to Psycho-Analysis*. London: Tavistock.

Winnicott, D.W. (1960) Countertransference. *British Journal of Medical Psychology*, 33: 17–21.

Woods, J. (2003) *Boys Who Have Abused: Psychoanalytic Psychotherapy with Victims/Perpetrators of Sexual Abuse*. London: Jessica Kingsley.

9

INFERIORISATION

Approaching a stigmatising reality in therapy

Antony Sigalas

Rashid sought therapy to cope with his chronic anxiety attacks.[1] Being the last born of a large family, he described his past life in Africa as difficult and deprived. Soon after he completed his primary education, he had to join the rest of his siblings in getting some work for extra financial support. His parents were also actively opposed to the political regime of his country, which made the family's circumstances even more challenging on a daily basis. Now, after having suffered a severe episode of anxiety in the middle of a busy London street, the paramedics who were called for help explained to him for the first time in his life that what he recalled as suffering from (since he was 12 years old) was a panic attack. Back in Africa, such attacks started when he was selling various things on the street without a licence, whilst trying at the same time to avoid the police officers who would repeatedly arrest him and confiscate his merchandise. He remembers how extremely sad and disheartened he was each time he was released back into the vicious circle of his daily hardship. Since his arrival in the UK, Rashid has not been able to find permanent work and his new life after his successful asylum application appeared to be challenged by the same level of adversity as the one he had left behind. He described his most severe anxiety attacks as mainly occurring in bed, just before he was about to fall asleep at night. Once he recovers from them, he stays awake until he manages eventually to get some sleep in the early hours of the morning.

Inferiorisation in a psychoanalytic context

In our clinical experience with culturally diverse clients, we witness a growing number of people from refugee and asylum-seeking communities like Rashid, who present themselves with overwhelming and unbearable personal and socio-economic realities. More and more, we see families that survived war and other conflicts being scattered all over the world with one family member arriving in the UK whilst the rest of the family remains back in their country of origin, or seeking asylum in another. In worse cases, family members are declared missing or dead. We see people tormented by memories of violent traumas and repeated experiences of loss who struggle in their new adjustments and in their roles as parents and partners, and as sons and daughters, in a host society that assumes that the adaptation of their personal identity out of the assigned status of the 'refugee' should be as smooth and problem free as possible.

However, this process of adaptation appears to be a rather complex personal experience that is often challenged further by a systematic pattern of *inferiorisation* with potentially detrimental effects on the individual's psychic self. In its wider context this neologism, employed by a number of writers (Adam 1978 and Eribon 2004, amongst others), describes the process by which mainly racial, cultural, socio-economic, political or religious constructs can be used to reinforce a hierarchy that allows an individual or a group to assume and exercise their supremacy over another. In its complexity, the adapting process necessitated by external realities is helpful to approach alongside an intrapsychic examination of the individual's early injuries, and within the structural frame of the triad of id, ego and super-ego.

Moving away from the argument regarding the actual organic origin of inferiority in the theory of individual psychology (Adler 1945), the emphasis here is rather on the failure to consider how one's subjected experience of inferiorisation impacts on the ego's efforts to manage the already primal sense of inferiority of the injured child in response to the perceived loss of love, or fear of castration (Freud 1933). Equally so, on the ego's efforts to develop its adaptive potential to the inner conflict between the ego and the id, seen as determinant of neurosis and always in relation to the external world (Freud 1947). What is specifically relevant to this investigation is the consequent sense of inferiority and guilt induced by a punitive super-ego/ego ideal that has not been extensively approached by the original theorists, when considering how the external experience of inferiorisation may impede one's adapting efforts. With the ego undeveloped and powerless in its early stages trying to deal with inner conflicts with the *inappropriate manner of repression*, whilst the super-ego torments it with anxiety, the inferiorising conditions, in contrast to Winnicott's *facilitating* ones (1990), can seriously compromise the prospect of gaining a healthier sense of self. As we often see evident in our clinical work, a neurotic self may carry the torment of a chronic anxiety and depression for a long period of time, usually with somatising symptoms. Prolonged inferiorisation significantly adds to such torments and it can even be projected onto the other when the ego is unconsciously driven to comply in its defence for survival, cross-contaminating in this way different strains of the 'virus' of inadequacy. Within the same family line, we see generations carrying the burden of such destructive projections. In turn, strengthening the self by trying to achieve a status of superiority over the other is a way of compensating, or overcompensating, for the Adlerian *inferiority complex*. A complex that can lead to an almost obsessive preoccupation needed to sustain a pseudo state of a healthy functioning, usually through the familiar striving for power (Adler 1945). Across cultures, such power has historically supplied the sad incentive to exercise the grandiose delusion of a nation's superiority over another.

After their arrival in the UK, people from different ethnic backgrounds are, despite their refugee status, expected to initiate their acculturation and as unrealistically soon as possible in order to adjust and presumably develop a sense of belonging to the host culture. Often their previous collective experiences, whether familial or societal, might have already contributed to their inferiorised state of being. Yet, trying to adjust and belong to a new collective reality can be as stigmatising as the previous one, inducing and re-enacting further states of inferiorisation. The consequence being a destructive and demoralising experience for one's self which simultaneously has to cope with inner conflict and traumatic memories. From the moment they arrive in the foreign country, their inferiorisation can be manifested at every step of the way. For some, it could take place in their initial contact with the challenging UK Border Agency, or with those healthcare professionals who appear to see 'the victim' in them through a pathologising lens, as opposed to 'the survivor'. Many more, experience inferiorisation via a disparaging society that reinforces their sense of otherness of not only as being foreign, but most of the time as partially inferior, inducing further feelings of despair, despondency, sadness, grief, anger, fear, guilt and what the existentialists call *ontological* insecurity.

From an early stage, Rashid's childhood was described as being affected by his family's challenging socio-political and economic circumstances. He acknowledged in fact that he had never felt secure in his life, which he thought did not allow him as a consequence to develop a confident sense of self. This lack of confidence was attributed to his growing up years under the very real and at the same time inherited fear of persecution, mainly induced by the undemocratic political power and its police. On the other hand, with his parents' inner resources stretched by their efforts to keep up with the challenges of the day-to-day life, Rashid described their commitment to their respective roles as limited to the 'basics' and their parental love failing to reach him. Yet, regardless of how basic that care was described to be, it seemed consistent enough to allow the formation of an *affectional bond* towards them who at times of crisis, along with his strong religious belief, remained an accessible source of comfort (Bowlby 1979). In his developmental adjustment, he managed to exercise cognitively a credible degree of resilience, as reflected in statements such as: 'you just had to get on with things – what other choices did I have?' Unconsciously, he also seemed to follow a pattern of coping via repression, dissociation and emotional dysregulation mostly manifested in his angry outbursts. In his own reflective thoughts during his sessions, he came to realise that over the years he had not ever considered himself worthy of any state of being other than the one of sadness and overall discontent. The very idea of starting a new life in an environment in which he could hopefully not feel scared or intimidated was almost unrealistic for him and yet very desirable. His journey to the foreign land not only ironically proved him right by showing him that wish fulfilments do not come true to those who are 'undeserving', but also reintimidated him by further experiences of inferiorisation that challenged his already depressed self. A self that was presented as dependent on a positive change to initiate a healing process, so that it would not continue to restrict itself by having to be only adaptive, but by starting to be creative, too (Guntrip 1985).

During the initial stage of the clinical work, Rashid appeared helpless in his chronic depressive mood and pessimistic way of thinking. Week after week, the client would also report on his persistent anxious state that he felt he could not manage. In his own prolonged struggle, his inner recourses were presented as extremely weak, even more so by the constant disappointment of the perceived failures, reinforced by his accusatory super-ego. Failure to change, to adjust, to let go, to forgive, to learn; failure to understand, to conquer his fears, to live independently with dignity, to settle and even failure to hope. Empathic reflections on the expressed self-reproaches seemed to gradually get the client's attention to his inner world, whose initial self-doubt regarding the prospect of reaching a transformative stage towards improvement in the relatively short period of time of his contract was very strong. This doubt was seen as explicable in the context of transference and his low self-perception, rather than indicative of resistance. However, once the emphasis was put on approaching the recurrent experiences of his inferiorisation, the client's improved level of engagement strengthened the potential for a breakthrough. The analysis of the self, in the context of 'not being enough' as a result of a deep-seated sense of guilt and unworthiness, gained a different meaning once the imposed inferiorisation was introduced as a contributing factor to his mental struggle. Moreover, the initial suffering associated with the perceived inadequate love in the parental experience seemed to have resurfaced in the collective one, when the demeaning and rejecting society reactivated the already engrained pattern of self-defeat and self-denigration.

Inferiorisation in a wider context

By comparison, the ubiquitous presence of inferiorisation can be examined in many different contexts. Eribon (2004), the French historian and social scientist, uses the term to describe the subjugated experience of sexual minorities by the normative heterosexual collective. The very experience of racism is founded on the disturbing notion of one's racial superiority over the other. Racial inferiorisation historically dehumanised ethnic and religious communities (Sartre 1973) and continues to do so to this day. Barry Adam (1978) specifically argues against the obliteration of the effects of a racist social structure in the 'self-esteem' studies of the subordinated minorities. As the list goes on, the position in the family, gender, social circumstances, mental health, learning and physical ability may determine the betrayal of the failure to relate to the other in a non-inferiorising, respectful way. This failure is also relevant and applicable to the experiences of domestic violence, bullying, sexual and economic exploitation, and of any other form of abuse. In our clinical work we can observe how society's inferiorising attitude feeds into the workings of self-destructiveness in addictive behaviour.

Accordingly, thinking about the 'other' reflectively in the therapeutic relationship assumes the awareness of the therapist's own frame of reference as being culturally diverse and separate from that of their client, besides the likelihood of their racial or ethnic differences. However, how openly can we consider whether such differences function in a way that could reinforce feelings of powerlessness and inadequacy in the client? Addressing the issue of racism in the clinical dyad could help the investigation to follow this route (Thomas 1992, amongst others), as could sexism (Eichenbaum and Orbach 1983, amongst others) and homophobia (Downey and Friedman 2008, amongst others). Similarly, can such feelings be reinforced by an austere monarchy of conceptualising human suffering that can be inappropriately imposed onto the culturally different experience, as mentioned earlier? Or by the countertherapeutic use of interpretation that not only limits the potential for facilitating the client's own self-discovery, but also damages to the extent of violation with an induced fear that Winnicott termed the fear of being *spiritually raped* (1990)? Broadly speaking, Britt Krause, whilst pointing out the inevitable categorisation of difference, reminds us of the importance to reflect on whether this very process is used to assist domination, or recognition (2012). In the clinical room, the applicability of this question needn't be too unsettling for us to raise in any context of difference, in order to recognise whether the imbalance of power has a potential underlying functionality to the detriment of the client's sense of worthiness.

The delusion of a dream

Watching the award-winning film/documentary *In This world* by Michael Winterbottom (2002), about a young boy's migratory journey to London from Pakistan with his uncle, one cannot help but feel amazed by the sheer determination of those two human beings in their efforts to achieve their goal despite the shocking conditions, the financial cost, the risk taking and the fear of the unknown. Their perceived goal was to build a better future in Europe. The assumed despair seems to be the main driving force for the vast majority of those who choose to undergo such horrific travels, with often disturbingly sad consequences as we hear reported on the news. Even for those who feel compelled to their decision making, one begins to wonder whether such choices are influenced by the fact that one part of the world has imposed the idea on the rest that what can be offered there is far better and more desirable than what can be found elsewhere. A Western world that has perhaps sold itself as far more liberal, fair, affluent, worthy and superior to other societies, and the very same that is experienced as having interfered so badly in, and in some cases irreparably damaged their perceived as less fortunate communities. A world that seems to have convinced not only the 'outsiders', but long before its own 'exclusive members' who in turn, whilst comfortably holding on to their privileged positions, have already conceded to its benefits as they try to fit in, and 'tick off the required boxes' in order to avoid being confronted by their own fears of inadequacy. Strikingly enough, it was the young boy in that film who poignantly reminded his uncle and the audience of the ephemeral reality of life: 'it was just a Walkman', he exclaimed, referring to the one possession that his uncle regretfully had to hand over as a bribe to an officer to avoid jeopardising their journey. Even though his music player helped him to feel connected to the life he left behind via its nostalgic tunes, its loss had to be put in perspective, as it stood so trivial against all the other greater losses that such journeys bring. And for many of those who succeed in reaching their desired destinations, their losses extend to the almost sadistic discovery of what a new life fails to offer after all.

Inferiorisation in a psychotherapeutic context

These are some of the clients that many of us see in our professional roles with our credentials as therapists promising the facilitation of our clients' healing potential, in an environment in which the presented experiences can be contained not only by our *therapeutic considerations*, but also by our *therapeutic care* (Papadopoulos 2002). The kind of care that steps away from the familiar ground of clinical intervention, and at times extends to our additional efforts to be helpful to our clients' housing, educational, medical, financial or asylum problems. These circumstances appear excruciating and may leave us challenged by the same sense of hopelessness as the one experienced by those who seek our help. Such therapeutic care can also strengthen our clinical interventions in alleviating our clients' hopelessness and inferiorisation, as we patiently witness their engagement in the clinical environment. An environment which is often used as that of a lost familial one for understanding, acceptance, relatedness, validation, holding, safety, reliability and care. Whilst we within our helping roles get credited with the knowledge gained by the sharing of their experiences and inspired by their demonstrated resilience and resourcefulness.

Working in a clinical setting such as the Nafsiyat Centre for over 15 years (Sigalas 2011) has given me the opportunity to feel part of a professional community committed to the clinical work with clients whose minority status required the respectful recognition of the cultural and racial significance of their presenting experiences. Whilst being inspired by its founder Jafar Kareem and by the practice of intercultural therapy (Kareem and Littlewood 1992), my colleagues and I have all been appreciative of the opportunity to find both a corner to voice what we believe needs to be voiced, and a platform for innovation and creativity. Our voices echoed those who openly and provocatively spoke about how racism impacts on daily life and in therapeutic interactions, both consciously and unconsciously (Money-Kyrle 1960; Lago and Thomson 1996, amongst others). Equally so, those who challenged the universal applicability of Western psychotherapy and emphasised how social conditions are as important in recovery as treatment (Littlewood 1992; Pedersen 1987, amongst others). Not to mention the ones who drew attention to the research findings indicating the prejudiced approach of mental health institutions towards Black and minority ethnic communities, and in particular to what Littlewood and Lipsedge identified as the failure to explore 'not on whether a patient is "orientated to reality" but to which reality and why' (1982: 10). It is within this intercultural frame of work that the suffering of inferiorisation when it is also respectfully addressed, and analytically contained in the therapeutic environment, enhances in my view the clients' potential for reviving their self-healing process.

Rashid's words come to mind when, in an attempt to describe his isolated state of being, he contrasted ironically the impressive synchronism of a very large flock of birds communicating in a split second its direction in the sky, to a small group of humans struggling to communicate with speech. As difficult as it may seem at the time they seek help, the therapeutic environment can be the space where efforts are put to enable our clients to feel that it is indeed possible to achieve such communicative 'synchronism' in their lives. Starting in their interaction with a therapist whose empathic engagement will not ignore states of inferiorisation in the client's attempts to convey the personal and cultural meaning of their experiences. Whilst initially comparing himself to a hopeless bird flying aimlessly on its own after having lost its way, Rashid gradually became aware that he had started to feel hopeful about finding his way back into 'a flock'.

Conclusion

A well-known newspaper recently used the logo 'countries have borders – stories don't' for its promotional campaign. This prompts us to concede that as stories can indeed be easily communicated nowadays even via a click of a button, they are also transcendental through generations and across cultures, and their universality rather than the unparalleled validity of their difference is what draws people together and helps them be grounded with their humility and humanity. In essence, as Slavoj Žižek (2008) argues, actual universality is not the sharing of basic values, but the sharing of the struggle to overcome 'the inadequacy within' each culture, as reflected in experiences such as *repression, exploitation* and *suffering* that can be very familiar and common to us all.

Note

1 This chapter was initially presented in part at Nafsiyat's 30-year anniversary conference at Regent's University, London.

References

Adam, B.D. (1978) Inferiorization and Self-Esteem. *Journal of Social Psychology*, 41: 47–53.
Adler, A. (1945) *Social Interest: A Challenge to Mankind*. London: Faber & Faber.
Bowlby, J. (1979) *The Making and Breaking of Affectional Bonds*. London: Tavistock.
Downey, J.T. and Friedman, R.C. (2008) Homosexuality: Therapeutic Issues. *British Journal of Psychotherapy*, 24: 429–468. Oxford: Blackwell.
Eichenbaum, L. and Orbach, S. (1983) *Outside In – Inside Out. Women's Psychology: A Feminist Psychoanalytic Approach*. London: Penguin.
Eribon, D. (2004) *Insult and the Making of the Gay Self*. Durham, NC: Duke University Press.
Freud, S. (1933) *New Introductory Lectures on Psycho-Analysis*. London: Hogarth Press.
Freud, S. (1947) *The Question of Lay Analysis*. London: Imago Publishing Company.

Guntrip, H. (1985) *Psychoanalytic Theory, Therapy and the Self.* London: Karnac.
Kareem, J. and Littlewood, R. (eds) (1992) *Intercultural Therapy: Themes Interpretations and Practice.* London: Blackwell Scientific.
Krause, I.-B. (ed.) (2012) *Culture and Reflexivity in Systemic Psychotherapy: Mutual Perspectives.* London: Karnac.
Lago, C. and Thomson, J. (1996) *Race, Culture and Counselling.* Buckingham: Open University Press.
Littlewood, R. (1992) How Universal Is Something We Call Therapy? In J. Kareem and R. Littlewood (eds), *Intercultural Therapy: Themes, Interpretations and Practice.* London: Blackwell.
Littlewood, R. and Lipsedge, M. (1982) *Aliens and Alienists: Ethnic Minorities and Psychiatry.* London: Penguin.
Money-Kyrle, R. (1960) On Prejudice: A Psychoanalytical Approach. *British Journal of Medical Psychology*, 33: 205–209.
Papadopoulos, R. (ed.) (2002) *Therapeutic Care for Refugees: No Place Like Home.* London: Karnac.
Pedersen, P.B. (1987) *Handbook of Cross-Cultural Counselling.* New York: Praegar.
Sartre, J.P. (1973) *Anti-Semite and Jew.* New York: Shocken.
Sigalas, A. (2011) Psychotherapeutic Work at Nafsiyat. In C. Lago (ed.), *The Handbook of Transcultural Counselling and Psychotherapy.* London: Open University Press.
Thomas, L. (1992) Racism and Psychotherapy: Working with Racism in the Consulting Room: An Analytical View. In J. Kareem and R. Littlewood (eds), *Intercultural Therapy. Themes, Interpretations and Practice.* London: Blackwell.
Winnicott, D.W. (1990) *The Maturational Process and the Facilitating Environment.* London: Karnac.
Winterbottom, M. (2002) In this World. Film. London: BBC.
Žižek, S. (2008) *Violence.* London: Profile Books.

10

FACE TO FACE

Psychotherapy in black and white

Charles Brown

This chapter outlines some aspects of the unfolding dynamic between therapist and patient in the analytic process. I give an account of transference dreams not often addressed in the psychoanalytic literature, and describe two patients' dreams of me – a Black male therapist. The first example given is when the therapist is dreamt of as he really is. In the second dream the therapist is transformed into something he is not. In discussing the unconscious dynamics of the interracial dyad I suggest that one reason for the appearance of the therapist in the patient's dreams is when there is a visible colour difference between the patient and the therapist. The literature regarding this difference between the therapist and patient is sparse and the process involved in including unconscious meaning of colour and its possible relevance to the work is rarely reported.

This chapter discusses how these sorts of dreams were mutually understood and explores what emerged from the recognition of the fact of a difference between the therapist and the patient. I go on to extrapolate the meaning of colour within the therapy, scrutinising how the complex issues and multiple levels of meaning were made use of and how colour related to the differentiation of the me and the not me in the therapist/patient dyad. From a relational perspective the dreams presented opportunities for the articulation of social identities, racialised subjectivities and ultimately for mutual recognition and growth.

Working in a racial and diverse cultural society the significance of colour and its meaning in the therapeutic encounter can impact on many levels both consciously and unconsciously. I contend that drawing these elements out in therapy can result in meaningful exchanges that may benefit the work.

First clinical example

A 46-year-old upper-middle-class mother whom I shall call Cecilia had been in three-times-a-week therapy for almost two years at the time of this dream. During the course of the therapy Cecilia had several dreams relating to me; this was the only one where I appeared as myself. She had sought therapy because she wanted to break away from a marriage where she felt empty and lifeless.

When Cecilia's mother became pregnant her parents were expected to marry as a matter of course. Her father was a heavy drinker and womaniser whose unpredictable drunken rages would terrify Cecilia when she was growing up. She described once coming upon her father with his hands around her mother's neck. Her mother was not someone who could talk about feelings and was experienced as being distant and authoritarian.

Cecilia had met and married her own husband when they were in a religious organisation. Her involvement in the organisation had come through a sexual relationship with a prominent and charismatic older married member of the organisation.

The couple left the organisation when their child was very young and she became a stay-at-home mother and adopted a celibate lifestyle. However, Cecilia maintained some of the friendships she had made in the organisation.

The therapy had been focused on Cecilia's depersonalisation, feelings of anger and inability to express herself apart from her response to the behaviour of others. She had little self-agency and felt that she could not do anything without apology.

The dream in question took place after Cecilia had been talking about her son who was preparing to throw a party for some of his friends. She had noticed that he had not invited a couple of his friends to whom she thought he was close. When she asked him about this he told her that he didn't want to invite them because he would then have to invite other people that he didn't want to be there. She knew some of her son's friends were drinking a lot and she was worried about his drinking.

In the following session Cecilia brought this dream.

> My son and I visit a museum but the entrance leads into the office part of the building and not to where the exhibitions were. I spend a lot of time trying to get out. It is night-time when we eventually came out onto the street. I start to walk quickly through the streets. After a while I notice that my son is no longer with me. I begin looking and calling for him. I see a group of Black men beating someone up. I can't quite see who it is as they are all over the person. I see you standing there watching it all and I ask you who is being beaten. You say teach me how to row, before moving away.

Cecilia's initial association was to her work environment where she felt that she had to subscribe to certain attitudes and particular beliefs. One of her colleagues, she added, had recently posted a disparaging Facebook comment about all the posh white boys that they had to work with. Further associations were then made to white privilege linked to the Oxford and Cambridge universities' annual boat race. As we discussed the dream further Cecilia said that I (as the dream therapist) was asking for something that she was unable to give. That is, if she wanted me to help her, she must do something for me in return. She said she could not change cultural history and make the playing field level between Black people and white people.

Cecilia said that she was feeling exposed and afraid to give voice to her words and her emotions in case it went off somewhere that would make me feel uncomfortable. The therapeutic space had become frightening and violently oppressive and unable to offer any possibilities to think or to be a space of safety. In the dream she was anxious that the gang in their rage might round on her. She then felt guilty and expressed her fear of being judged by me, as in the dream.

The use of the therapist's colour, stripped of his analytic function and reduced to a racialised subject, can take place not only in the Oedipal situation but also in the socially constructed psyche. That is to say, in both the symbolic and the real. Cecilia was able through our discussions and thinking to acknowledge some shared experience between us.

This meant that rather than colour being limiting in the therapy, recognition and acknowledgement allowed more authenticity whilst furthering the development of trust between the therapist and the patient within the analytic relationship. The possibility of thinking together, of two worlds meeting and of having a therapist who could mediate between the black and white drama of it all because he had a foot in both worlds, supported Cecilia in obtaining a solid sense of self. The therapist's capacity to acknowledge her anxieties, that is to say, between feelings about white guilt on the one hand and Black rage on the other opened up possibilities for the work that had hitherto been unavailable. Thus, both were participants in finding connections that allowed thinking across that divide and learn something that could help us both in gaining further understanding.

Second clinical example

Irene, a woman in her mid-30s, had sought treatment to address her depression and difficulties around sex and sexuality. She began attending twice-weekly appointments. Using the couch (which she referred to as 'the bed') immediately stimulated intense transference feelings.

Irene's description of her mother was of an overinvolved, critical and unempathic woman. Irene felt her mother was completely wrapped up in her husband and that her father neglected her because her mother needed him. Irene's father was described as a very practical man but she felt that he did not understand her, often leaving her feeling interrogated by him and not heard. Whilst she had told her family that she was gay, she described herself to me as being bisexual.

When Irene was three years old her parents attempted to move her into a room of her own. This resulted in a hysterical outburst that so alarmed the parents that a doctor was summoned. The doctor suggested that the child remain in the parental bedroom.

After university, she went back to live with her parents for a short while. She then moved into shared accommodation but this did not work out and she wanted to return home, but her mother said that it was time she flew the nest.

The dream that I discuss here occurred during the latter part of the first year of therapy.

Irene had attended a friend's wedding where she had seen a good-looking man. She thought that the good-looking man might have come to dance with her. She was disappointed when he did not. She then felt that she had to make do with dancing with her female friend. The next session Irene brought this dream: 'I came to therapy and was surprised to see that you were a blond-haired white female.'

Discussing associations to the dream Irene said that whilst she did not recognise the woman in the dream, she acknowledged that it might be me, as she had come to her therapy in the dream.

In thinking about the dream she spoke about being her mother's confidant and her experience of rejection by her father. She would feel guilty if she were to say anything about her feelings because of her parents' own troubled childhoods. Irene's relationship with her mother was as a passive participant in the marriage as her mother took to talking to Irene about her sexual life. Irene found this pattern repeated in her relationships with her friends and their partners in whose relationships she would take up the role of the voyeur and confidant.

Irene's parents had been in the habit of walking around the house naked when she was growing up. In addition she had come upon the primal scene.

Irene went on to tell me that recently when her mother was showing her holiday photos they went through each picture in detail. When Irene asked, in turn, if she would like to see her photos of a recent visit to a European city, her mother said yes, but after seeing a few said she was tired and went to lie down. Her father said he would like to see the pictures but as they were going through the pictures he began to comment on each image. He offered advice and made remarks on the lighting and the setting or something else that he was then able to relate back to himself.

There seemed to be no place where Irene felt relationally attended to. Never having had a sexual relationship meant that the whole area of intimacy was fraught for her.

In the dream, Irene had transformed me into her preoccupied and self-absorbed mother who would bake her cakes, give her sweets and take her into her confidence. I felt that, as the therapist, I could not have a space in the mind of Irene who would invariably feed herself immediately before and after our appointments. Irene would often say that she had no feelings at all towards me and that the therapy was a service that she paid for and as such could not be construed as a relationship at all.

As a result of discussing the dream, Irene's competitiveness and anger towards her mother could be acknowledged. As her defences against relating and relationships were explored and clarified, she became gradually but noticeably softer in her general appearance and she became more vulnerable in her interactions with me. For example, she found that she was able to weep, for the first time, in the presence of another.

Irene's denial of the reality that I was Black and what that might mean for her was used to defend against her own feelings about sexual desire, desires that she had projected onto me. This was one reason why she dreamt of me as a blonde-haired, white woman – another reason was that she was defending against her sexual wishes by changing my sex and colour to white, which could not respond to her with a similar erotic gesture. Desire was linked in her mind with the trauma of exclusion and rejection connected with the overeroticised atmosphere in her family home where she was exposed to parental sex in a way that she found distressing. Irene's unconscious associations to my skin and her sexual fantasies were overlaid by idealised whiteness.

Discussing the dream helped Irene recognise that after breaks in the therapy she had begun to miss our sessions, and that she missed me. She had also been able to engage with a non-white personal trainer, whose name she would invariably pronounce with an exaggerated accent. When I commented on this Irene was able to think about and take back her projections and acknowledge her underlying hostility and acknowledge again her sexual attraction to dark skin. Irene became more accepting of my presence in the therapy and was able to admit the presence of men in the world.

Irene spoke about a trip she had taken where the tour guide was a Black man who told Irene that he had recently ended a relationship. He would frequently mix up his ex-partner's name with Irene's own. She associated the Black tour guide with me, her therapist. It then emerged that the tour guide also shared his name with me. During this session, Irene noticed that I was wearing a wedding band and wondered whether I had got married during the therapy.

Discussion

A review of the literature reveals that discussions about race and culture in relation to dreams have been limited. This includes discussions in which a specific clinical phenomenon such as transference, countertransference or resistance is being examined. There is a sense that difference will be problematic in the work. Similarly, the literature does not have much to say about patients' dreams of the therapist. When it is discussed, the focus is on the therapist's failure in technique or the pathology of the patient.

Traditionally, when the therapist appeared as himself in the patient's dream it was viewed as being due to a technical error on the part of the therapist, mismanagement of the analytic frame or the therapist's similarities with important figures in the patient's past (Harris 1962; Langs 1980; Rosenbaum 1965; Gillman 1980; Feldman 1945).

Freud (1900) ascribed the presence of colour in the dream to a re-enactment of something in the memory. Calef (1954) agreed that colour could serve as a symbol for an old sensory impression that could become part of the resistance, revealing its presence in the formation of the images of the dream. In the same paper Calef also commented that many colour dreams in the literature exposed primal scene material.

Blum (1964) considered the appearance of colour, like all dream elements, was shaped by structural conflicts. He also noted that the meaning of colour in the dream may be genetically overdetermined and complex:

> color may have a role among the many other variables in the differentiation of self from object or in identification with the object. The individual's awareness of his own complexion, skin color ... relate color not only to the body image but also to self-representation and identity.

Recent perspectives link up these types of dreams with the therapeutic participants. Eyre (1988) suggested that when the therapist is used as a dream symbol it heralded a sign of change and movement in the work. Kavanagh (1994) held that dreams of the therapist must take into account not only when such dreams occur in treatment, but with which patient and which therapist.

Leary (1995) has pointed out that race and ethnicity have been treated as if they are qualities possessed only by people of colour, and that when one thinks of the majority culture, one fails to recognise that it is also a definable culture with limitations and parameters just like all other cultures. Ideas about black skin can be imbued with many stereotypical meanings that also carry individual personal meaning. This individuality of symbols reflects the person's unique qualities and experiences (Rosenthal 1977–8).

When the patient and the therapist have different colour skins the dissimilarities can lead to an impasse that occurs when the patient holds a particular culture-specific value and can be left feeling misunderstood. Curry (1964–5) suggested that 'When the therapist is Black and the patient is white certain fantasies, myths and beliefs are mobilized' which consequently shape the transference.

I have found that the Black male therapist often finds himself dealing with dreams, wishes and fantasies stimulated by the reality of the colour of his skin. Several authors have supported the view that colour has a profound influence on the analytic process and is often used as a transference resistance by patients (Myers 1977; Highlen and Hill 1984; Holmes 1992; Yi 1998).

Myers (1980) has written about these kinds of dreams. He suggested that female patients, who presented dreams of the therapist turning white, had fathers who were seen as rejecting their daughters' emerging sense of femininity and sexuality during the Oedipal phase. The mothers were perceived as having been rejected by their own fathers and a bond was formed between the mothers and daughters. According to Myers, the situation of a narcissistic humiliation occurring at the hands of the father led to the transformation of the father/therapist into the protecting or neutral mother figure in the dreams. Some of Myers' ideas are pertinent and applicable, particularly in the case of Irene, with its themes of super-ego criticisms, inhibitions and prohibitions. However, I expand the clinical picture and emphasise the influence of the cross-racial dimension of the therapeutic encounter.

The racial dynamics between the Black male therapist, the white female patient and the impact of attitudes each of them hold with regards to colour will highlight the need for the patient to become aware, perhaps for the first time, of herself as a racial being when trying to locate herself using the Black male therapist as a reference (Miller and Josephs 2009). It is inevitable that categories pertaining to race will be present in the therapeutic space, even in the absence of obvious racial or cultural difference between the two participants in the room.

The meanings assigned to colour as it emerges in the transference can greatly enrich the analytic process and prove beneficial to the treatment when they arise. Tang and Gardener (1999) observed that when the variables of race '[a]re considered along with traditional clinical material, a more helpful and complete analytic picture can emerge'. In addition to this, I would assert that exploration of these issues during the therapy might provide a connection with core conflicts, transference and resistance.

References

Blum, H.P. (1964) Colour in Dreams. *International Journal of Psychoanalysis*, 45: 519–529.
Calef, V. (1954) Colour in Dreams. *Journal of the American Psychoanalytic Association*, 2: 453–460.
Curry, A.E. (1964–5) Myth, Transference and the Black Psychotherapist. *Psychoanalytic Review*, 51D(4): 7–14.
Holmes, D.E. (1992) Race and Transference in Psychoanalysis and Psychotherapy. *International Journal of Psychoanalysis*, 73: 1–11.
Eyre, D. (1988) The Use of the Analyst as a Dream Symbol. *British Journal of Psychotherapy*, 5(1): 5–18.
Feldman, S.S. (1945) Interpretation of a Typical and Stereotyped Dream Met with Only during Psychoanalysis. *Psychoanalytic Quarterly*, 14: 511–515.
Freud, S. (1900) *The Interpretation of Dreams*. Translation by A.A. Brill. Ware: Wordsworth Editions.
Gillman, R. (1980) Dreams in Which the Analyst Appears as Himself. In J. Natterson (ed.), *The Dream in Clinical Practice*. New York: Jason Aronson.
Harris, I. (1962) Dreams about the Analyst. *International Journal of Psychoanalysis*, 43: 151–158.
Highlen, P.S. and Hill, C.E. (1984) Factors Affecting Client Change in Individual Counseling: Current Status and Theoretical Speculations. In S.D. Brown and R.W. Lent (eds), *The Handbook of Counseling Psychology*. New York: Wiley.
Kavanagh, G. (1994) The Patient's Dreams of the Analyst. *Contemporary Psychoanalysis*, 30: 500–509.
Langs, R. (1980) The Dream in Psychotherapy. In J. Natterson (ed.), *The Dream in Clinical Practice*. New York: Jason Aronson.
Leary, K. (1995) Interpreting in the Dark. *Psychoanalytic Psychology*, 12: 127–140.
Miller, E.A. and Josephs, L. (2009) Whiteness as Pathological Narcissism. *Contemporary Psychoanalysis*. 45: 93–119.
Myers, W.A. (1977) The Significance of the Colors Black and White in the Dreams of Black and White Patients. *Journal of the American Psychoanalytic Association*. 25: 163–181.
Myers, W.A. (1980) A Transference Dream with Superego Implications. *Psychoanalytic Quarterly*, 49: 284–307.
Rosenbaum, M. (1965) Dreams in Which the Analyst Appears Undisguised: A Clinical and Statistical Study. *International Journal of Psycho-Analysis*, 46: 429–437.
Rosenthal, H.R. (1977–8) A Clinical Note on the Manifest Content of Dreams. *Modern Psychoanalysis*, 2: 228–243.
Tang, N.M. and Gardener, J. (1999) Race, Culture, and Psychotherapy: Transference to Minority Therapists. *Psychoanalytic Quarterly*, 68: 1–20.
Yi, K.Y. (1998) Transference and Race: An Intersubjective Conceptualization. *Psychoanalytic Psychology*, 15: 245–261.

11

EMBODIED INTERCULTURAL GROUND

Carmen Joanne Ablack

Phenomenological awareness

Metaphor, symbols, movements and allegory, to tell stories, share word stories and to convey something of what I am experiencing in the room with clients and supervisees are part of my approach.[1] Use of phenomenological awareness in my integrative gestalt body psychotherapy approach is foundational and it is this phenomenological awareness I will use here to explore my ideas about embodying intercultural ground.

Phenomenological awareness is (put simply) the act of focusing on your body-mind experiences whilst having them; your experiencing of your sensations, affects and thoughts and how you are affected by situation and context in any one moment, i.e. the full environmental experience. Phenomenological method in psychotherapy involves speaking out these experiences as intervention and to support relational dialogue. Your awareness of breathing and allowing your whole body-mind to engage with your felt sense of the words as you read as well as engaging with your responses arising to any meaning making you are doing in response to the thoughts and ideas is phenomenological engagement.

I begin by writing briefly about my background and my reflective learning from this, noting signs of what led me to the ground of emerging embodied intercultural experience and noting my embodied intercultural phenomenology as I write. In expanding on these concepts I identify some themes and possible clinically informed theoretical positions about my work and more widely on what might be needed in the psychotherapy task. I focus specifically on the concepts of dignity and ignominy including a brief case vignette, and write about embodied intercultural phenomenology and awareness as a necessary development arising from working with relational awareness.

'To embody' goes back to 1548 formed from English *em* and body, and embodiment first appeared in the writings of Carlyle in 1828. 'Intercultural' has not quite made it to my copy of *Chambers Dictionary of Etymology*, however, I understand 'inter-' to mean variously among, reciprocally and between (APA n.d.). It is in these senses that I use the term intercultural, with acknowledgement of *cultural diffusion*, in use by 1912; *cultural diversity* by 1935; *cultural imperialism* by 1937; *cultural pluralism* by 1932; *cultural relativism* by 1948, as relevant to historical understanding of cultural (as cited by Harper, www.dictionary.com/browse/inter-).

Some beginnings

I first started learning about facilitating from supporting others whilst at school, becoming conscious about learning as I assisted first-year art classes whilst a sixth former, watching and learning about different ways in which individuals needed to be responded to and seeing all the ways I could find to do this ... I was experimenting – finding out about being with another whilst supporting them.

Later, working voluntarily with young women school non-attenders, I was discovering embodiment of these relationships through the unfolding ground by being with both my bodily awareness and inviting them to be with theirs. We danced, we sang, we painted and laughed and cried together. I used my body awareness as an instrument of understanding in a mixture of intuition and trusting unknowing in equal measure. I was sometimes overwhelmed and awed by the effect that simple interventions, like movements of hands and feet to the beat, could achieve. Studying psychology and sociology at university at this time and trying to make sense of what I was experiencing and being in the world as emerging grown-up me was like many students an exciting and confusing time.

Earlier as a teen in another culturally different world of black, white and brown, of Irish, English and Afro-Caribbean, geographically somewhere between Kilburn and Maida Vale, I was learning to inhibit my spontaneity and to draw away from really showing my body's intuitive authentic moves. For fear – it was the 1970s and I was skinny with hair in long plaits – I looked like a 'Paki' and I was treated like a 'Paki' got treated in that area at that time. I sometimes was under serious threat; my body (or at least its strength, agility and speed) saved me from the end of a fist or a knife or from grown men doing worse to me than just holding me down in broad daylight and spitting in my mouth whilst young mothers watched, children in prams.

It was an ugly time and I was left feeling like an ugly teen who either would die or would just manage to survive, there seemed at times no other option. It was outside my mother's experience to know what to do with a child on whom so much had impacted, so sensitive and so stubbornly scared. We went through a difficult stage and experienced a cross-cultural missing for many years on the back of such events and my inability to speak and her inability to really help me with them was painful for both of us. I made a decision many therapists will recognise from their work, quite early on, to just not tell her again about any of it. Part of the opposite of 'embodied intercultural' is 'experience denial' of the ground that is forming for the other and with the other in such narratives.

Unready for the sheer wanton violence of the daily racism of school and living in the UK in 1972, I think now that she could not face what felt like betrayal by a country she had seen as also hers. My experience had not been her experience of living and working here as a young Black woman during the war 'supporting the war effort' of the mother country. I was to learn decades later, not long before she passed away, that my dad had faced similar actual threat at knifepoint to his own life as a Commonwealth scholarship student in the 1930s. His trauma from this and his experiences of being a young Black man who was part of the Second World War effort, I now believe, added to his incapability of really taking in how threatened his children were *in reality*, 40 plus years later. He necessarily froze parts of himself, his awareness, and was less able to meet us in our experiencing, thus affecting our self-states and senses of identity as ongoing processes (Wright 2016); or our ability to understand our *selves-in worlds*, where an awareness of 'selves' and 'worlds' is interdependent and describes different aspects of our experiences (Sheehan 2016: 109–29).

Reflecting on these earlier personal moments in preparation for the talk I reconnect with a familiar polarity, one which I name here as the 'dignity-ignominy polarity' or a 'survival event process' of minority existence. Both my parents, and many from minority cultural/heritage/socio-economic and other non-majority groups, live or lived their lives in their own versions of this polarity event. And now the resonances I experience – with the identification dilemmas faced by those abused over time, or now coming forward or the individual, group and community attacks (physically, mentally and psychologically and emotionally) in the dividing of communities atmosphere currently – cannot be avoided and are part of the considerations informing the emergence of my understanding of embodied intercultural ground.

Sitting in 'chaos'

Often I can sit still in apparent chaos, finding a way through by simply looking, waiting, feeling and welcoming my own embodied phenomenological processing. A part of this phenomenological processing is how I am engaging with and being affected by the environment – remembering that environment includes other people, the situation and the context. Whenever I got the chance as a child I loved to 'sit' amongst the 'chaos' of the playground looking at and feeling the patterns being made, literally feeling movements in the air as they happened. I also loved to play right in the centre of this, sometimes adapting to others and sometimes as the innovator. As an older teenager, helping younger pupils who were scared and disoriented, I became a still point, a 'place' to share fears or anxieties that felt too dangerous for sharing with the peer group and teachers.

My experiences – as a child growing up in and amongst many cultures, in different countries, of being a student and years later back in London of being a teacher, manager, psychotherapist and supervisor within the context of minority experiences and situations – have led me time and again to explore the meanings and processes of this 'dignity-ignominity' polarity event. I am using 'event' as understood in Gestalt field theory – there are only events; things are not things fixed forever in time and space, but rather are events in the phenomenological field defined by situational contexts (Wollants 2012; Hodges 2003). As situational contexts affect the 'thing' becoming other than it was, there is the moving form of 'event-*ing*', and I as therapist am utilising phenomenological tracking making enquiry into my unfolding awareness, into that of the client, in the moments of contacting and attending to shared between awareness that is neither just you or I. Event phenomena are being described through a poem written in 2013, inspired by the privilege of working with clients who were learning to live with their unique 'traumatic event-*ing*' and being with our relational-situational sensing in the here and now:

Situational One

As I walk along the shore feeling the sand gyrate gently between my toes,

I come to recognise a sudden cold, odd feeling in my feet,

They start to freeze in the sunshine …

I look down …

My toenails are turning bluish of hue and my toe-tips paling in the sunlight,

Blood contracts and I am lost in a sense of no time, no space, no contact,

But for the grating sand grains on the skins of my separated toes

and in the numbing of feet that are apparently mine;

Suddenly a cry from above cuts through,

I finally take a breath and feel the rush of air into my mouth,

A sickly staleness comes into my awareness, I cough convulsively and

my stomach finding a rhythm in this – heaves the toxicity between my teeth

out, out onto the sand,

to be washed away by the coming waves.

Horrible, horrible smell.

Situational Two

Delightful, delightful release;

Emptied, breathing again,

I feel the sand gyrate gently against and between my toes,

I come to recognise my warmth in my feet

Sun rays on my whole body,

I become fascinated by the warmth, cold, warmth in my feet

as the waves lap across them and move away;

I am in contact with the waves, the feel of them on my body

The sense of them in my body,

I sense my whole self, embracing the moment,

Situation aware, I come to feel some sense of being in motion

I am with the changing waves, my moving breath

and the sand gently gyrating against my toes,

here,

in this moment,

in this time,

Simply awaiting the next event-ing of ever unfolding me-ing.

(Situation One, Situation Two, *Carmen Joanne Ablack, March 2013*)

Dignity-ignominy as an embodied process

When attending to intercultural possibilities, my experience is one of unfolding self-respect, self-esteem, poise, pride, self-possession and self-worth – 'dignity'. Often in conjunction with polarising 'ignominy' – presence of humiliation, discomfort, shame, senses of disgrace and dishonour and embodied in the narratives shared between the clients and me. This work requires evaluative self-reflecting where essences and energies of shame and humiliation are welcomed as essential elements needing 'voice' and an understanding of their overarching presence in processes of identity. This identity process experiencing occurs as embodied intercultural ground creating happens.

VIGNETTE PART 1

Surita, a children's medical practitioner became increasingly ill over several years with no explanation showing through the endless tests done. Finally with some disgust she admitted to herself she had the condition known as ME, a condition she had not quite believed in as a medical practitioner – this showed up as an ongoing process event of shame for her in therapy. When she started with me she had been medically retired for a few years and had already been in therapy. She was from the outset dryly funny, with a lovely touch of appreciating the absurdities of life generally and specifically.

She had utterly changed her life in order to accommodate and try and 'move on' from her medical condition. She came through a referral from another therapist who felt she 'needed to think about her body'.

First meeting, the initial meeting was somewhat like a whirlwind, Surita had so much to convey ... my immediate impressions were of liveliness and underlying fragility, she laughed with the abandon of a child as she talked about all she had gone through, almost bouncing in the seat of the couch as she looked and spoke with me. She also had a delicate voice that she dropped into as she spoke about her sense of knowing that she had not quite found what she needed in terms of meaning ... meaning from therapy, meaning from living with her condition, meaning of being who she is now rather than who she was.

I ventured a response, inviting her to just take in me, the room, the space created already and see what that was like, see what if anything she was drawn to saying ... I was wanting to get a sense of if and how she experienced subtleties and shades of being present already with me, and was curious as to what she did notice, what she considered, what she wanted to say in response and what was not yet present.

She visibly breathed more deeply, started to look slowly, slowly, at different things in the room, including looking at me without smiling between each area of room or object considered. She then said that she felt she 'might find some things here to reflect me, ... some that will inspire me and ... [deeper breath] some that will challenge me ... I want you to challenge me ... I need to find out why, what this all means and I want to know if I can actually recover ...'

She found she needed to rest for 24 hours after each session (not go out, speak to no more than one person, take her time), this was different to her previous experience, the attention to embodiment was new and needed pacing.

A few sessions later we are talking about an image from the past that she had on the way to therapy, a brief glimpse of her mother sitting next to her somewhere outside when she was about two and a half or three years old, sitting near water and just ignoring her ... letting her play and talk to herself, just listening to the sounds around her ... but with her mother unengaged,

'...*she just did not take any notice that I was with her ... I remember feeling bad about wanting her attention, ... wanting her to hear what I was hearing, feel the stones and the other things I was finding... but feeling bad ...as if I was intruding on her by wanting this ... it often felt like I was intruding ... if I asked for her attention...*'

And as you tell me this ... ?

She becomes very still, and as I feel a sensation of warmth in my belly and cold in my legs, I note that she is squeezing her legs hard together...

Just notice your legs.........

A silence and then

'*Sh..sh..sh.. I..I... I am not here ... I have gone far into my world listening to the sounds ... and she is left sitting on the ground ... sh ... sh ... sh...*

I remember ... she didn't even notice that I fell as I moved to the sounds. It was as if she was frozen in time ... and I was moving.'

> She is breathing slowly, her face has relaxed and her eyes are closed;
> I notice my breath is more in my belly and my head is tilted as if listening for something just out of range of hearing ...
> ...
> And now ... as you remember that time ... that moving to the sounds?
> *'My mother could not be with me ... I can feel how my legs were really tightly held when you asked me to notice, I think that I did that inside myself a lot... as if I had to hold on ... no ... hold in who I was for fear that I would be too "alien" for her ... and we of course were "aliens", my family I mean ... we were aliens to where we were, and she was alien to me and I to her ...'*
> And in sensing and being with sensing 'alienness' you notice what? ...
> *'Ah God ... [her eyes open fully and she looks at me] ... God it was so difficult to be here and to feel how much she wanted to be home ...'*
> You could feel how much she wanted to 'be home' ... and it was so difficult for you to be here when you felt she wanted to be there...?
> *'She could not see me without seeing that she was not home ... I became her "not home" child [tears, gentle, quiet, sobbing] ... I tried so hard to be like she told me she was as a child ... I forced myself to behave like she said she did for her mother ...'*

'Anamenesis' as remembering

Ross Brown (2009) captures something of what is happening at this point that is worth drawing attention to. Brown is writing about the effects of sound and silences:

> sonic ghosts are not only in my head [he is talking of thoughts and 'imagined or recalled' sounds]; there are also bodily sensations, corporeal imaginings of aural feelings: the recollection of the internal vibration of standing by the sea or the roadside ... the complex emotional arrangement of vibrations, flushes, prickling skin and adrenal activity of engaging with music.

Brown continues with Augoyard and Torgue's description of 'phenomena they call *anamnesis*: the physical recollection – literally the re-*membering* – of sound through the body'. He says this can be triggered empathically by perceiving with our senses and through imagined or remembered sounds 'one might view it as an embodied form of memory experienced in the aural body ... hearing and remembering ... overlap'.

Additionally, I want to highlight a connection between Brown's writing above and Peter Philippson in *The Emergent Self* (2009: 133) on Goldstein's coining, definition and understanding of 'self-actualisation' as 'self-formed in its action'. Philippson reminds us that self-*ing* is a process, happening through engagement with, and to my understanding is *always* present. What becomes crucial is the level of awareness, the depth of phenomenological enquiry and the relational-situational matrix in which all this is happening.

Totton and Priestman (2012) summarise this well, 'If we explore embodiment we encounter relationship; if we explore relationship we encounter embodiment'. They posit the centrality of the 'interplay' between embodiment-relationship and relationship-embodiment in their work. I would identify with this as an important aspect of all truly relational work, and further it cannot be explored and understood fully without the intercultural ground of the relationship being in the matrix also.

VIGNETTE PART 2

[More tears, more loudly ... and then she is also shaking a little, it has a rhythm, and she starts a sinuous movement of her spine]

'My body never moves like this ... this is something new ...'

Something new, how is that for you?

'Okay... I think...'

Okay... you think? ... And your legs ... how are your legs as you move newly?

'My legs are... um they are speaking [she smiles] saying... your mother won't like this ... [she laughs a little] ... oh no mama, really, really would not like this ... it's too ... um ... um'

It's too? ... You are too...?

[I move a little like she is doing, our eyes meet and she smiles at me, then grins fully ... I am very moved by her / by us in this moment.]

'But [what looks like an amazed smile and then a grin] ... I'm not too ... ...

I _am_ this ... I am my movement ... I am this ... in my body ... it is my body [sounding declarative] ... it is my body that can move ...'

Your body that can move ... that can move like this ... your movement?

[A longer silence as she continues to explore her movements.]

What's your sense of your movement's nature ... you are ...?

'I am not held, ... I think... I am not my mother's childhood ...'

[Also declarative.]

[She stops moving and is breathing a little fast.]

She cries... 'I was not my body either ... I gave it away...'

You ... gave it away?

'No... that's not quite it ... I had to be in her place, ... her space ... be like she wanted me to be, ... needed me to be ... it was too scary for her if I ... was not? ... She couldn't meet me ...'

She _couldn't_ meet you? She could not meet _you_...?

'We should have been able to create a new place ... in this new place ...

I wanted her to help me be in this new place ... I wanted meeting ... as I had to go to school and had to find my place. ... I wanted her to want to be with me **in**

> *this new place... her body, her thoughts, her feelings ...**her love for me, the child me, to be here with me in this new place.'***
> [She cries really hard now.]
> [I wait, ... aware of my own spine, pulsing, resonating; ... and also aware of the sense of resonance with my own missing need of being met by my mother;
> I breathe and recentre on being with her whilst allowing my sensitivity/awareness of my own feelings to further open my heart to her ...]
> *'Do you understand? ... Do you get what I mean? ...'*
> What I am getting [as I put my hand deliberately on my heart] is that, ... is that you wanted her to ... um ... to understand it was a new place for you too.
> You wanted her to bring her love for you to ..., to you, to *both* of you in this new place ... that you had to go out into the world and be at school and you wanted her to understand this ... what this was like for you...
> *'Yes, yes, ... for both of us ... love for us both ... so we could face the new places we each had to be in at least together...somehow'.*
> As you speak now, I am aware of a sense of ache in my chest just here [I point to myself above my left breast] ... I am aching...here ... are you aware of your chest or your body right now?
> *'When you touched your chest I felt like a sense of longing ... a sense of a fluttering in my heart ... as if a gate was opening and all feelings were tumbling out ...*
> *I longed for her to see me ... I longed for her to understand what it was like for me ... I wanted her to get my world too ...'*
> You wanted her to get your world ... and you wanted her to create a new way of meeting in the world you both found yourselves in ... meet with you [she nods and smiles at me and nods again] ...
> You wanted to create a new ground, so to speak ... shared between you ...?
> *'Yes, that's it ... I like "new ground" ... I wanted us to be able to start on new ground by creating a shared way of doing it ... of being ... that would have made me feel safe and I would have known I mattered... ...I think that is what matters to me now as an adult...that I get to be met and to ... you know...'*
> And the ground here with me as we look at this... are you met enough by me here?
> *'Hmm... that's a good one.'* [She smiles.] ...
> You're welcome, I try ... [laughing quietly]
> *'Yeah, ... you and me ... we meet ... I feel like you are here with me but not like I have to be something, ... not much anyway, sometimes I can feel that ... but that's <u>not</u> us ... It's more when I'm not here (present) letting you meet me... hmm, ... there's always more ...'*
> But maybe not now ... we are close to time for us to complete today.

I hold such respect for the courage and sensitivity of this woman. I feel I learned more and more about being human, about being in relational embodied intercultural ground every time we met.

Finally, I want to share here a couple of thoughts and ideas from specific therapeutic literature that informed my thinking as I wrote this chapter and thought about working together with this client. Krause (1998: 174–5) offers

> meaning is never unattached, but must always be articulated by persons embedded in particular relationships in particular spaces and at particular times. That it is the therapist's job to understand this detail. And this in turn implies that meaning like culture is heterodox [heterodox meaning not following the usual standards or beliefs].

She adds meaning, like culture, is therefore, 'always changing and shifting and in the process of being created'.

Fairfield (2004) writing about groups says when we limit our way of working to too interpretative a frame we are risking missing subtle dynamics, nuances and multiple layers that belong to the whole field. I would add, after rereading Brown (2009), we also risk the sterility of 'repetition' of what we know or think we know against the potential of listening and hearing 'new sounds' in the relational field.

Whilst interpretative and transferential understandings also may be useful in looking at my vignette, following Fairfield I have chosen to focus on the 'opening of the gate' the client spoke of, to being available to allowing something else, new places and moments of meeting, allowing for systemic meanings unfolding co-creating new ground. For me this is the event-*ing* embodied intercultural ground, where phenomenology and awareness are arising from working with relational awareness and relational awareness arises from phenomenological processing.

Note

1 This chapter derives in part from a talk I gave to the Association of Jungian Analysts in 2013.

References

Ablack, C.J. (2013) Do You 'Do Difference'? Embodied Intercultural Ground. An unpublished talk given to the Association of Jungian Analysts on Tuesday 26 March 2013 (part of Cutting Edges: Analytic Psychology, a series of talks initiated by Gottfried M. Heuer).

Brown, R. (2009) Noise, Memory, Gesture: The Theatre in a Minute's Silence. In C. Counsell and R. Mock (eds), *Performance, Embodiment and Cultural Memory* 203–220. Newcastle: Cambridge Scholars Publishing.

Fairfield, M. (2004) Gestalt Groups Revisited: A Phenomenological Approach. *Gestalt Review*, 8(3).

Hodges, C. (2003) Creative Processes in Gestalt Group Therapy. In M. Spagnulo-Lobb and N. Amendt-Lyon (eds), *Creative License: The Art of Gestalt Therapy*, 249–259. Vienna: Springer.

Krause, I.-B. (1998) *Therapy across Culture*. London: SAGE.

Philippson, P. (2009) *The Emergent Self: An Existential- Gestalt Approach*. London: UKCP Karnac.

Sheehan, J. (2016) Self and World: Narrating Experience in the Supervisor/Supervisee Relationship. In A. Vetere and P. Stratton (eds), *Interacting Selves: Systemic Solutions for Personal and Professional development in Counselling and Psychotherapy*. London: Routledge.

Totton, N. and Priestman, A. (2012) Embodiment and Relationship: Two Halves of One Whole. Retrieved from: www.academia.edu/7424506/Embodiment_and_Relationship_Two_Halves_of_One_Whole. Also as a chapter in C. Young (ed.), *About Relational Body Psychotherapy*. Amsterdam: Body Psychotherapy Publications.

Wollants, G. (2012) *Gestalt Therapy: Therapy of the Situation*. London: SAGE.

Wright, S. (2016) *Dancing between Hope and Despair: Trauma, Attachment and the Therapeutic Relationship*. London: Palgrave.

12

INTERCULTURAL PSYCHOANALYTIC PSYCHOTHERAPY AND GENERATIONALLY TRANSMITTED TRAUMA

Lennox K. Thomas

This chapter looks at intercultural psychoanalytic psychotherapy with patients who have experienced trauma which has affected their functioning over several generations. What was left in the wake of large-scale traumatic events has not traditionally been an area of interest for psychoanalytic psychotherapy. Whilst each event differs, the common factor has been areas of altered psychological functioning for patients. A relatively new form of psychotherapy developed by Jafar Kareem in the 1970s – intercultural psychoanalytic psychotherapy (Kareem 1988) – was interested in difference. Kareem was concerned with context, culture and race in psychoanalysis at a time when minorities were not considered suitable for the talking therapies. He feared that conventional psychoanalysis, having been an innovative and radical form of psychological treatment for the emotionally tortured, was becoming a closed shop to ethnic, cultural and sexual minorities. A serious alternative to hospitalisation for the wealthier classes in the early 20th century, analysis had now become complacent. Kareem felt that the talking therapies should be available for all at a time when establishment psychotherapy had shut its eyes to minorities. This was at a time when Asians, Blacks and other internally colonised people were living in the land of the coloniser and experiencing severe difficulties in the mental health system, in education and in the criminal justice system. African Caribbean people are still between six and twelve times as likely to be admitted to a psychiatric hospital as compared to the general population (Harrison et al. 1999). Separation appears as a repeated pattern, as indeed forced separation was during enslavement, and this has an impact on the development of secure trusting relationships (Thomas 2014). Sixty percent of children are born to single-headed households which is an early indicator of future family impoverishment, and the children of these families are themselves more likely to become teenage parents. Kwame McKenzie (2006) posits the idea that the day-to-day grind of racism, abuse and self-medication with drugs and drink contributes to the stressors that push Caribbean people to the door of the acute psychiatric services (Littlewood and Lipsedge

1997; Harrison et al. 1999). This poses a considerable challenge to psychotherapists and other community mental health workers and social workers.

Intercultural psychotherapy has had an influence on the interrogation of psychotherapy and has been a catalyst for several articles in professional journals (Morgan 1998; Rose 1998; Uwahemu 2004). Intercultural ideas began a dialogue on diversity in psychoanalytic psychotherapy and encouraged people from Black and minority ethnic communities to join the profession. Holding on to the principles of psychoanalysis, intercultural therapy has not ignored such concerns of minority populations as those featured in the work of Fletchman-Smith (2000) and Akhtar (2005). Because of racism and colonisation, the consulting room is enriched with issues of trauma, culture, struggle and adaptation. Intercultural therapy has encouraged patients and therapists from different backgrounds and cultures to find a way of working together. Depth psychological treatment had not paid much attention to ethnic and cultural difference and what transference, counter-transference and pre-transference might yield when differences are considered in the consulting room.

Once considered, it is difficult to ignore the historical relationships that exist between coloniser and colonised groups and the psychological barriers of racism that need to be deconstructed in order to achieve good therapeutic engagement. There have been many gains from an intercultural approach; the curiosity and exploration of difference in the consulting room has led to a series of Tavistock Clinic workshops and the book *Thinking Space* by Lowe (2013). This examination of the therapeutic process has inevitably led to curiosity about 'intracultural' issues, gender, sexuality, class and power in psychoanalytic therapy. There are many issues that sometimes arise in therapy from the meeting of people from seemingly the same backgrounds that give rise to a host of transferential situations. I will explore these ideas here.

Recognising trauma

Therapists have always worked with trauma, Freud's early cases all featured patients who had traumatic experiences from which they were recovering. In more recent years, therapists have been confronted with the traumatic experience of those fleeing totalitarian regimes, political and other persecution. Drawing on the interests and preoccupations of this wider population, psychotherapists have been increasingly challenged by the big issues of despair, loss of home identity and of finding a meaning to live. Post-traumatic trauma in many of these patients has led to greater thinking about trauma in other areas of our work. Trauma describes an event or series of events that have life-changing effects on those involved. The emotional fallout from this can seamlessly be passed on to later generations if it is not processed. The traumatic event could be both physical and psychological and when subjects have not been able to recover to pre-trauma states, this leaves them in the process of 'adaptive' behaviours in an attempt to achieve recovery. Examples of historical trauma are the capture and enslavement of Africans for over 400 years in the Caribbean and Americas, the slaughter of tens of thousands on the Indian subcontinent after the 1947 partitioning of India, the internment and murder of Jews in Europe by the Nazi regime and the starvation and death of Irish people during the 19th-century potato famine. The stories are alive in families who were touched by these events, and in some the subject has become taboo and elaborate means have been employed to avoid their historical pain. Work on generationally transmitted trauma in African American communities has come from the United States, from DeGruy-Leary (2005) and Reid et al. (2005). They specifically refer to this as post-traumatic slavery Syndrome or post-traumatic slavery disorder. Others have written about holocaust trauma and more recent tragedies in Bosnia (e.g. Laub 1992).

Whilst many therapists work in their own communities, some have been able to recognise therapeutic issues across cultures. Neil Altman (2000), a white New York psychoanalyst, was able to work therapeutically in poor Black and Hispanic communities with issues of community disorganisation and its effect on young patients. He said that his was a split practice, working with the poor and disenfranchised whilst also treating the Manhattan privileged. Both served to enrich each other with the material and challenges they threw up for him as an analyst and a person. American psychotherapists and clinical social workers who have worked in mostly Black or Hispanic communities have noted the issues and behaviours that they considered adaptive as plantation behaviour, as if little has changed since their emancipation from slavery. It is interesting that not all people from traumatic backgrounds experience post-traumatic trauma and some appear to have been spared this. It might be the case that sound developmental experiences and family resilience have helped in their survival.

The capacity for healthy dissociation in trauma usually buys time until the trauma can be processed at a later date. Other people are affected by the trauma of their parents or grandparents who survived the horrors of the concentration camps, only to expose their children to their dysregulated emotions, drawing them into the cycle of traumatised behaviour. Kareem had worked with child survivors of the camps in Austria just after the Second World War and later in Israel. He was to witness their trauma, and hard-won recovery in some cases. The psychotherapist Ruth Barnet wrote about the experiences of the children of Holocaust survivors in the 1970s, having worked as a therapist with many confused young people in the United Kingdom.

Stephen is one such person who was born of parents affected by the Shoah. He had been in many different therapies, group and individual, for 30 years before he began treatment with me.

Stephen

Coming to therapy at 55, Stephen said that he had been depressed all of his life. He requested weekly therapy and was hard work in the early sessions, always regretting that our therapy time was soon over. I suggested that he might be able to use an additional session and he agreed to come twice. Stephen's story unfolded over a long period of time because he was often silent, almost frozen in the consulting room, and incapable of giving a sequential account of his early history. The meaning of his silence would not become clear until several months later. He began to talk about his work and his relationships with his colleagues in the laboratory where he worked. As he became agitated about his feelings of grievance at work he would excitedly flap his arms about and speak so quickly that it was difficult to understand his words. A senior scientist, he felt that his junior staff were not sufficiently committed to their work. He had reported being bad-tempered with people and rigid in his views, believing that they should honour their word, mean what they say and say what they mean. This seemed to be a repeated motif in Stephen's story. He had inherited a tidy sum from his parents and did not need to work, but was a dedicated employee who took pleasure in his work and the meaning it gave him. Devoted to his wife, they often argued over what he considered to be the fecklessness of his young adult children who lived off the family money struggling with addictions and showing no intention of working. I learnt that Stephen often woke at night full of emotions, sadness and despair. He had found that the only way for this to pass was to creep downstairs and listen to moving classical pieces through headphones. After being moved to tears and shaking he would get temporary relief and return to bed. I learned that he had done this for many years.

Whilst these were Stephen's presenting issues, his depression and how he functioned with other people, it was not until hearing his developmental history that some conclusions could be drawn about childhood patterns and how he was raised.

The first born of two, Stephen has a sister three and a half years younger. Both his parents were secular Jews, his father English and his mother Dutch. In his teens he learnt that all of his maternal family had been sent to concentration camps where they died leaving his mother devastated for several years. She only escaped because she was a student at an English university. He said that she was always depressed and sat Shiva for the rest of her life. She was in bed for a lot of his childhood and the home was run by a competent but uninvolved housekeeper.

Child development and transmitted trauma

Krystal (1978: 96), in *The Psychoanalytic Study of the Child*, describes the mothers in such situations as closed off and the child identifying with the automotive dead self, always trying to please. There are similar findings from work by Grubrich-Simitis (1981: 433), who said that Holocaust survivors' children can sometimes feel unable to experience themselves as being alive. This transmission was cold unaffectionate behaviour, avoidance and mystery about the past and an unapproachability. It seemed that Stephen's family were not too different in the way that they sought to protect their children from the family experience and also shield themselves from the pain of remembering. Without knowing their histories, offspring parents and grandparents are locked in a collusive silence. The subject of the war was closed off in Stephen's home and it was at his father's funeral when he was 53 that he learned that his dad had been in the Royal Air Force during the war. It also clarified for me why Stephen was so quiet in the early months of therapy; he had grown accustomed to being kept in silence. Stephen did not see himself positively reflected in his mother's eyes as a young child and I suspect that his early ability to comprehend others had been seriously affected. Stephen presented as someone on the autistic spectrum, unable to read other people's emotions or intentions. It would seem that the deficits from his early developmental relationships was taking on the appearance of Asperger's syndrome, but his behaviour is in keeping with someone who was raised in a mausoleum. When he visited friends' homes as a teenager he realised that there was something very odd about his own home. It seems that Stephen just did not have that secure childhood attachment which helps us to learn interactional skills as infants. The codes and nuances of behaviour and the ability to meta-cognitise (use a theory of mind) were not available to him, most likely because his primary carer had been so emotionally shut down with grief. Given the events in his childhood it is not surprising that he developed a caretaker self as a child, as described by Winnicott (1960), and has now been depressed for so many years.

Some children of African and Asian descent raised in a white society have masks or proxy identities (Thomas 1998; Uwahemu 2004) in order to protect themselves and to present what they consider a better part of themselves to the world. This invariably plays down their difference, Asianness or Blackness, in order to fit into white society without too much difficulty. The wearing of the proxy is ultimately damaging to the child and can lead to personality disintegration. In a study of identity issues in schoolchildren the African American psychologists Clarke and Clark (1947) famously found that Black children showed a marked preference for white dolls and a rejection of the Black dolls whom they resembled. Later replicated in the United Kingdom by Davey and Norburn (1980) with similar results, these studies seemed to ask many questions about the prevalence of prejudiced attitudes among schoolchildren, absorbed from the society around them. An important outcome was the question of the degree to which Black children had internalised negative self-identities and proxy self-issues had affected them.

Post-traumatic slavery trauma

Many African Caribbean adults in intercultural therapy report that they were 'rockers' when they were young: children who would bounce back and forth in an armchair in rhythmic motion to soothe themselves, attention and comfort being unavailable. Parents having to work long hours and the inadequacy of good childcare left many children understimulated and starving for contact. This has had far-reaching consequences, some resorting to rocking in adulthood at times of stress. This affected adult relationship and some recognised that they were hungry for affection, but found it difficult to give affection in return, the playful trusting part of themselves having been shut down. The broken attachments and emotional distance once learned during slavery were partly caused by mothers knowing that their children would be taken away and sold. A practice of over 300 years is passed on through generations of babies born into families preparing them for a forced separation: the learnt behaviour of female slaves that has passed down the generations, keeping an emotional distance between themselves and their children Fletchman-Smith (2011: 49). The risk that children could be sold at any point resulted in many growing up emotionally avoidant with insecurities, not shown what being loved feels like. This gets perpetuated so that many children in the family experience the deficit of emotional closeness. By not fully knowing, or not trusting any remnants of parental affection, the trauma of cold avoidant childhood is repeated (see Thomas 2014). Breaking the spell requires remembering, wishing to be different and working through. Daring to question some family patterns and values is one of the strategies to break transmission to the next generation. Being repeatedly played out through the generations it is not surprising that a frequent complaint from Caribbean parents and children is about the difficulty of being openly affectionate. Professionals who are familiar with Gregory Bateson's double-bind theory (1973) will be aware of how modes of communication in families gets passed on. A positive effort has to be made by a family member to disentangle themselves from the confusing communications in order to break the pattern. The use of the genogram helps to understand the roles, relationships and parenting styles opening the possibilities for re-evaluation and change.

There was a deliberate attempt in the American and British colonies to subdue and degrade the African so it is unsurprising that they, too, in the main, saw themselves as an inferior people. The brutal behaviour from the plantation can be seen in some present-day Caribbean families, just passed down the generations without curiosity of where the violence came from. Caribbean experiences of trauma have contributed to fragmented internal states which reflect the damage inflicted on them as a people and a need to make sense of themselves in the world. Engaging with these issues in psychoanalytic intercultural therapy is a considerable challenge.

Professor Freddie Hickling, a psychiatrist and psychotherapist (2007), conducted his large group 'Explanations' with hospital patients. He describes these as history, psychoeducational entertainment and educational social action. His project at Bellevue Hospital in Jamaica seemed to educate and inspire mostly poor, oppressed people who were confined to hospital wards. For the first time in the history of psychological medicine a connection has been made between plantation behaviour, family adaptation and transmitted psychological trauma. Hickling's work was not without controversy in Jamaican mental health circles. There was a lot of political disapproval and his non-traditional approach was associated with and mired in the cannabis debate which was then raging on the island. His explanations sought to connect inpatients to the social, communal and historic trauma by the use of the arts and music. Professor Hickling had been involved in studies into schizophrenia at the Institute of Psychiatry in London and he practised community psychiatry in the West Midlands in the 1980s. His influence was considerable in the probation field as well as in community mental hospitals. He collaborated with the newly formed Nafsiyat Centre and shared platforms with us during the Department of Health-funded research that was being carried out at the Centre with patients from Black and minority ethnic communities (Acharyya et al. 1989). Hickling's own findings revealed that young British Caribbean people were five times more likely than their parents to experience mental ill health and felt that cannabis use was one contributor, as well as the experience of racism and discrimination. He makes an interesting link between oppression and mental illness and drew attention to the European colonisation of New Zealand as a further example. Being actively able to resist the psychological conditioning of hundreds of years of European colonisation, he felt, was the only way that Africans and other people of colour could create a blueprint for minority mental health.

Acknowledging past trauma

Rituals around traumatic events have developed to mark them as a shared commemoration, such as the Seder family meal at Passover. This has marked the deliverance of Jewish people for thousands of years and is an important demonstration of resilience as much about the future and the need not to forget. The Seder has been constant and seen Jewish people through the trauma of centuries of pogroms and extermination camps in Europe. Sometimes it is difficult to forget the trauma because it is seared into the memory of the community and the fear can be triggered by a variety of events. The mentally frail 86-year-old David, bachelor uncle of a Jewish colleague, whispered to his great nephew and niece that they needed 'to always have a bag packed ready because you never know when they will come'. Uncle David was a child of a similar age when the same words were said to him in Poland in the 1930s. This provoked anger and fear in his nephew, who felt that his uncle was frightening the children. My colleague could not deal with the fear that was evoked in him because he had been shielded from much of the talk of war by his parents. The persecution had moved into a fourth generation to the relative security of north London, and the fear seemed as fresh as 1938. On reflection, my colleague could forgive his uncle by recognising his own fear and concern. He now realised why his uncle had not been able to have relationships and settle down, his fear about the future playing a large part in restricting his life. The psychoanalyst Vamik Volkan (1997: 43) describes the mechanism of transmission of trauma as the older generation externalising their traumatised self onto a child's personality. Consequently, the child becomes a container absorbing the unworked parts of the previous generation's trauma. This happens because the trauma cannot be metabolised by those before them, they are either frozen with fear, operate denial about the events or put a brave face on it for their own survival. The child is then left with the unprocessed emotions and often a family silence about the past. The effects of historical trauma are far reaching. Some are in living history and will come to the attention of psychotherapists. We know about people who have buried their experiences of childhood abuse, only to recall the events in adulthood when they are seemingly better able to deal with it. With the largest numbers of people becoming exiled since the Second World War, experiencing loss of family members and witnessing their deaths, there will be an increased demand for psychological services. So powerful can be the trauma, particularly for children, that it appears to have gone away, but it remains incubated until the young person is able sometimes to deal with it.

Hearing a loud noise like an explosion just after collecting his children from primary school, Ali, a refugee from Iraq, grabbed his children and dived behind a hedge. After a few minutes, he realised that it was a car backfiring and not a bomb exploding as he had been familiar with in his native Basra from which he had fled six years earlier. In his therapy group with other traumatised men, he is ashamed and tearful at not being able to talk to his confused children about what happened. He said that he felt stupid and ashamed and did not realise that he was still so affected by the bombings he had experienced in Iraq. Ali said that he had tried so hard to put the past behind him, his rape humiliation and then hasty escape from Iraq, and was surprised to be confronted with it around the corner from his children's school. He realised that he had to find a way to explain his behaviour to his children because to them it would seem odd even though they asked no questions. He feared that his triggers to trauma were already being absorbed and passed on to his children, and this was the last thing he wanted to happen.

Sushelia

Sushelia decided to begin psychoanalytic psychotherapy because of her distress about her distant relationship with her mother. As a teenager, she had read her parents' old letters and discovered something that she should never have seen. She wondered if she could ever talk about this in her family because of the secrets. She felt that she was a reminder of shame in her family given that Asian families were organised along the lines of honour and shame.

A married professional woman Sushelia came to therapy in her late 50s. She wanted a therapist who was not like herself from an Asian background because she thought that her family would be judged and felt that she could get on well with someone from a European or African background (having lived in Africa since her infancy). In the past few years she had become preoccupied with something that she could not share with her husband or her family. Her parents were separated for a couple of years soon after their marriage because of the partition of India and Pakistan (Ghosh 2013). Her father was pursuing a university course several hundred miles away from Gujarat where he lived with his family and new wife. She was born during their separation and suspects that her father was not her father. She said that despite this, looking taller and different from her Hindu family, she was always her father's favourite 'darling little Susu'. She was followed by two boys and a girl, they all got on well together but she was never close to her mother. It was not until at 15 going through her parents' old letters that she discovered that her mother had been raped by Muslim men when the house was broken into and robbed at the time of Partition. Her mother was suicidal but was reassured by her father and his family that killing herself would destroy them all, and they vowed to love the baby as their own. Her mother was reclusive and very religious, spending hours cleansing and doing puja. She said that Baba, her father, must have lived with terrible guilt feelings – that he should have been at home to protect his family. From what was said about her parents as young people, her mother was warm and lively before her ordeal. Sushelia has only known her mother as depressed and withdrawn and she would like to let them all know her discovery in order to take the burden from their shoulders, but fears that they would feel betrayed by the way she got this information. She told her therapist that she did not want her parents going to their graves not knowing how much she appreciated them for keeping her and loving her because many children conceived in this way were given to missionaries even if the mothers did not kill themselves. Low-caste families had kept 'cuckoo children' but the middle classes had to think about their honour. The family left India for Uganda soon after India became independent when Sushelia was a baby. She said that her father's mother was kind and loving when she was alive, and felt like her real mother. In her early 20s, the family left Uganda for the United Kingdom. She said that she had been secretly searching the web for information about babies who were born after partition rapes.

Sushelia thought that the secret in her family was so dangerous that it could kill her parents, and certainly her mother, if it was brought out into the open. She always had a difficult relationship with her mother and thought it was because she was followed by her brother who was adored by the family. As a result of this she made a point of not favouring her own son over her daughter. She said that she was quite depressed after each birth and often wondered how her mother might have felt giving birth to her, an unwanted child and a constant reminder of what had happened to her. When she found out the secret she felt responsible for her mother's feelings of shame and pollution. We can only speculate on what Sushelia saw in her mother's eyes and what was mirrored back to her. She might not have been able to read her mother's face, and it was her good fortune to have had a loving grandmother who had less complicated feelings towards her. Some families can unwittingly pass on toxic states of mind to their children. The 1947 Partition saw thousands of women raped, and again in 1971 with a repeat of this atrocity during the war between Pakistan and breakaway Bangladesh. Jaswant Guzder, a Canadian psychoanalyst (Guzder and Krishna 2005), has discussed issues of shame, honour and purity as themes in psychotherapy with women from the Indian sub-continent. This and family loyalty can be critical organising issues in the treatment of Indian diaspora women. Sushelia settled into intensive therapy with a white British female therapist. She was able to explore her feelings towards her parents and the need to have it all 'in the open' subsided. She said that the situation had existed before she was born and she was not going to harm her parents by bringing it all up. Her therapy explored her feelings of inferiority in her family and her distance from her mother. She believed that she was loved because it was so easy for her parents to have given her away like many others. She had a happy marriage and children and believed that she was a lucky woman.

War, persecution and cumulative oppression has contributed to the generational transmission of trauma. Kuriloff (2014) discusses the difficulty for postwar France in remembering the war and described professionals and the population carrying on as if nothing had happened. The desire to get over the disruption of trauma can lead to a premature recovery and a wish to brush it all under the carpet, only to be surprised by its reappearance. Georges Devereux (1978) and Franz Fanon (1967) were to draw attention to this lacuna in French mental health, particularly in post-trauma work with Jews and Africans.

Whilst trauma might have begun for African Caribbean people with capture in Africa, followed by violence and enslavement in the colonies, this has set off patterns of behaviour that persist today and are transformed into multiple contemporary problems affecting families and communities. Members of postslavery communities have adapted a survival mode yet the trauma has left them more likely to go to prison than to college; the fear that successful members would walk away from their community changed after a good education. Continental Africans are often puzzled by what they see as the casualness of their Caribbean and American cousins not fully recognising the damage that was done to them during hundreds of years of enslavement. Unlike the Seder, there is no unifying remembrance for the African Holocaust. Consciousness raising and the instilling of African pride was something that Marcus Garvey introduced at the beginning of the 20th century and was taken up by the National Association for the Advancement of Colored People in the United States.

The Wells family

The Wells family could not recognise a single traumatic event that they shared as a family apart from the out-of-control beatings they received from their mother, known as 'murderations' in the family. They all felt some form of cumulative trauma and distress after her death. Their father's considerable loss of memory due to dementia left them feeling emotionally damaged and lost. The oldest boy and the youngest, Maureen, had been struggling with mental health problems. They recognised that their recently depressed mother came from a family of angry floggers and this had passed down the paternal line to her. Their great grandfather was the son of a plantation slave in Jamaica who was regularly beaten by his father, and who in turn beat his sons badly. This behaviour had been repeated down the line to their mother, Leonie, the granddaughter who scared the life out of them as children when their father was not around. They reported scary sayings from their mother: 'if bacra don't get you obeah will'. They felt that they were ruled by fear and 'divide and rule tactics' to keep them in line. The family came to therapy because Maureen was fast approaching a breakdown some months after the funeral and because they could not feel at peace with their dead mother. The two adult daughters and two sons wanted to lay to rest their unhappy childhood and perhaps get to an understanding of their mother. They learnt from a surviving aunt that their mother had been badly treated by their father and that his bullying and violent behaviour was what she had inherited as learned behaviour. It was important for them to talk about how they felt and what they did to regulate their emotions when at risk of feeling overwhelmed. Mental illness had also passed down three generations and seemed to affect the children who were selected out for this particular cruelty.

It is interesting to note that some Caribbean people laugh and joke about 'the beatings' and wear their survival of them as a badge of honour. Others would join in with the camaraderie of a group that survived an ordeal. Some have said that it was wrong and they could not treat their own children in this way but others have said that it did them no harm. These words of resilience can sometimes mask incubation of the trauma or capitulation out of fear and loyalty to their parents. Going on to repeat this harsh treatment with their own children is an indication that they were not over it. Working with three generations or more of Caribbean families is likely to reveal post-traumatic transmission if it continues to exist in the family. This together with the scars of migration and loss and the adapted psychological mechanisms to cope with racial prejudice and the emotional cost this has incurred for some Caribbean families: 'Certainly slavery, and then migration, have impacted further on maternal and paternal functioning, leading to deficits in the care and control of children' (Fletchman-Smith 2011: 82).

In these families, current psychological and social functioning might have been significantly affected by their past. Together the family might have the patterns available to them to look at their history and how life events were shaped. These patterns that are passed down can be damaging like the preference for lighter-skinned children, the admiration for longer, silkier hair and for European facial features. Those who do not possess these attributes often know their place on the pecking order of family and grow up without the necessary affirmation and self-confidence leaving them vulnerable in the outside world. This drip feed of negative information nurtures low self-esteem and self-hatred which can often be seen in intracultural therapy. The Black therapist will be able to recognise internalised racism in their patient as described in Rose's (1998) *Daring to Work with Internalised Racism*. This can be accompanied by intense envy of other successful Black people and shame if this secret is openly discussed. One of the problems with generational transmission is the belief among some Caribbean people that these plantation behaviours are part of their culture, having little regard to how it was formed. For example, the pattern of enslaved women being treated as breeding machines to increase the master's workforce was just an economic decision to produce plantation labour. Even in present times discovering the identity of a father can sometimes be treated as a 'need-to-know' matter by the mother. A child is often told that their father did not raise them, so they did not need to know him. Fletchman-Smith's book (2011) discusses psychological patterns and issues related to African Caribbean parenting and makes some comparisons with Oedipus (who of course did not know his father). Plantation patterns of unknown fathers must inevitably lead us to the question of why the perpetuation of this pattern is not good for Caribbean communities. Even when the families have been able to change their material position in society, like the Caribbean family of Leoni Wells, the psychological damage can be unaltered and passed on.

The professional task

Living in a multicultural environment makes it difficult to have the security of already made identities and appropriate ways to be. Psychotherapy has become sensitive to culture and difference but it has not become a safe enough work because of power imbalances in the consulting room. It is important that the professional is able to remain reflective and boundaried about what emerges from the patient, whether this is anger, pain or shame. The work of the therapist is not done unless they have made a connection with the nature of social and psychological adjustment that might have taken place (Fanon 1967). Psychotherapists working across cultures will be very likely to encounter patients who have experienced trauma or secondary trauma. In the complex relationship, the therapist will be helping the patient to access emotions and memories of things that might have left an emotional scar. Whilst this is at the hands of parents or members of a shared community, their parents would have been victim of a similar event that dates back several generations and was connected to a history of adapted family behaviour. White therapists and Black patients can find themselves falling into old familiar behaviours towards each other, so powerful is the lure. We can learn much from the relational school of psychoanalysis (Aron 1991) about the co-created relationship between the patient and the therapist. In as much as the issues of the internally colonised patient need to be addressed, low self-worth and restricted attainment, the descendants of colonisers also need to deal with their sense of white entitlement which might not have been an issue addressed by their own therapy. Forgetting the painful history of our master/servant relationship has meant that collectively we have not considered its complex and haunting long-term effects on the therapeutic relationship. Therapeutic relationships will inevitably be affected by difference, social class, culture, skin colour, education and other differences between the client and therapist (Thomas 1998, 2013). Too often, professionals view the scrutiny of generational transmission of trauma as middle-class interference that undermines the Black patient's culture and coping strategies. Professionals can find themselves not addressing the trauma, by side stepping the issues for their own protection or wishing not to humiliate the patient. This stance also protects them from accusations of possessing prejudiced attitudes. Black therapists might not be able to access this material if they have not explored their own family history, traumatic or otherwise. The cumulative trauma of slavery and oppression makes it difficult for generational matters to come into an assessment without some sense of cultural competence. The therapist needs to be aware of the effect of the process on the patient and what they say about bringing about behavioural change, or heightening awareness. Therapy is not effective if the issues of trauma and transmission are not addressed with the patient, and therapists and their supervisors need to exercise due diligence in this regard. What motivates transference and countertransference across ethnic lines always needs to be explored in supervision because of the complex stereotypes and sexual stereotypes in the interactions. Dealing with the trauma of slavery will inevitably involve the white therapist in some form of self-examination and increased reflexivity. Historically, white people have wielded psychological capital over black and brown people as a result of enslavement and colonial oppression. Transference, countertransference and pre-transference issues need to be closely examined because the psychotherapy profession has been slow to see this relevance (Curry 1964). The paradox that has not been addressed is why those with self-claimed superior minds and morality chose to perpetrate such inhuman acts for such a long time. The developing of such a lack of empathy for Blacks and others required centuries of distorted doctrine. This is borne out by the recent pattern of killing African Americans at prayer in church.

Conclusion

Many mental health professionals have stated that racism and its generational transmission have had an impact on the psychological health of Black and other people from trauma backgrounds. Others might say that the system of slavery has harmed white people too, giving them a false sense of superiority and leading them to be indifferent to the suffering of others at their hands. The hundreds of years of slavery and its attendant hardships have been seen as the core reasons for disproportionate mental ill health and other social failings in postslavery communities. The view is that descendants of enslaved people have not recovered from the damaging psychological effects of this which blighted their lives. Post-traumatic disorder is embedded in family behaviour passed on unmodified from one generation to another, just like a family cake recipe: as part of the family system it is difficult for professionals and families alike to identify. Multidisciplinary approaches, intercultural psychotherapists, family therapists and social workers would have much to contribute because often more than one family member is affected. Appearing to be repeated destructive cycles that are difficult to break out from, the unworked traumatisation of indifferent parenting, separation patterns and other behaviours coming out of colonisation and slavery needs to be explored. Post-traumatic slavery disorder is the sequel to many years of African enslavement. Jewish trauma has been described as a post-Holocaust masking of the persecution of Jews for hundreds of years before. War and ethnic or religious violence has led to the displacement and trauma of many people in the past 40 years. Rape and sexual violence as torture has been increasingly considered as a systematic aspect of modern war. As psychotherapists working across cultures we are still learning about trauma and its generational transmission.

References

Acharyya, S.Moorhouse, S.Kareem, J. and Littlewood, R. (1989) Nafsiyat Psychotherapy Centre for Ethnic Minorities. *Psychiatric Bulletin*, 13: 358–360.

Akhtar, S. (ed.) (2005) *Freud along the Ganges: Psychoanalytic Reflections on the People and Culture of India*. New York: Other Press.

Altman, N. (2000) *Psychoanalysis and the Inner City*. New York: Analytic Press.
Aron, L. (1991) The Patient's Experience of the Analyst's Subjectivity. In S. Mitchell and L. Aron (eds), *Relational Psychoanalysis*. New York: Analytic Press.
Bateson, G., Jackson, D., Haley, J. and Weakland, J. (1973) Towards a Theory of Schizophrenia. In G. Bateson (ed.), *Steps to an Ecology of Mind*. New York: Paladin.
Clarke, K.B. and Clark, M.P. (1947) Racial Identification and Preference in Negro Children. In T.M. Newcomb and E.L. Hartley (eds), *Readings in Social Psychology*. New York: Holt, Rinehart & Winston.
Curry, A. (1964) Myth Transference and the Black Psychotherapist. *Psychoanalytic Review*, 51: 7–14.
Davey, A.G. and Norburn, V. (1980) Ethnic Awareness and Difference in Primary School Children. *New Community*, 8: 206–212.
DeGruy- Leary, J. (2005) *Post Traumatic Slavery Syndrome*. Milwaukee, OR: Upton Press.
Devereux, G. (1978) *Ethnopsychoanalysis: Psychoanalysis and Anthropology as Complementary Frames of Reference*. Berkeley, CA: University of California Press.
Fanon, F. (1967) *Black Skins White Masks*. London: Penguin.
Fletchman-Smith, B. (2000) *Mental Slavery: Psychoanalytic Studies of Caribbean People*. London: Karnac.
Fletchman-Smith, B. (2011) *Transcending the Legacies of Slavery*. London: Karnac.
Ghosh, P. (2013) Partition of India and Pakistan: The Rape of Women on an Epic, Historic Scale. *International Business Times*, 16 August.
Grubrich-Simitis, I. (1981) Extreme Traumatisation as Cumulative Trauma: Psychoanalytic Investigations of the Effects of Concentration Camp Experiences on Survivors and Their Children. *Psychoanalytic Study of the Child*, 36: 415–450.
Guzder, J. and Krishna, M. (2005) Sita Shakti: Cultural Collision in the Psychotherapy of Diaspora Indian Women. In S. Akhtar (ed.), *Freud along the Ganges*. New York: Other Press.
Harrison, G.Holton, A.Neilson, D.Owens, D., Boot, D. and Cooper, J. (1999) Severe Mental Disorder in Afro-Caribbean Patients: Some Social, Demographic and Service Factors. *Psychological Medicine*, 19: 683–696.
Hickling, F.W. (2007) *Psychohistoriography: A Post-Colonial Psychoanalytic and Psychotherapeutic Model*. London: Jessica Kingsley.
Kareem, J. (1988) Outside in … Inside out … Some Considerations in Intercultural Psychotherapy. *Journal of Social Work Practice*, 3: 57–71.
Krystal, H. (1978) Trauma and affects, *Psychoanalytic Study of the Child*, 33: 81–116.
Kuriloff, E.A. (2014) *Contemporary Psychoanalysis and the Legacy of the Third Reich*. London: Routledge.
Littlewood, R. and Lipsedge, M. (1997) *Aliens and Alienists, Ethnic minorities and Psychiatry*, 3rd edition. London: Routledge.
Lowe, F. (2013) *Thinking Space: Promoting Thinking about Race, Culture and Diversity in Psychotherapy and Beyond*. London: Karnac.
McKenzie, K. (2006) *Mind Your Head: Improving the Mental Wellbeing of Men and Boys*. Conference presentation, Wembley.
Morgan, H. (1998) Between Fear and Blindness: The White Therapist and the Black Patient. *Journal of the British Association of Psychotherapists*, 5: 48–61.
Reid, O.G., Mims, S. and Higginbottom, L. (2005) *Post Traumatic Slavery Disorder*. Charlotte, NC: Conquering Books.
Rose, E. (1998) Daring to Work with Internalised Racism. *Journal of the British Association of Counselling*, May: 92–94.

Thomas, L. (1998) Psychotherapy in the Context of Race and Culture: An Intercultural Therapeutic Approach. In S. Fernando (ed.), *Mental Health in a Multi-Ethnic Society: A Multi-Disciplinary Handbook*. London: Routledge.

Thomas, L.K. (2013) Empires of Mind: Colonial History and Its Implications for Counselling and Psychotherapy. *Psychodynamic Practice*, 19: 117–128.

Thomas, L.K. (2014) *Attachment in African Caribbean Families*. In A. Danquah and K. Berry (eds), *Attachment Theory in Adult Mental Health*. London: Routledge.

Uwahemu, A. (2004) The Proxy Self: A More Acceptable Version of Me. *British Association of Counselling and Psychotherapy Journal*, 15: 44.

Volkan, V. (1997) *Bloodlines: From Ethnic Pride to Ethnic Terrorism*. Boulder, CO: Westview.

Winnicott, D.W. (1960) Ego Distortion in Terms of True and False Self. In D.W. Winnicott (ed.), *The Maturational Process and the Facilitating Environment*. London: Hogarth Press.

13

BEYOND THE FAMIL(Y)AR: THE CONSTRUCT OF THE SELF OUTSIDE THE DYAD

Intercultural therapy as an opportunity to explore the social self

Francesca Zanatta

In this chapter, I will explore the possibility of an alternative framework for considering the formation of the self beyond the familiar schemes and conceptualisations of the individual, as determined by the dyadic experience. Expanding upon the tenets introduced by the work of theorists interested with the social aspects of being, particularly George Herbert Mead (1956) and Roy Wagner (1975), I will argue for an approach that considers the self as a dynamic product of social interactions and networks. My thinking presented here should be viewed as work in progress, as the exploration of a substitute ending, as in a choose-your-adventure sort of story. Respectful of the theoretical sets I will be critiquing, I do not wish to undermine the importance of these perspectives, but to encourage a more profound level of critique and revision of these. The goal of this exercise is two-fold. Firstly, I wish to stress the 'fatalistic' essence of the vast majority of psychological perspectives on the formation of the self. I then wish to highlight the possibility of modelling therapeutic interventions as social-ecological explorations, aimed at advocating for the patient as recommended by Burman (2007), rather than labelling and controlling. In the psychoanalytical fashion, I will introduce my reflections through two case studies from my professional experiences in working with children and families.

An unfinished revolution

One of the many challenges of working with children in care is the incessant questioning of the taken-for-granted aspects of life. A common point of inquiry is the validity of the positive correlation between lack of/experience of a broken family and the fragmented individual. When asked this question, weary of providing a definitive answer, I normally refer back to positive narratives of other young people, rather than seeking refuge and support in theories. Throughout the years, I have come to the conclusion that my choice of response is mainly informed by the fact that a sort of deterministic ethos seems to underlie the vast majority of psychological theories on this matter. In other words, the 'psy-sciences' generally hold and promote the belief that certain early life experiences are inevitably linked to specific outcomes. If parents fail to perform as expected in their roles, if something does not go as it should, then the child's growth and development is permanently wrecked; or in the words of a young care leaver, 'my mother broke me when she left, there is nothing you can do to fix me'.

Whilst it could be argued that Freud is the father of this psychic determinism (Székely 1979), attachment theory has undeniably placed infant determinism at the heart of policies, interventions, popular debates and shared beliefs (Guldberg, 2009). It is perhaps the longevity of attachment theory or its presumed roots in scientific observations (LeVine 2015) that granted its indisputability.[1] Rather than challenging its credibility, the numerous oversimplified and romanticised applications of the theory[2] have promoted its marketisation (Burman 1997) and fortified the popular *psychomythologies* (Lilienfeld et al. 2010) derived from it. The latest developments of the theory warrant consistent maternal sensitivity[3] over all powers in the shaping and making of not simply the psychological but also the physical development of the individual. Hills (2012: 167) confirms in fact that 'all the existential conditions of alienation besides poverty (detachment, aloneness, meaninglessness and dependencies) come from deeply held disappointment at not being cared about'. Similarly, yet strengthened by selected medical evidences correlating attachment to the physical formation of children's brains, Gerhardt (2004: 1) proclaims that a triumphal 'full biological explanation of our social behavior is becoming available'. As the argument develops, Gerhardt clarifies that poor attachment is not the sole root of all evils; maternal stress levels during the pregnancy are also to be deemed responsible for later troubles. It is therefore a combined set of issues, mostly related to maternal dysfunctioning, that leads to a 'troubled, poorly attuned mother–infant relationship, expressed physiologically in a continuation of elevated cortisol levels (Turp 2006: 307). As previously mentioned, the impact of these discoveries stretches beyond researchers and practitioners. Not too long ago at a dinner with friends, an expectant acquaintance sought my *expert*[4] approval for her decision not to return to work after her baby's birth. The woman had first heard about attachment theory through her couples' therapist, who had mentioned it after having traced the origins of my acquaintance's husband's infidelity to his inadequate and unsolved relation to his mother. The fear of her child growing with the same scars as her husband had convinced the woman of the importance of her ongoing and loving physical presence in the baby's life, at least for the first two to three years of its life. Incapable of providing an honest reply I diverted and spent the remainder of the evening picturing a puzzled Shulamit Firestone questioning a disappointed Judith Butler on the return of '*pumpkin shitting*'[5] to fashion.[6]

This episode forced me to consider the role of attachment theory in the dilemma on the connection between women's and children's rights, and ultimately in the formation of the self. Different perspectives provide contrasting interpretations as to why feminists have failed both ends of the dyad, leading to an increased number of broken selves in our society. Gerhardt (2004) suggested that feminism, blinded by women's eagerness for liberation from the captivity of the household, accomplished only a half-revolution. Whilst mothers were set free from their biological expectations, the future generation of selves were failed, left abandoned in the care of precarious, mercenary parent figures, surrogates of motherhood. A possible subproduct of Ainsworth et al.'s (1971) maternal sensitivity, in Gerhardt's vision the parenting that matters is solely mothering, 'in theory, anyone can do it … but the baby's mother is primed to do these things for her baby' (2004: 38). Such a statement might appear dissonant and obsolete in the age of artificial reproductive technology, same-sex adoptions and queer families, phenomena that have galvanised a research strand aiming to revisit and ultimately overcome 'heteronormative and bio-normative assumptions' as much in parenting as in the formation of the self (Sander-Staudt 2016: 461).

Located on the other end of the critique of feminist theory, bell hooks (2000b: 135) also shares her disappointment at the incomplete revolution deriving from the reductive wish to escape the 'cult of domesticity'. The focus of this second commentary is, however, significantly different; the limitation of feminism is not identified in the act of rejecting maternity, but on the fixation on mothers as the sole responsible sources of love and care for children. Expanding on the feminist challenge against the determinism of biology, bell hooks argues for overcoming the idea of the exclusivity of motherhood. The author anticipates that ending the myth of the superior value of motherhood would enable the realisation of equality in parenting and associated responsibilities, and ultimately across genders at large. Moreover, hooks suggests that it would pose an end to the phenomenon described by LeVine as the 'pathogenic potential of mothers',[7] an issue that 'once the speculation of few psychiatrists, became part of the common culture in America and Britain' (2015: 56). Granting figures other than mothers an actual, equal and meaningful opportunity in the upbringing of infants would also signify a first step towards a fundamental change in the way we understand the socialisation of children and the formation of the self. If we agree that 'interaction, it turns out, is the high road from merely human to fully humane' (Abrams 2004), expanding capacity for meaningful attachment beyond the dyad could allow for other figures in the life of the infant to play a prominent role in the formation of the self. Moreover, Black feminist theorists have identified in the practice of community parenting an act of resistance against inequalities and an opportunity for the self to develop as more confident and resilient (Hill Collins 1994; Reynolds 2005; hooks 2000b).

From the dyad to systems of individuals

In the foreword to a recently published collection of essays exploring variations to dyadic attachment (Otto and Keller 2014), alongside praising the value of elements of the original theory, Lamb (2014) reminds the reader of the importance of considering culture in the formation of social experiences and relationships. For however revolutionary it might sound, the recommendation is not new; over 20 years ago, in the first edition of a preceding book, the editors Jafar Kareem and Roland Littlewood, with the contributions of the other authors, emphasised the importance of considering that 'social and political phenomena are powerful forces ... determining the lives of individuals who live in a particular society' (Kareem and Littlewood 1992: 19).

The acceptance of the role of culture and the social world in the formation and shaping of the self has been a slow process and is yet to reach a sufficiently wide audience or to be incorporated in practice and beliefs, as demonstrated by Gerhardt's publication (2004). As also argued by Meehan and Hawks (2014), the paucity of studies addressing attachment outside the dyad has thus far significantly impacted on the capacity to explore how this might feature in children's lives and development. From a cultural perspective, this oversight precludes the recognition and validation of alternative forms of child rearing, not only outside but also within Western society. As mentioned before, globalisation (Clark 2010) and the proliferation of non-nuclear, non-normative families (Sander-Staudt 2016) in recent times call for an urgent update of the theoretical framework in use. The romanticised version of Western childhood advertised in theories and policies appears archaic and relevant to a disappearing minority, as also indicated by James and James (2008).

As part of my doctoral dissertation, I explored the compositions, interactions and dynamics of African Caribbean families living in London. This exercise gave visibility to the necessity to revisit the significance of the dyad and to take into consideration the numerous factors at work in the life of a child and the formation of the self. One of the fascinating aspects of collating data within the West Indian community is the complexity of the various factors at play. Culture, financial circumstances, class, gender, history of migration and much more visibly interplay in the shaping of the everyday experiences and identities of these children, placing a strong emphasis on the importance of keeping an intersectional approach in the exploration of their lives and selves. In researching the existing literature, I started noticing a connection between the standards indicated by the likes of attachment theory and the numerous stereotypes that have been attributed to families from this background (Fitzharbert 1967). In light of these stereotypical, comparative visions, West Indian families have been perceived as characterised by poisonous dyads,[8] featuring single mothers providing the child with inadequate care, instable presence and limited sensitivity (Chamberlain 2004; Foner 1979; Clarke 1957). Essentially, stereotypes of the Black matricentral family have represented for years the opposite of the Western ideal of family: disempowered fathers, insufficiently dedicated mothers, and differently nurtured children. The debate on whether these perceived differences derive from African heritage (Sudakasa 1996) or slavery (Frazier 1948) maintains the focus on a comparative analysis of the dyad, failing to acknowledge the full range of factors of relevance in the lives of these families. Conversely, Black feminism promotes a holistic approach to the family experience, offering the opportunity to focus on the bigger picture, rather than being constraint to comparisons against what is believed to be the normative. One of the points of emphasis identified through this process is the centrality of the public, the social in the experiences of all of the family members alike (Reynolds 2005; Collins 1994; hooks 2000b). On the basis of this theoretical framework, in my field work I opted for conducting observations on family compositions and children's socialisation within but also outside the boundaries prescribed by their normative definitions. Thanks to the suggestion of one of my key informants, Leah, I had gained knowledge that 'the best way to understand their [a person's] role in the child's life is to go to the child's birthday party', and I started attending birthday parties and similar events, aiming to engage with the broader social network around the child. The resulting observations substantially overturned the data collected on previous occasions, focusing within the boundaries of *placed parenthood* (Allen and Taylor 2012). The resulting picture greatly differs: parents are present in their own way and within their realistic capacities (determined mostly by external factors such as employment, housing, relations, etc.), whilst extended family networks provide ongoing support and offer flexible presences, as and when needed. I will further explore this statement through the study of Destiny's family composition.

Destiny

Destiny would proudly call herself a single mother, whilst also acknowledging that 'I ain't doing all the job on my own. Does it sound bad if I admit that my children are who they are not just because of me?' (Destiny, field work notes). Destiny and her four children were living in a small council flat surrounded by friends and what Destiny referred to as their 'London family'; both the fathers of the children were not actively involved in their lives and Destiny would rely on friends for help. The father of the two eldest was living in Jamaica, whilst the other was in London, alas not on good terms with Destiny. When I first met her, Destiny was in a relationship and her partner had expressed the wish to be more involved in her children's lives, a situation that evolved during the ethnography and eventually resulted in the two taking separate ways. In light of my initial observations, the children's family network looked as in Figure 13.1.

From the initial conversations with Destiny, I gathered that her mother, Mrs D, was highly involved in the upbringing of her children. This piece of information helped me identify Destiny and her mother as significant figures in the children's lives, as depicted in Figure 13.2.

A few months later, Destiny invited me to her daughter Siobhan's birthday party. The occasion functioned as an opportunity to gain a better understanding of the *family*; a large number of cooperating and coexisting realities gravitated together, creating a functional and equilibrated system of connectivity. The party soon became a metaphor for the division of responsibilities in place in the intricate network of people around Destiny's children. Although the connection with F1 (father of Mario and Sherell) did not offer any additional social capital, the 'absence' of F2 was filled by the presence of Mrs Fiona, who at the party supported Mrs D in the blessing of their granddaughter and in maintaining a high level of respectability for the family. In the family's everyday life, Mrs Fiona would often pick up the children from school and escort them to after-school club and

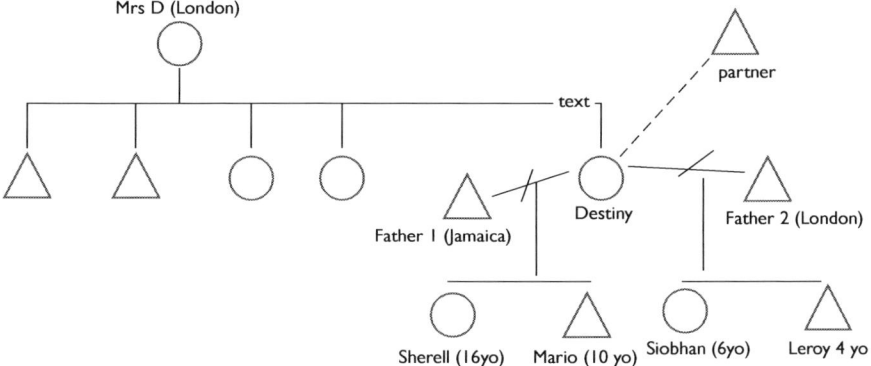

FIGURE 13.1 Destiny's family

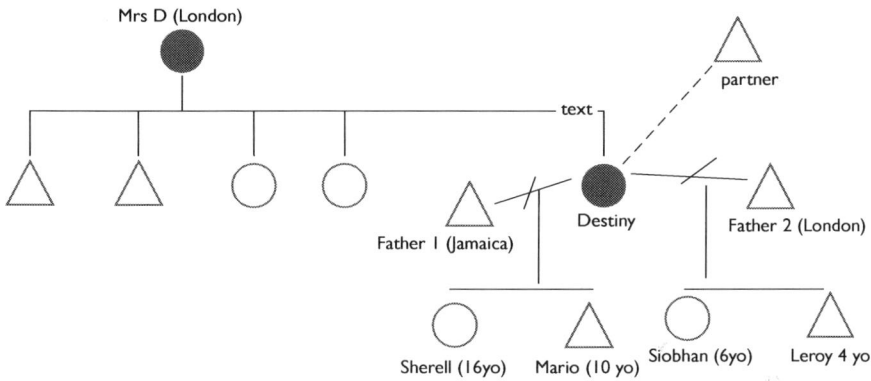

FIGURE 13.2 Destiny's family (members responsible for children in grey)

activities. At the party, Clifton and Ono, Destiny's younger brothers, had taken responsibility for the music and the barbeque (which was taking place outside the venue in proximity to the kitchen). Both of them were very present in the children's lives, though Ono had the stronger presence as being responsible for taking Mario to football club. Yvonne, Destiny's younger sister, was in charge of looking after the younger children. Yvonne, who had a ten-year-old child, was not employed and was therefore left in charge of Leroy whilst Destiny was at work. Even distant relatives had a role, at the party as much as in the everyday life. Marcelle, Destiny's half-sister living in Jamaica, had organised for some food specialties to be delivered in time for the party. On a day-to-day basis, Marcelle and her children would keep in contact via Skype and function as hosting family during the children's[9] trips to the island. The system did not, however, stop at the extended family; Shandrice (Sherell's godmother), Aunt Hatty-Ann and Neisha all had a specific role, at the party as in the children's lives (Figure 13.3).

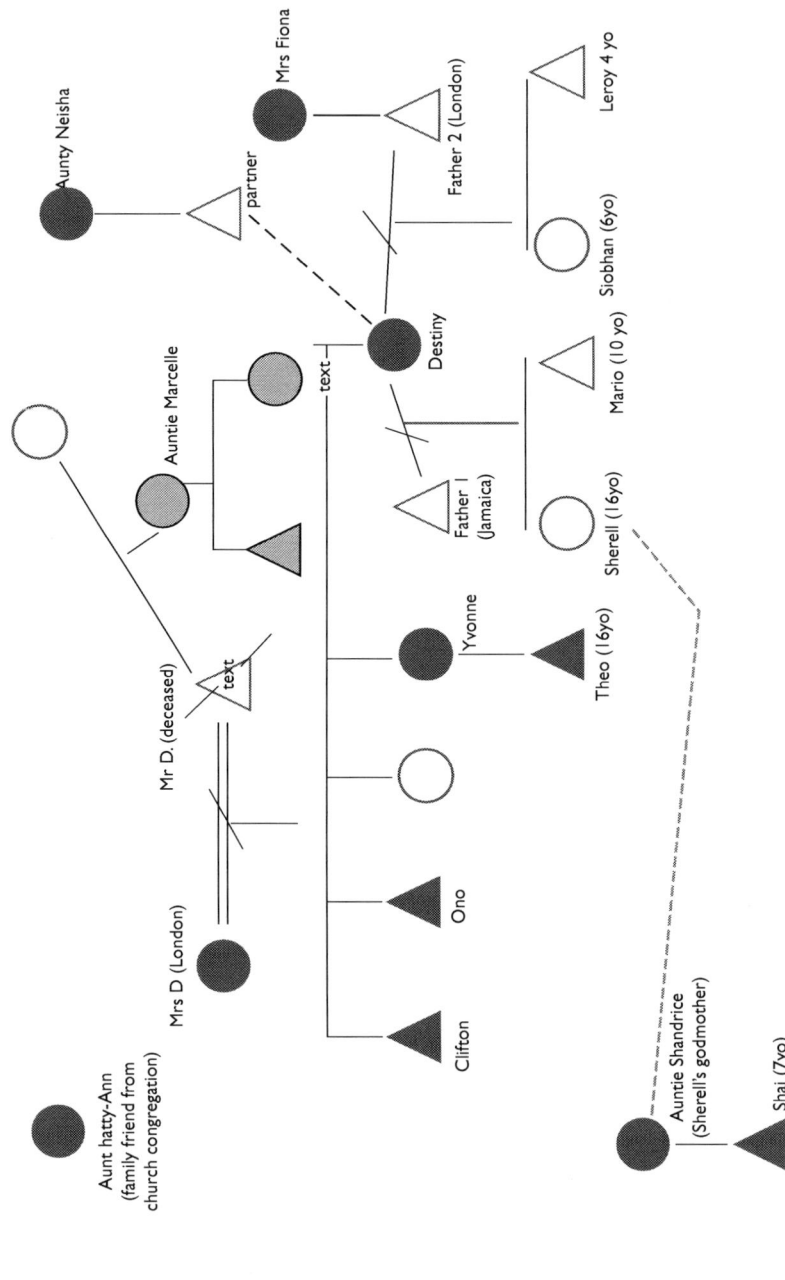

FIGURE 13.3 Destiny's systems (members responsible for children in grey)

The significance of the systems composing this *family* is conveyed in the solemnity of the blessing of the cake, and of the child, when Mrs D asked for the whole *family* to congregate around the child. Words do not do justice to the visual impact of this moment: a room full of people, mostly not related by blood, gathered in silence around Siobhan wishing her the best for her future and committing to offer guidance and support in her journey through life. Though Destiny might not fit the ideal of caring mother and there did not appear to be a consistent, predominant attachment figure, the children were part of a complex and wide system of connections and care. Reynolds (2005: 87) comments on the power of this sort of shared parenting, emphasising how 'Caribbean women feel and share a collective responsibility for children and other vulnerable members of the Black community, to whom they are not biologically related'. This picture echoes the idea of community parenting,[10] described in length by bell hooks (2000a), who also promotes this as the parenting alternative of the future. This family's picture offers a perspective that transcends both the concepts of community mothering (Reynolds 2003) and of shared mothering (Olwig 1999), by giving emphasis to the myriad of characters and factors influencing and shaping children and the formation of the self. This family's picture offers a perspective that transcends the Western idea of the self and its formation.

The self and its systems

In her contribution to the volume *Unmasking Race, Culture and Attachment in the Psychoanalytical Space*, Eleftheriadou (2006) laments the limited space allowed for 'racial/cultural material ... within the therapeutic arena'. It is important to emphasise that this issue is not solely manifest in restrictions in communication and exploration of culture-related matters. The adoption of normalising frameworks stemmed from a specific socio-cultural background, such as the concept of the dyad, also reinforces the creation of therapeutic environments within socio-cultural vacuums. As denounced by Billington (1996: 53), 'narrow and value-laden' definitions of 'childhood', 'self' and 'family' are adopted by Western psy-sciences with an unspoken intent to control individuals, 'through procedures of regulation and pathologisation'. This tendency has been discussed by Wagner (1975: 54) in his book on the creation of 'culture', in which the author highlights the human tendency to 'apply the conventional orders and regularities of our sciences to the phenomenal world in order to rationalize and understand it'. In a similar fashion, it can be argued that the psy-sciences promote the application of standardised frameworks, charged with socio-economic determinations, to contain, make sense of and ultimately control forms of being (Billington 1996; Alldred 1996). I will unpack this critique with a case study of a young child I observed as part of her assessment team.

Anna, a lively three-year-old second-generation Jamaican Briton, was referred to the family project I was working at for assessment and with the idea to engage her parents in a mediation process. Anna had recently moved out of her mother's home, Felicia the mother being afflicted by multiple sclerosis, to live with her father. The child's social worker had requested a psychological assessment, concerned that the recent changes in the child's life would have an impact on her wellbeing. After the first observation, the psychologist expressed concerns with regards to Anna's apparent unwillingness to leave her father's side, even for play. In my notes, I summarised my colleagues' commentaries as follows: 'nonverbal? Insecure, incapable of leaving father and unwilling to engage in social exchange with play worker. Trauma? Evident lack of interest in surroundings' (personal notes). The other practitioners involved agreed that Anna evidenced signs of a disrupted attachment, as it was clear she had suffered from the abrupt separation from her mother, and were concerned for the child's development. The information perceived with regards to Anna's family were placing the child in a sort of broken family picture, composed solely by her mother and father. As the sessions continued, Anna started opening up and engaging with both the environment and the practitioners. Most importantly, as the observations continued the team started gathering further details about Anna's family system, which counted not only her mother and father but a paternal aunt, Patricia, and her teenage daughter, Georgia (Figure 13.4). Moreover, Anna attended a playgroup regularly, with either a friend of Patricia or her father's new partner, and every Sunday she would spend the day in the local church.

Anna seemed undisturbed by the limited contact with her biological mother, she started calling Auntie Patricia 'Ma Patricia' and her father's new partner 'Ma' Mary'. Anna's living arrangements and daily routines placed her 'living' across four households,[11] each hosting figures of importance in Anna's universe, as depicted in Figure 13.5.

Anna appeared content, but the concerns with regards to her disrupted attachment with her mother continued nevertheless. The practitioner's focus shifted from the possible outcome of the limited contact between mother and daughter to exploring the cause of Anna's limited interest in seeing her mother. After a session at the centre,[12] a colleague sought Aunt Patricia's views on Anna's circumstances,

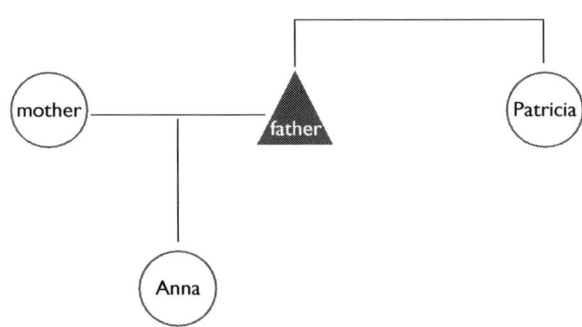

FIGURE 13.4 Anna's presumed family

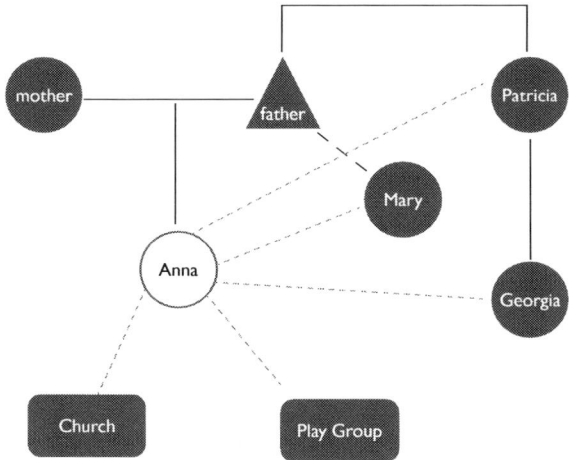

FIGURE 13.5 Anna's system of care

to which the woman replied 'she only gets upset when she is here because you keep telling her she should be'.

The preoccupation of the practitioners involved with regards to the necessity for Anna's mother to be involved in order to prevent causing any harm to the child's development ironically became the issue mostly disturbing Anna's life.

The making of the self

> The self, as that which can be an object to itself, is essentially a social structure, and it arises in social experience.
>
> *(Mead 1956: 204)*

Attachment theory identifies in the attachment figure the social tool that enables the child's self to emerge and take shape. In order for this process to occur in a 'healthy' manner, it is necessary for the attachment figure to exhibit a certain type of sensitivity towards the child, for this sensitivity to be of a certain quality and to maintain consistency and be present reliably throughout time, hence my colleagues' preoccupation for Anna's development (Ainsworth and Bowlby 1991; Morelli and Henry 2013). A visual representation of the 'ideal' circumstances for Anna's self to develop would probably be as in Figure 13.6.

Throughout the years, existing critiques of attachment theory have promoted changes in this framework. Feminism has challenged the necessity for the mother to function as the main figure of attachment (Oyewumi 2000), opening the main 'circle of influence' of the child to other persons. Culturally informed reviews of the theory have fostered the opening of this circle to a wider spectrum of possible figures, allowing greater fluidity and acknowledging the presence of culture as a force impacting on these interactions (Hrdy 2009). Further to this, anthropological

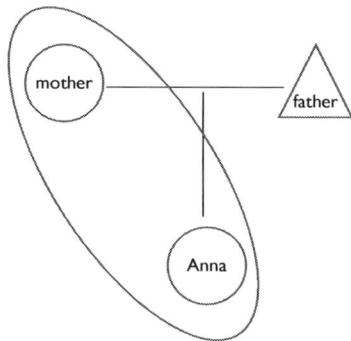

FIGURE 13.6 Attachment conducing to development of healthy self

research has challenged the universality of concepts such as maternal sensitivity and ideals of quality mothering, making space for cultural variations and different perspectives of childrearing priorities and experiences (Rogoff et al. 2013). These advancements in the theorisation of attachment would therefore validate the family system as depicted in Figure 13.5. Nevertheless the emphasis on a circumscribed, dyadic or non-, experience of a relation in which the child/self is solely a recipient remains for, as stressed by Gerhardt (2004: 18), 'the baby is an interactive project not a self powered one'.

This fidelity to ideas placing emphasis on the development of the 'natural self' as confined within a specific period of time, a set of interactions and one directionality of influencing, invests 'adults' with the power to determine and shape, dismissing children as sole recipients of development. The mono-directionality of this exchange is overcome with the conceptualisation of the self as resulting from interactions, as part of a process that requires the presence of both the self and the other (Mead 1956). In Mead's schema, the self and the audience are subjected to reciprocal influences, both prior to, during and after the interaction. In preparing for the interaction the self considers and plans its actions, Mead refers to these as 'gestures', engaging therefore in a conversation with itself, which leads to the shaping of the self per se. The importance of recognising the role of self in its own shaping is essential as, as explained by Mead (2013: 124): failure to do so would result in the formulation of 'obvious absurdities'. Mead's vision of the social self recognises, for children, the possibility to be active in the shaping of their selves. The acceptance of self-reliance licenses the self of a certain agency, regardless of age, as suggested also in Wyness' (2014) interpretation of age as category, functioning as a mere feature of the individual, as gender and race. Removing age from being a determinant in the formation of the self opens a debate on whether childhood is the core period for this process and therefore whether only interactions with parents shape the self. Stretching the development of the self beyond a specific period forces the recognition that a broad number of factors must be at play in this mechanism, and that the self might not remain constant throughout the years. Moving away from this conceptualisation of the self as one, permanent and innate, in his exploration on the formation of the self, Wagner (1975: 80) suggests that 'our theories of child development and the expectations they bring about are simply masks for the collective invention of the "natural" self'. In Wagner's work, the self, socially defined as in Mead's work, is far from natural. The self is in fact an 'inventive process' (Ingold 2016: xi), 'created by consciously articulating the conventional controls of Culture, by attempting to predict, control and process it' (Wagner 1975: 80). Ultimately Wagner's perspective offers culture a dominant role in the formation of the self, both as concept and as reality, eliminating the focus on the relation with specific pre-determined others, and widening the interest on all the others interacting with the self (see Figure 13.7).

The vision of a self that is (in itself) the product of its context, 'culture', as much as the outcome of dynamic and multilayered interactions with itself and others, 'social', enables a complete shift in the concept of development from a more practical angle.

Firstly, this vision invalids the deterministic perspective that incapacitates the overcoming of traumatic experiences. Secondly, it recognises the ambiguous dynamics at play between agency and social influences, allowing for the self to become different selves coexisting in the various contexts of relevance to the individual. Lastly, it urges the recognition of the role of culture and all of its components, rejecting the choice of not acknowledging this in the therapeutic setting (and in life in general for that matter).

Reflections for practice

Ribbens admonishes her readers of the 'danger of describing social contexts as though they exist independently of the people who construct them' (1994: 8). in a similar manner, the conceptualisation of the social self as detailed above emphasises

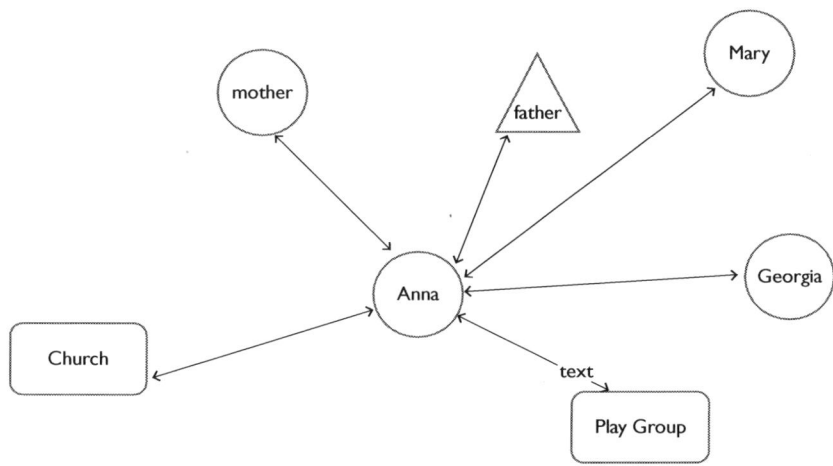

FIGURE 13.7 System in interaction with Anna's self

the dangers of describing people as existing independently of the contexts and people that construct them.

Mead (2013) defined a social act as 'a complex organic process implied by each individual stimulus and response involved in it'. In recognising the self as a social act, we would not only allow the emphasis on the sole responsibility of parents to be lifted, but also share this among the whole of society, similarly as suggested through the concept of community parenting (hooks 2000b). Additionally, children's agency would be recognised and valued, enabling them to be perceived as equal citizens rather than as incomplete humans.

A question that ought to be asked is whether persisting with the idealisation of a natural self that develops solely through attachment of specific figure(s) is a mere act of control, an attempt to maintain individuals attuned to society and its requirements for conformity. Moreover, it is important to reflect whether this model of formation of the self is an attempt to concentrate responsibility within a circumscribed social unit, evading our necessity to reflect on the impact that social inequalities have on a daily basis and in the long term in the shaping of the self.

Notes

1 The suggestion that attachment theory might not actually be scientifically valid is seldom welcomed by interested ears in psychological circles.
2 In recent years, attachment has in fact not just been adopted as a working framework in practice with children, for example, supporting pupils in schools (Bomber 2007) and through social work practice (Schofield 2002), but also with parents, through programmes such as attachment-focused parenting (Hughes 2009).
3 Consistency of the three key tenets of attachment as indicated by Ainsworth (1971).
4 Her words.
5 How Firestone notably described the experience of giving birth, to her disgrace without having actually experienced it.
6 In my imaginary cartoon, Butler's response would read 'fear not, it's only a performance'.
7 LeVine refers to the tendency to identify mothers as the root of their children's problems
8 Interesting to note how the lack of a father figure, a character mostly ignored in psy-theories of child development, becomes of great importance and deemed as pathological in the experience of Caribbean families.
9 Both Sherell and Mario had spent a few summers in Jamaica living with Marcelle and visiting their father from time to time.
10 hooks (2000a) elevates the concept of community parenting to a further level of engagement of the wider society, as in her version everyone is responsible and contributing to the group.
11 Her father's house, Aunt Patricia, Mary's house and the house where she attended playgroups.
12 Anna was referred for play therapy and regular observations to track her progress.

References

Abrams, R. (2004) Minding the Baby: Review of *Why Love Matters: How Affection Shapes a Baby's* Brain by Sue Gerhardt. *Guardian*, 17 July. Retrieved from: www.theguardian.com/books/2004/jul/17/highereducation.booksonhealth

Ainsworth, M.D.S. and Bowlby, J. (1991) An Ethological Approach to Personality Development. *American Psychologist*, 46(4): 333–341.

Ainsworth, M.D.S., Bell, S.M. and Stayton, D.J. (1971) Individual Differences in Strange Situation Behavior of One Year Olds. In H.R. Schaffer (ed.), *The Origins of Human Social Relationships*, 17–57. London: Academic Press.

Alldred, P. (1996) Whose Expertise? Conceptualizing Resistance to Advice about Childrearing. In E. Burman, G. Aitken, P. Alldred, R. Allwood, T. Billington, B. Goldberg, A. Gordo Lopez, C. Heenan, D. Marks and S. Warner (eds), *Psychology, Discourse, Practice: From Regulation to Resistance*. London: Taylor and Francis.

Allen, K. and Taylor, Y. (2012). Placed Parenting, Locating Unrest: Failed Femininities, Troubled Mothers and Rioting Subjects. *Studies in the Maternal*, 4(2):1–25. Retrieved from: http://doi.org/10.16995/sim.39

Billington, T. (1996) Pathologizing Children: Psychology in Education and Acts of Government. In E. Burman, G. Aitken, P. Alldred, R. Allwood, T. Billington, B. Goldberg, A. Gordo Lopez, C. Heenan, D. Marks and S. Warner (eds), *Psychology, Discourse, Practice: From Regulation to Resistance*. London: Taylor and Francis.

Bomber, L. (2007) *Inside I'm Hurting: Practical Strategies for Supporting Children with Attachment Difficulties in Schools*. London: Worth.

Burman, E. (1997) Psychology: Market, Metaphor and Metamorphosis. *Culture and Psychology*, 3(2): 143–152.

Burman, E. (2007) *Deconstructing Developmental Psychology*. New York: Routledge.

Chamberlain, M. (2004) Caribbean Kinship in a Global Setting. *Caribbean Studies*, 32(1), 73–98.

Clark, R. (2010) *Childhood in Society for Early Childhood Studies*. London: SAGE.

Clarke, E. (1957) *My Mother Who Fathered Me*. London: George Allen Unwin.

Collins, P.H. (1994) Shifting the Center: Race, Class, and Feminist Theorizing about Motherhood. In E. Nakan, G. Chang and L. Forcey (eds), *Mothering: Ideology, Experience and Agency*, 45–65. New York: Routledge.

Eleftheriadou, Z. (2006) Revisiting the Concepts of Racism and Culture. In K. White (ed.), *Unmasking Race, Culture and Attachment in the Psychoanalytic Space*. London: Karnac.

Fitzherbert, K. (1967) *West Indian Children in London*. London: Bell and Sons.

Foner, N. (1979) *Jamaica Farewell: Jamaican Migrants in London*. London: Routledge.

Frazier, E.F. (1948) *The Negro Family in the United States*. Chicago, IL: University of Chicago Press.

Gerhardt, S. (2004) *Why Love Matters: How Affection Shapes a Baby's Brain*. London: Routledge.

Guldberg, H. (2009) *Reclaiming Childhood: Freedom and Play in an Age of Fear*. London: Routledge.

Hill Collins, P. (1994) *Black Feminist Thought: Knowledge, Consciousness and the Politics of Empowerment*. New York: Routledge.

Hills, J. (2012) *Introduction to Systemic and Family Therapy*. London: Palgrave Macmillan.

hooks, b. (2000a) *Feminism Is for Everybody: Passionate Politics*. New York: Routledge.

hooks, b. (2000b) *Feminist Theory: From Margin to Centre*. London: Pluto Press.

Hrdy, S.B. (2009) *Mothers and Others: The Evolutionary Origins of Mutual Understanding*. Cambridge, MA: Belknap Press.

Hughes, D. (2009) *Principles of Attachment-Focused Parenting: Effective Strategies to Care for Children*. New York: Norton.

Ingold, T. (2016) Foreword. In R. Wagner, *The Invention of Culture*, 2nd edition. Chicago, IL: University of Chicago Press.

James, A. and James, A. (2008) *Key Concepts in Childhood Studies*. London: SAGE.

Kareem, J. (1992) The Nafsiyat Intercultural Therapy Centre. In J. Kareem and R. Littlewood (eds), *Intercultural Therapy: Themes, Interpretations and Practice*. London: Blackwell.

Kareem, J. and Littlewood, R. (eds) (1992) *Intercultural Therapy: Themes, Interpretations and Practice.* London: Blackwell.

Lamb, M. (2014) Foreword. In H. Otto and H. Keller (eds), *Different Faces of Attachment: Cultural Variations on a Universal Human Need.* Cambridge: Cambridge University Press.

LeVine, R.A. (2015) Attachment Theory as Cultural Ideology, in H. Otto and H. Keller (eds), *Different Faces of Attachment: Cultural Variations of a Universal Human Need.* Cambridge: Cambridge University Press.

Lilienfeld, S., Lynn, S.J., Ruscio, J. and Beyerstein, B.L. (2010) *50 Great Myths of Popular Psychology: Shattering Widespread Misconceptions about Human Behavior.* Chichester, Malden, MA: Wiley-Blackwell.

Mead, G.H. (1956) *On Social Psychology: Selected Papers, Edited and with an Introduction by Anselm Strauss.* Chicago, IL: University of Chicago Press.

Mead, G.H. (2013) *Mind, Self and Society: From the Standpoint of a Social Behaviourist.* e-book, Heptagon.

Meehan, C.L. and Hawks, S. (2014) Maternal and Allomaternal Responsiveness: The Significance of Cooperative Caregiving in Attachment Theory. In H. Otto and H. Keller (eds), *Different Faces of Attachment: Cultural Variations on a Universal Human Need*, 113–140. Cambridge: Cambridge University Press.

Morelli, G. and Henry, P.I. (2013) Afterword. In N. Quinn and J.M. Mageo (eds), *Attachment Reconsidered: Cultural Perspectives on a Western Theory*, 241–249. New York: Palgrave Macmillan.

Olwig, K.F. (1999) Narratives of the Children Left Behind: Home and Identity in Globalized Caribbean Families. *Journal of Ethnic and Migration Studies*, 25: 267–284.

Otto, H. and Keller, H. (2014) *Different Faces of Attachment: Cultural Variations on a Universal Human Need.* Cambridge: Cambridge University Press.

Oyewumi, O. (2000) Family Bonds/Conceptual Binds: African Notes on Feminist Epistemologies. *Signs*, 25: 1093–1098.

Reynolds, T. (2003) The Success of Our Mothers: Caribbean Mothering, Childrearing and Strategies in Resisting Racism. In D. McCalla (eds), *Black Success in the UK: Essays in Racial and Ethnic Studies.* Cambridge: Cambridge University Press.

Reynolds, T. (2005) *Caribbean Mothers: Identity and Experience in the UK.* London: Tufnell Press.

Ribbens, J. (1994) *Mothers and Their Children: A Feminist Sociology of Childrearing.* London: SAGE.

Rogoff, B., Mistry, J., Goncu, A. and Mosier, C. (2013) Cultural Variation in the Role Relations of Toddlers and Their Families. In M. Bornstein (eds), *Cultural Approaches to Parenting.* Hoboken: Taylor and Francis.

Sander-Staudt, M. (2016) Frontiers in Parenthood: Queer Mothering, Maternal Ambivalence, Adoption, and Reproductive Technology. *Hypatia*, 31: 460–465. DOI: doi:10.1111/hypa.12231

Schofield, G. (2002) *Attachment Theory: An Introduction for Social Workers.* Norwich: School of Social Work and Psychosocial Studies, University of East Anglia.

Sudakasa, N. (1996) *The Strength of Our Mothers: African and African American Women and Families.* Trenton, NJ: African World Press.

Székely, L. (1979) A Discourse on Sophocles: Freud and Determinism. *Scandinavian Psychoanalytic Review*, 2: 67–81.

Turp, M. (2006) Why Love Matters: How Affection Shapes a Baby's Brain, by Sue Gerhardt. *Infant Observation*, 9(3): 305–309, DOI: doi:10.1080/13698030601074476

Wagner, R. (1975) *The Invention of Culture*, 2nd edition. Chicago, IL: University of Chicago Press.

Wyness, M. (2014) *Childhood.* Hoboken: Wiley.

14

THE CHALLENGE OF RACISM IN CLINICAL SUPERVISION

Isha Mckenzie-Mavinga

This chapter outlines some essential points about the context of supervision as a reflexive process. In particular, the role of defences and postracism as a defensive discourse that often causes this challenge to remain hidden. Ultimately, this chapter will support a dialogue about the challenges of racism and encourage exploration of responses to the challenge within the context of clinical supervision and working with verbalised and unspoken racial content. This chapter will also address aspects of supervision in the context of clinical work with supervisees, racialised content of client material and dynamics of racism in therapy and supervision. The subject of racism and clinical supervision comes to mind for several reasons. First, comments from some supervisees about not feeling able to take their work with black clients to white supervisors. The impact of Eurocentric thinking and racism ripples through to the supervisory relationship and affects the intercultural relationship between therapist and supervisor.

This brings into context what may get transferred to the client–therapist relationship. If this process goes unchallenged the supervisee denies her or himself an opportunity to work through a possible parallel rupture in supervision that may reflect the client–therapist interrelationship. Clients may also lose out on the benefits of being fully supported through the challenge.

Supervision is generally experienced as an opportunity to share the therapist's relational process and their use of supportive skills in their client work. This aspect of therapeutic work supports safety and continuity between client and therapist. A space for the therapist's self-reflection and personal and professional development is provided. Supervision can also be used to explore areas of concern and vulnerability that arise for the therapist during client work. This is always done with concern for the client's safety, emotional and physical wellbeing and social progress. When material about oppressions emerge in the client work, it can sometimes evoke feelings of naiveté and identification with, or defence against the feelings associated with particular oppressions. The oppression of racism is one such challenge that often induces these responses both in life and in therapeutic interchange. It is clear that internalised racism and Eurocentric assimilation may underpin some of the responses to this challenge.

I will take a look at how the challenge of racism can arise in the clinical triad and some ways that it can be explored and supported. Throughout this chapter I will refer to several concepts as a framework for discussion about the influence of racism in practice. These concepts I have named 'the black Western archetype', 'ancestral baggage', 'recognition trauma' and 'a black empathic approach' (Mckenzie-Mavinga 2009, 2016).

Another reason for concern about racism in the supervisory process is that the taboo of racism and the impact of Eurocentric assimilation processes create a discourse about race equality that suggests we are in a phase of postracism. This perception has resulted in an assumption that we live in a period of acceptance, tolerance, understanding and harmony with our differences.

Although people do generally live harmoniously, for most of the time this perspective may be far from the truth. It only takes an insurgent uprising or some exposure to the contradictions of diversity to unleash prejudices and homogeneous racist thoughts into the mindset of individuals and communities to perpetuate negative stereotypes. An example of this was the post-Brexit period in 2016 that unleashed micro-conversations akin to the 'keep Britain white' discourse in the 1950s: visible notices saying 'no blacks, no Irish, no dogs'.

In addition to white racism, this time around the discourse included concerns about non-British Europeans. Trainees and therapists expressed their concern about the impact of such post-Brexit responses. As working European migrants, some were concerned about their status as British citizens.

Howitt and Owusu-Bempa (1994) suggest that racism has merely changed its clothes and that a belief in the discourse of 'postracism' serves to stagnate any change to institutional racism and the growth of anti oppressive practice in psychology and psychotherapy. Therefore, inevitably, relationships with clients and clinical supervision become affected. In order to move through this postcolonial perception therapists and supervisors must have a dialogue about this elephant in the room.

In addition to withholding presentation of black clients' racialised material and indeed the taboo of racism, a trickster shadow promotes silence and denial about diversity and the impact of racism. This silence and denial can distract from empathy and the learning process, thus marginalising the cultural components of personal development and the therapeutic process. One way that this can happen is when fear or denial of exploring the impact of racism leads to misinterpretation of racism or a dilution of key issues by generalising concerns.

Defences and denial of racism can lead to a distorted gaze. When this happens therapists may question their worthiness about working with the challenge of racism. Therapists who feel they cannot bring black clients to supervision need to be encouraged to believe that they can achieve transcultural competency in their clinical work, with the hidden nuances of internalised and unconscious racism. Emotional content attached to facilitation of racial issues must therefore be acknowledged and supported in clinical supervision. To facilitate this supervisors and therapists must be aware of and able to conduct a dialogue about racism in supervision and the therapeutic setting.

The concept of internalised racism has thus become a feature of ongoing efforts to understand how the hurt of racism impacts on the unconscious psyche and internal process of developing personal identity. Internalised racism may influence how this particular dynamic intersects with other oppressions and how this in turn impacts on the relational contexts of supervision. For example, some black counsellors addressing black issues with white clients felt inadequate and feared rejection by white clients. Some white counsellors were concerned about being effective with black clients, particularly with the impact of racism and their ability to empathise with this oppression. Bibi (a British, Asian, Pakistani, Muslim woman who trained in combined psychodynamic and person-centred counselling) tells me:

> I'm being supervised for my private work. I value my supervision. When I have presented issues of difference in supervision the dialogue has often seemed to merge into a general discussion about humanity. It is as if we cover the cracks up instead of risking discomfort and maybe talking about the awkwardness in the room. There is something avoiding in it, but also something comforting because it is saying there is a higher good. But I feel the higher good can only be fulfilling if we include all the difficult bits too and stop trying to 'skip that bit'. As a child I witnessed my parent's experience of racism and thinking back, they would have been the same age that I am now. These were bleak and nasty experiences. Having eggs thrown at your front door and dogs set on you because it is known that you do not have dogs inside the home, being verbally abused, called Pakis and stuff like that. There is going to be residues of that happening now in different forms and at varying levels, whether conscious or subconscious.
>
> There is always that something hidden looking down on. I often need to ask myself: is it just me projecting an inferiority complex relating to race issues here with this person or is there actually something to be worked on? As an associate, doing volunteer counselling here, I have felt on my own with black issues and I have had to work on my own black clients here. It would have been lovely to have some support with this in supervision. As an associate I felt I taught in supervision and this is a very interesting concept to me. It is not just about me breaking new ground. Let's all break new ground.

Isolation for the black practitioner is one of many disempowering experiences. As expressed by Bibi there is an inner and outer struggle going on, without adequate facilitation.

As Lago and Thompson note (1996: 81):

Counsellors, are much less likely to attend to clients who talk about the history of their own people. (Examples of this would include clients' stories of forebears, ancestors, religious, ethnic and tribal history and so on.) In many cultures the connection between past and present history makes it necessary for counsellors to understand clearly the client's historical context as a way of understanding their present behaviour.

Paulette (an experienced white Jewish female counsellor trained in person-centred counselling) asks:

> How appropriate and when is it appropriate to ask questions related to race and ethnicity? People were not aware of black issues or areas like disability at the time I trained. There was not much inclusion in those days. There were no black students and the issues addressed, due to the make-up of the group, were class and sexuality. I think people were less conscious. When I worked as a trainer, the course aimed to be inclusive, but it was hard to deal with issues of racism in a way that was not divisive. There was ill feeling and groups got polarised. It felt dangerous and difficult at times. My later experience of having a black colleague helped me to see that racist attitudes can cling to us from early conditioning in a society that has not yet learnt to be inclusive and so have a lot of those racist ideas. I realised that this could be true even for me as a Jew who had fought racism from my earliest days. I attended a white awareness group that was very valuable and where I learned that with compassion it is possible to explore the hurts, which lie behind racist feelings. I had been able to use what I learned especially with white people, dealing with their own racism. I put attention on their heritage being accepted and heard. I became more open to exploring the effects of racism with trainees and clients, but I'm still timid about explicitly addressing these issues.

Paulette's pertinent question seems to reflect her wish to understand how and when to use her voice in addressing black issues in the therapeutic setting. I have heard this question asked many times during training and supervision sessions. D'Ardenne and Mahtani (1989), in their important documentation of transcultural counselling, emphasise 'the active and reciprocal process' involved with their approach, as opposed to 'inter cultural or cross cultural' approaches. They suggest that 'counsellors in the transcultural setting are responsible for working across, through and beyond their cultural difference'. I have found this approach useful in my own understanding of black issues. The authors state that counsellors are no different from others in not wishing to acknowledge their own racism or cultural prejudices. They also suggest that white counsellors may be less culturally skilled than their clients due to their different learning experience of coping with a hostile and alien environment. If this is the case, how do supervisors manage this dilemma?

It is known that racism often gets re-enacted in negative and self-demeaning ways that can cause low self-concept and feelings of powerlessness. We also know that, similarly to other oppressions, it becomes institutionalised and we know that racism can be covert and overt and cause physical and mental problems.

Exploring the phenomenon of racism can be seen as a discovery process in a heuristic sense, because the process of learning in clinical supervision is like a journey into meaning. Both supervisor and therapist will need to travel through their responses and emotions about racism, to create a mutual experience that can benefit clients. This process includes self-challenge and willingness to change thinking and behaviour that may otherwise further oppress clients. Therapists may need to have feelings and fears about the challenge of racism validated. Internalised racism may need to be identified and self-challenge supported.

A black supervisee (I will call her Julia) frequently refers to her own stereotyping and how this may influence her relationship with clients. She is aware that this may be caused by her internalised racism and her internalisation of other negative stereotypes. We discovered that this concern distracts from empathy with the client. The use of concepts such as 'ancestral baggage' and 'recognition trauma' to define the process of personal development associated with this was helpful and supported the challenge.

We are all subject to the process of ancestral baggage as what gets passed on intergenerationally is key to each individual's cultural make-up.

Moustakas (1990) views the initial stage of curiosity and concern about a phenomenon 'as immersion': becoming connected to the phenomena and exploring its universality as though it were a shared concern.

This supervisee became curious and concerned about the impact of racism on her clinical work and supervision. Julia had terminated previous supervision where she did not feel supported when working with black issues. She wanted to be more forthcoming in her supervision and client work and to stop feeling that she was editing her work and therefore missing perspectives that might be important for black and Asian clients. I felt that it was therefore my responsibility to model being explicit about racism and encourage her to openly explore the impact on clients and herself.

In one of our early meetings she shared concerns about a client who was presenting trauma as a result of racism at work. The client was expressing a sense of disbelief and fear of madness, yet she was aware how racism manifests and how it had an impact on her. Julia became aware of a parallel process. The client's partner had named 'racism', but Julia had not been used to the term being voiced during her training, so she was avoiding it. Julia was aware that the client needed a safe space to explore the term and her experience of racism. During that meeting, I named it, which brought a sense of relief to Julia. She expressed that she had been trying to blot out her experience and subsequent feelings. We were then able to name her associated rage and locate some empathy for the client. I have named the rage associated with black clients and racism 'black rage' (Mckenzie-Mavinga 2016).

Those powerful feelings associated with awareness of the impact of racism I have termed 'recognition trauma' Mckenzie-Mavinga (2009). Recognition trauma is a process that once acknowledged can be explored and worked through, because the feelings have been given voice and expression. Often feelings related to the impact of racism are denied, causing numbness and low self-esteem. The feelings become internalised and sometimes they become self-harming or get projected in negative ways towards others (Cross 1971).

Harbouring racism can compound other oppressive experiences, such as sexism or homophobia, that clients may have experienced during their lifetime. If therapists have a picture of clients' ethnic and cultural background it may support their knowledge of the client's experience and ways of coping with racism. Identifying a client's history of oppression and racism and their ways of coping can offer insights about their emergence from recognition trauma. I call this a black empathic approach because it is based on feeling responses that genuinely acknowledge and connect to black issues and a context of racism. This approach emanates from gained understanding of the impact and experiences of racism and individual coping skills. This action can also produce information about whether the client has enough cultural collateral (awareness and positivity about their cultural background, Byfield 2008) to build positive insights about their identity and support their empowerment.

Julia was able to locate a black empathic approach by facing self-imposed restrictions, imposed initially by her training, that were causing her fear of naming racism. Rogers (1961) used the term 'locus of evaluation' to describe an experience of inner knowing. Although he advocated a person-centred approach to client work, it is clear that therapists need to consider whether this approach is enough to address aspects of oppression such as racism, which may lay hidden due to assimilation, taboo and institutionalised racism.

In a heuristic sense, the supervisory experience becomes a place for 'incubation' of thought and feeling, leading to 'illumination' and greater consciousness of self in relation to the client and her or his material. The client's storyline can be altered or repaired by the therapist's motivation to get more deeply connected to the phenomena of racism as experienced by her or him. In other words, making an effort to express an empathic connection specifically linked to the experience of racism and the empowerment of those impacted by it. This is what I mean by a black empathic approach.

Heuristics emphasise self-disclosure to encourage participant or co-researchers to share. This gives greater connection to the subject under observation, and influences the journey from personal to general and vice versa. Therefore, terms used to describe an experience may give others access to the experience. This can create acceptance and understanding if taken on board in supervision.

The idea of self-disclosure may seem problematic to some traditional therapeutic approaches, but if we are to find new ways of thinking that support the challenge of racism it is important to consider aspects of disclosure that may work. Skin colour diversity and gender are often taken-for-granted aspects of disclosure. It is the therapist's responsibility to mediate levels of disclosure with clients. There are also some hidden aspects of identity, for example, hidden disabilities and sexuality, and mixed-heritage individuals who appear white.

Based on visual knowledge, on meeting me, clients occasionally express curiosity about my background. A client asked me what island I came from. Knowing that she is Jamaican I took this to mean what island in the Caribbean do I come from. I see this as a way of locating a connection between us as black people. If I respond using a psychodynamic interpretation such as 'it seems my background is important to you', this may seem distancing for a client rather than connecting with them, because I am aware that our connection as black women may be key to safety for this client. In a community where bonding between black people can support the impact of racism and create empathy this consideration is important. Attention to this type of interchange can be a useful starting point for a black empathic approach.

Julia could see that her client was a black woman, and vice versa. She was also aware that the client had an African heritage. These were initial points of disclosure and connection. She was also aware that this information could sometimes create identification with the client. She was also aware of the client's powerful feelings of wounding from the experience of racism, yet both Julia and the client talked around the experience of racism without naming it. On becoming aware of this omission and the fear connected to naming it, Julia felt more empowered to empathise and work with the client's rage.

Denial and isolation caused by fear of addressing racism can reinforce taboo about this theme. Hidden nuances become activated and create a defence that may prevent individuals from acknowledging racism, even though they may have alluded to it as the cause of their distress. This taboo often gets perpetuated during training, and trainees may then feel excluded from a dialogue that can support them with their client work when the impact of racism may be apparent.

Moustakas (1990) addresses the power of tacit knowledge and the idea that we can find meaning based on the knowledge that something exists. He calls this 'the illumination process'. The reflective process of therapy requires us to know the meaning of themes and experiences that clients portray. This brings us knowledge that we can then connect to a client's life journey. Denial and disbelief about the impact of racism can thwart this experience and perpetuate a taboo about listening and accepting these experiences. The supervisee and the supervisor will need to validate their levels of tacit knowledge about racism as this process will assist their ability to work with the challenge of racism in therapy. The explication phase of the heuristic process allows space to examine discoveries and organise thinking about the next phase. The supervisory process presents a space for this kind of examination and it can support therapists to develop their approach to the challenge of racism. Supervision in this respect honours an educative process for personal development purposes. This process may challenge client, therapist and supervisor.

Taboos about this subject can often silence the client, the therapist and the supervisor, therefore it is not enough to assume that multicultural awareness or intercultural experiences can offer an active response to the challenge of racism. This may pathologise clients, as though the problem of racism does not really exist and therefore it does not need attending to. This is what I call 'the trickster shadow' that can form into negative stereotypes of black people and their experience of racism.

The trickster shadow can perform harmful negative perceptions of self and other. For example, individuals who were taught that they had to strive to be better than white people. This comment can create situations where individuals may not feel good enough and therefore overwork or internalise stereotypes that can keep them in denial about the impact of racism on their lives. A sort of head-down, soldier on regardless attitude can not only cause overwork to prove their worth, it can cause the hurt of racism to get buried until individuals become overwhelmed with their feelings about oppression. This sometimes manifests in harshness towards self and others and limited self-care. The passing on of this way of being I have called 'ancestral baggage'.

Some components of ancestral baggage are based on what may be called 'black Western archetypes'. These are negative images and unconscious concepts that perpetuate Western socio-cultural aspects of racism. For example, 'the lazy black boy'. This concept fuels perceptions of black people that reflect a negative gaze reflecting perspectives that they are only fit for menial work, low salaries and jobs that do not hold responsibility.

Fanon talks of consciousness in terms of relinquishing the self as object, but echoes the hopelessness attached to finding the black self through the gaze:

> I came into the world imbued with the will to find a meaning in things, my spirit filled with desire to attain to the source of the world, and then I found that I was in the midst of objects. Sealed into crushing objecthood, I turned beseechingly to others. Their attention was liberation, running over my body suddenly abraded into nonbeing, endowing me once more with agility that I thought lost, and by taking me out of the world, restoring me to it. But just as I reached the other side, I stumbled and the movements, the attitudes, the glances of the other fixed me there, in the sense in which a chemical solution is fixed by a dye. I was indignant; I demanded an explanation. Nothing happened. I burst apart. Now the fragments have been put together by another self.
>
> *(Fanon 1986: 109)*

Julia was curious about how she could cope with her thoughts about the stereotype of the angry black woman. She was aware of the client's shame and her own anger about the client's situation. She was also curious about the use of a person-centred approach and how she could reconcile the need to acknowledge racism to the client if the client had not mentioned the term. In the session with this particular client Julia felt a strong sense of identification with the client's concerns about being seen within a stereotypical perception of the angry black woman, as aggressive rather than experiencing hurt. This was causing her to identify with the client rather than empathise.

We discussed a black Western archetype based on slaves carrying their rage about racism until safely within the familiar (family), where they could sing, dance, chant and reconnect. This archetype of aggressive black women can be seen to influence withholding of the client's anger and the therapist's inability to empathise with this state, which perpetuates disconnection. On the other hand, the black client's anger has often been interpreted as a mental health concern. Jung advocated that archetypes should be exposed and brought to light, so that we can see more clearly how to change attitudes and inhibiting processes.

Only when all props and crutches are broken, and no cover from the rear offers even the slightest hope of security, does it become possible for us to experience an archetype that till then had lain hidden behind the meaningful nonsense played out as the anima. This is the archetype of meaning, just as the anima is the archetype of life itself (Jung 1972: 32).

As Julia became more familiar with her own internalised racism, she realised how this sometimes prevented her from empathising with clients. She noticed that she would switch into a sort of campaigning approach that ignited her own rage and distracted her from staying with the client's feelings about racism. In her supervision she asked the question 'how do I contain my own angry black woman, when I am working with a client who is angry about racism?'.

Raising this question in supervision brought to the surface Julia's anger and hurt about her own experiences of racism that she felt she had toned down in her own therapy. This gave her insight about greater expectation of her therapist to hold her black rage, and therefore a realisation that identifying with the client in this way was preventing her empathy with the client's anger specifically about the impact of racism. I call this distracted empathy. Her challenge was to acknowledge that connecting empathically and specifically to the client's feelings about the experience of racism may assist her own holding of the client. It was also necessary to evaluate whether a rigid use of the person-centred approach may perpetuate denial of powerful feelings associated with racism.

On another occasion when Julia was working with a white middle-class client she found herself being overcurious and almost accusatory about a member of the client's family. Therefore, she was not allowing the client to come to her own conclusions about the situation. She caught herself labelling the client's relative rather than letting the client continue her story and encouraging her to share her feelings. In supervision she questioned the impact of a Black Western archetype of the 'Mammy' influencing her responses and ways that she occasionally rescues clients. I asked Julia whether she experienced a parallel in her relationships with white women in the world. She shared with me that she was raised in a white area and that therefore she feels very cosmopolitan.

Insights about the role she performs when in white spaces came to the surface. The challenge of resisting the urge to take on and take care of her white female client became apparent. There was another challenge about how her assimilation processes were becoming entangled with her responses to clients. She was already concerned about the influence of her training and her use of a person-centred approach and there were fears about integrating what I call a 'black empathic approach', where she might achieve a relaxed confidence about taking the initiative to acknowledge racism and work with it.

In Julia's previous thinking a good therapist strives to use her assimilation of traditional theory and her life experience. Her reflective process brought to consciousness an imbalance causing her to lean more towards assimilation and push her life experience into the background.

In conclusion, I view this approach as a transcultural model that works using a black empathic approach. As in feminist therapy this approach can be integrated across all models. A black empathic approach may present useful contradictions to a status quo of denial, silence and fear of addressing the challenge of racism. Inevitably, this may evoke a discourse of acceptance and active interplay with clients, supervisors and supervises impacted by racism.

Some therapists are turning to physical therapies, neuropsychology and behavioural approaches to help resolve neurosis trauma and anxiety. Evidently these approaches assist individuals to participate more actively in developing attitude and coping skills. However, maintenance of reflective introspection on the therapist's and supervisor's specific awareness of racism must be considered in supporting and empowering individuals impacted by racism. Using this approach, levels of cultural collateral and a backdrop that attends to ancestral baggage can assist therapists to move clients forward in their empowerment. There are certain pre-requisites for race awareness and active responses to racism in supervision. In particular, a mutual vision for supervisors and supervisees as shared via history of the everyday impact of racism on the personal development of individuals is necessary. This can create a foundation for the use of a black empathic approach.

Here are some useful pointers that I think can be considered when addressing the challenge of racism in supervision.

1. Ruptures evoked by cultural or racial issues need to be explored in supervision.
2. Be aware of seeing your own cultural assumptions as a norm.
3. Be aware of guilt, shame and overcompensation as a result of racism on the agenda.
4. Racism can be viewed as an aspect of intersecting oppressions.
5. Consider that each identity group and individual may have their own developmental process and history of racial oppression.
6. Consider integrating traditional therapeutic approaches with a black empathic approach.
7. Be aware that the use of parallels can mirror dominant power structures, i.e. assuming a feminist approach may actually support a racist position.
8. Splits and ruptures that occur as a result of racism may reflect the dominant culture, they are not necessarily in the mind of the individual and therefore not necessarily pathological.

9. Recognise and address conflicting parts and the pressure to choose one identity over another. For example, mixed-heritage people, cultural conflicts within different generations or conflicts about cultural assimilation.
10. Develop acceptance of visible and invisible oppression and be open to the idea that racism can create trauma and retraumatisation.
11. Screen early experiences of racism and individual coping skills that may influence responses to racism.
12. Be aware of cultural disposition, i.e. gender, ethnicity, spirituality, that may influence responses to racism.
13. Get a history of the traumatic event (when, where, how, who?). What happened immediately after?
14. Be aware of internalised responses to racism.
15. Look at the impact on the storyteller rather than the story.
16. Be aware of recognition trauma (the powerful feelings associated with acknowledging the experience of racism or of being a member of the perpetrator group).

References

Byfield, C. (2008) *Black Boys Can Make It*. Stoke-on-Trent: Trentham Books.
Cross, W.E. (1971) The Negro to Black Conversion Experience: Towards the Psychology of Black Liberation. *Journal of Black Psychology*, 5: 13–31.
D'Ardenne, P. and Mahtani, A. (1989) *Transcultural Counselling in Action*. London: SAGE.
Fanon, F. (1986) *Black Skin White Masks*. London: Pluto Press.
Howitt, D. and Owusu-Bempa, J. (1994) *The Racism of Psychology*. Harlow: Harvester Wheatsheaf.
Jung, C. (1972) *The Archetypes and the Collective Unconscious*. London: Routledge and Kegan Paul.
Lago, C. and Thompson, J. (1996) *Race, Culture and Counselling*. Maidenhead: Open University Press.
Mckenzie-Mavinga, I. (2009) *Black Issues in The Therapeutic Process*. London: Palgrave Macmillan.
Mckenzie-Mavinga, I. (2016) *The Challenge of Racism in Therapeutic Practice*. London: Palgrave Macmillan.
Moustakas, C. (1990) *Heuristic Research*. London: SAGE.
Rogers, C.R. (1961) *On Becoming a Person: A Therapist's View of Psychotherapy*. London: Constable.

INDEX

abuse, physical 146–7
abuse, sexual 105–110
Acharrya, Sourangshu 95
Achebe, Chinua 40, 48
Adams, Barry 114
Africa, West 40–59
African 3, 40–59, 111
Alleyne, Aileen 76
Altman, Neil 139
anamnesis 132
anthropology, social 2, 5, 10, 12, 96
ancestral baggage 168, 171, 174
anxiety 5, 7, 111
Arabian 5
Asian, South 4, 5, 16, 30, 84–93, 139, 144–5
assessment 24–39
attachment 7, 41, 153–166
Augoyard, Jean 132
Austin, John 89

Baldwin, James 54
Bangladeshi 3, 16
Barret, Ruth 139
Bateson, Gregory 13, 142
Bion, Wilfred 57
Black and Asian Therapist Network 78
'Black empathetic approach' 7
Blum, Harrison 123
Bourdieu, Pierre 96–97
Bowlby, John 7, 41
Brown, Ross 132
bullying 42
Burman, Erica 152

Burnham, John 14, 15
Burnett, Jon 11
'bush Black' 48

Calef, Victor 123
Caribbean 42, 56, 142, 147, 155
Carlyle, Thomas 127
catharsis 50
children 152–165
Christianity 49, 103
Clark, Kenneth 141
Clark, Marnie 141
class, social 3
colonialism 42–44
colour 5, 121, 122
colourism (shadism) 27
contact boundary 72
counter-transference 105–110, 148
cultural competence 31
'culture' 5, 46, 95–98, 109, 127

D'Ardenne, Patricia 170
DeGruy-Leary, Joy 139
depression 5, 7, 49, 63, 75, 106, 140
depressive position 75
detention, compulsory 2
Devereux, Georges 146
dignity 130
dissertation failure 78–79
double consciousness 49
dreams 119–125
Du Bois, William 56
Durkheim, Emile 10

eating disorder 2
Egyptian 5, 101
Einstein, Albert 95
Eleftheriadou Zack 159
embodiment 127–136
empathic approach, Black 168, 176
envy 41, 51, 66–67
Eribon, Didier 114
ethnic matching 2, 69
Eyre, Dean 124

Fairbairn, Ronald 90, 91
Fairfield, Mark 135
family 153, 167
family therapy 16, 21
Fanon, Frantz 3, 4, 54, 174
Fletchman Smith, Barbara 70, 138, 147
Foucault, Michel 11, 15
Foulkes, Michael 64
fractals 96
Freud, Sigmund 85, 123, 138, 153
functionalism 13

gender identity 28, 31, 47,62–69, 115
Gerhardt, Sue 153–154, 162
Ghana 42–44, 46–48, 52
Gramsci, Antonio 3, 26
groups, therapeutic 4, 13, 61–82
Grubrich-Simitis, Ilse 140
Guzder, Jaswant 145
guilt 5, 7, 60, 65, 114

hate crimes 3, 11
Hickling, Frederick 142
Hindu 21, 107
Holocaust (Shoah) 6, 140
honour 64
hooks, bell 154, 159, 164
Howitt, Dennis 168

identity, subdominant 7
identity models 32, 33–36
immigration 40–59
Indian 5
inferiorisation 5, 7, 111–118
internalised colonial object 7
internalised opposition 7, 24
internalised oppression 26, 27, 28, 29
internal working model 41–42
intercultural therapy – passim
intercultural therapy 94–104
Iraqi 144
Irish 6, 30, 55, 139
Islam 17, 30, 66, 95, 105–7, 144

Jamaica 146, 159
James, Alyson 155
Jews 55, 140, 143, 144

Kareem, Jafar 1, 100, 116, 137, 139, 154
Kavanagh, Graham 124
Klein, Melanie 75
Krause, Bitt 135
Krystal, Henry 140
Kuriloff, Emily 146

Lago, Colin 169
Lamb, Michael 154
language 89
Larsen, Nella 47
Lipsedge, Maurice 116
Littlewood, Ronald 116, 154
Lowe, Frank 136
Lucey, Aideen 55

Macpherson Report 10
McFalls, Laurence 11
McKenzie, Kwame 137
McKenzie-Mavinga, Isha 74, 88–89
Mahtani, Aruna 170
Marley, Bob 46
masculinity 47
Mead, George Herbert 152, 162, 164
memories, implicit 77
metaphor 127–136
motherhood 67, 127–8, 131, 154–5
Moorhouse, Sharon 7
Moustakas, Clark 171
multiculturalism 3
myalgic encephalomyelitis 130
Myers, Wayne 124

Nafsiyat Intercultural Therapy Centre 1, 69, 116, 143
NICE 12
Nkrumah, Kwame 56
"non-White" 83

Owusu-Bempa, Kwame 168

Padmore, George 56
pain, physical 66
Pakistan 30
Pandolfi, Mariella 11
"passing" 3, 28, 41–59
Pentecostalism 49
Perls, Fritz 72
phenomenological awareness 127
postmodernism 3, 25, 36
postracism 168

poverty 26
Priestman, Alison 133
prejudices 95
pretransference 109
privatisation 3
projective identification 8, 86
psychotic illness 2

"race" 61–82
race relations 8, 12
Race Relations (Amendment) Act 8, 12
"racial violence" 1, 3, 4, 11
racism 1, 7, 11, 25, 85, 92, 114, 115, 168–177
Rastafari 45, 57
Ratlansi, Ali 46
recognition trauma 7, 74,88, 168, 171, 177
refugees 5
Reid, Omar 139
repression 112
Reynolds, Tracey 159
Rodney, Walter 56
Rogers, Carl 172
Rose, Eileen 147

schooling 43
Sekyi, Kobina 53
self-disclosure, therapist 172–173
shame 60, 79–80, 131
Sikh 4, 85
slavers 6, 24, 45, 46, 52, 53–54, 56, 141–3

sorcery 19
suicide, attempted 2
supervision, clinical 7, 167–177
Sylhet 18
symbolic violence 12
systemic psychotherapy 13

tabiz 19
Thiongo, Ngugi-wa 43
Thomas, Lennox 55, 109
Torgue, Hentry 132
Totton, Mick 133
trainers 72
trauma, transgenerational 137–151
Turkish 4, 61–70
Turner, Victor 50
Tylor, Edward 95

violence, Black on Black 25
Volkan, Vamik 143

Wagner, Roy 152, 159, 163
West Indian 3–4, 6
White cultural values 32
Winnicott, Donald 55, 69, 99, 112, 115, 141
Winterbottom, Michael 115

Yoruba 24

Žižek, Slavoj 117

Printed in Great Britain
by Amazon

85653467R00111